Why Collingwood Matters

WHY PHILOSOPHY MATTERS

Series editor: Professor Constantine Sandis,
University of Hertfordshire, UK

Why Philosophy Matters focuses on why a particular philosopher, school of thought, or area of philosophical study really matters. Each book will offer a brief overview of the subject before exploring its reception both within and outside the academy and our authors will also defend different provocative outlooks on where the value of philosophy lies (or doesn't, as the case may be). Why Philosophy Matters is accompanied by an ongoing series of free events (talks, debates, workshops) in Bloomsbury. Podcasts of these events will be freely available on the series page.

Books in this series

Why Iris Murdoch Matters, Gary Browning
Why Medieval Philosophy Matters, Stephen Boulter
Why Solipsism Matters, Sami Pihlström
Why Climate Breakdown Matters, Rupert Read
Why Cicero Matters, Vittorio Bufacchi

Also available from Bloomsbury

Collingwood's The Idea of History, Peter Johnson
R. G. Collingwood: A Research Companion, James Connelly, Peter Johnson and Stephen Leach

Why Collingwood Matters

A Defence of Humanistic Understanding

Giuseppina D'Oro

BLOOMSBURY ACADEMIC
LONDON · NEW YORK · OXFORD · NEW DELHI · SYDNEY

BLOOMSBURY ACADEMIC
Bloomsbury Publishing Plc, 50 Bedford Square, London, WC1B 3DP, UK
Bloomsbury Publishing Inc, 1385 Broadway, New York, NY 10018, USA
Bloomsbury Publishing Ireland, 29 Earlsfort Terrace, Dublin 2, D02 AY28, Ireland

BLOOMSBURY, BLOOMSBURY ACADEMIC and the Diana logo
are trademarks of Bloomsbury Publishing Plc

First published in Great Britain 2024
This paperback edition published in 2025

Copyright © Giuseppina D'Oro, 2024

Giuseppina D'Oro has asserted her right under the Copyright, Designs and
Patents Act, 1988, to be identified as Author of this work.

Cover image: Kaleidoscope building with autumn foliage
(© Silvia Otte / Getty Images)

All rights reserved. No part of this publication may be: i) reproduced or
transmitted in any form, electronic or mechanical, including photocopying,
recording or by means of any information storage or retrieval system without
prior permission in writing from the publishers; or ii) used or reproduced in
any way for the training, development or operation of artificial intelligence (AI)
technologies, including generative AI technologies. The rights holders expressly
reserve this publication from the text and data mining exception as per
Article 4(3) of the Digital Single Market Directive (EU) 2019/790.

Bloomsbury Publishing Inc does not have any control over, or responsibility for,
any third-party websites referred to or in this book. All internet addresses given
in this book were correct at the time of going to press. The author and publisher
regret any inconvenience caused if addresses have changed or sites have
ceased to exist, but can accept no responsibility for any such changes.

A catalogue record for this book is available from the British Library.

A catalog record for this book is available from the Library of Congress.

ISBN: HB: 978-1-3501-8571-5
PB: 978-1-3504-2862-1
ePDF: 978-1-3501-8573-9
eBook: 978-1-3501-8574-6

Series: Why Philosophy Matters

Typeset by Integra Software Services Pvt. Ltd.

For product safety related questions contact productsafety@bloomsbury.com.

To find out more about our authors and books visit www.bloomsbury.com
and sign up for our newsletters.

To Mark and Ceri

Contents

Preface		x
1	The struggle against scientism	1
2	Philosophy as disentanglement	27
	Disambiguating the concept of cause	27
	Humanistic and scientific explanations	34
	Confining science to its own explanandum	39
	Scientism, narrow and broad	41
	Explanatory pluralism in place of epistemic relativism	43
	Sources of dissatisfaction	47
	A child's question	51
3	Causal exclusion and the elephant in the room	55
	Rationalizing explanations (of actions) and nomological explanations (of events)	55
	Reframing the questions of the philosophy of mind	60
	The question of the place of mind in nature	63
	Non-reductivism and the elephant in the room	66
	Davidson's challenge	72
	History, not psychology, as the study of mind	80
	Rationalizations can predict, but they predict in a different way	82
	The curse of King Midas	85
4	The 'limits' of science	89
	There is nothing spooky about 'actions'	89
	Soluble and insoluble mysteries	91
	Is consciousness the last stop?	95
	The gap is semantic, not epistemological	100
	Murder mysteries and scientific mysteries	103

5	History as the study of mind	107
	The past is an ambiguous term	107
	The past as another country	110
	Re-enactment and the problem of other minds	116
	Scissors-and-paste history	120
	How to misunderstand others. Historically	123
6	The past as it always was	129
	The 'different kinds of past' claim *versus* the 'many pasts' claim	129
	The decline of speculative philosophy of history and the epistemic priority of the present	132
	An aprioristic revisionism and evidence-based revisions	135
	Re-enactment and the content of thought	137
	On the alleged asymmetry between scientific and historical knowledge	141
	Narrative construction and the empiricist myth of the given	145
	The past *as it was* and the past as it is *in itself*	147
7	Beyond scientism and historicism	153
	What it really takes to overcome scientism	153
	Inverted scientism	155
	Avoiding historical fundamentalism without reintroducing the spectre of pure being	157
	No asymmetry between the epistemic and the moral case	161
	There is no epistemological coup	163
8	The historical past and the nature/culture distinction at the time of the Anthropocene	165
	Old and new challenges to explanatory pluralism	165
	The old challenge and the nature of Collingwood's explanatory pluralism	166
	The Anthropocene challenge to the nature/culture distinction	170

	The same boring old conceptual distinctions?	177
	Humanistic history and the historical future	187
9	The manifest and the scientific images	191
References		200
Index		209

Preface

Amongst neglected philosophers Collingwood is in one sense arguably the best known. Often philosophers are neglected because their name is unfamiliar. One has simply never heard of them. This is not the case with Collingwood whose name is fairly familiar but whose philosophy has not had a significant impact in contemporary debates. This neglect is surprising not least because metaphilosophy (a reflection on the nature and goals of philosophical inquiry) has recently undergone something of a revival and Collingwood wrote what are arguably the two most extensive treatises of the twentieth century on the character and role of philosophical reflection: *An Essay on Philosophical Method* and *An Essay on Metaphysics*. In the light of this revival one might have expected that his views on the role and character of philosophical analysis would have been revisited, but this has not happened. One of the reasons for this neglect may be due to the fact that the conception of metaphysics he defends is very different from the predominant conception of the nature and task of metaphysical inquiry. Collingwood thought metaphysics to be a logical, not an ontological inquiry, and the task of conceptual analysis in metaphysics to be that of uncovering presuppositions, rather than attempting to limn the nature of being. The end of the twentieth century, by contrast, has witnessed a return of what might be called heavy-duty metaphysics and with this a philosophical atmosphere that is not naturally receptive to his message. But even these considerations are not sufficient to explain the situation. There have been several attempts to rethink ontological questions beyond the confines of a traditional conception of metaphysics that have become highly topical and popular in philosophical circles, but Collingwood's views have not informed them, in spite of the fact that, amongst the attempts to rethink the role of conceptual analysis in metaphysics, he stands out as championing the positive contribution that philosophy can make, rather than simply highlighting primarily its destructive role in exposing the errors that a commitment to a conception of metaphysics as the science of pure being can lead.

Another reason for this neglect may have to do with the fact that while there is now an extensive and growing body of literature on Collingwood, Collingwood studies have, understandably, tended to focus on the internal development of his thought, rather than enlisting him up as an ally in a particular cause. This was the view of W. H. Dray, whose work mobilized Collingwood in order to challenge the idea of the unity of science. In a note that he asked to be read at the 2007 conference on Collingwood and Twentieth Century Philosophy in Montreal, which he could not attend for health reasons, Dray urged Collingwood scholars to reach out beyond the closed walls of Collingwood's scholarship. This book responds to this exhortation and seeks to explain why he matters. It argues that what Collingwood has to say matters because it sheds light on the nature of the relation between scientific knowledge and humanistic understanding. Collingwood shows that the progress of natural science does not pose a threat to humanistic understanding because the natural sciences and the humanities seek answers to different questions. And since they answer different questions they cannot be said to compete with one another. The main thesis of this book is that what Collingwood has to say matters because he addresses one of the most urgent questions since the rise of modern science, namely whether the day will come when the humanities will wither away as a result of scientific progress. Because this is not a book about debates within Collingwood scholarship, I have not spent a great deal of time rebutting what is still a prevalent reading of Collingwood as a historical relativist or radical historicist, a reading which, in my view, still constitutes one of the greatest obstacles in the way of appreciating the nature of his argument against scientism and the significance of his contribution to our understanding of what it is that we do, when we do metaphysics. I defended Collingwood against the charge of historical relativism/radical historicism in *Collingwood and the Metaphysics of Experience* (2002), where I argued that this interpretation is in large part due to a failure to recognize the continuities between his earlier and later metaphilosophical treatises. While I still stand by that claim, the focus here is on *An Essay on Metaphysics* and how this later contribution to the nature and role of philosophical analysis enables us to understand the relation between the humanities and natural science, as well as the relation between philosophy and science. As this book tries to show, these two things go together: a conception of philosophy as the underlabourer of science can only generate very emaciated defences of the autonomy of the human sciences which hardly deserve to be called 'non-reductivist'. Formulating a form of non-reductivism that is genuinely pluralistic from an explanatory point of view requires one to rethink nothing less than the role and character of philosophical analysis. Exploring Collingwood's conception of philosophy, asking what it does, and how it helps us to undo certain conceptual tangles, is fruitful not least because it shows that there are very different ways in which the argument for non-reductivism could be formulated. As an undergraduate I was attracted by the philosophy of mind; it seemed something relevant and interesting to focus on. But I moved away because I was left with the distinct impression that very little was actually said about the mind in the philosophy of mind. I was left dissatisfied by all the non-reductivist options that were presented and could not quite grasp how, for example, 'multiple realization functionalism' could be hailed as one of the most promising forms of non-reductivism. Years have gone by and the situation does not seem to have changed. Panpsychism may have taken the place of multiple realization functionalism as the most promising critique of physicalism, but that does not seem to have reintroduced the concept of mind into the philosophy of mind. One of the things this book tries to show is that there is a different way to approach the concept of mind, and it turns to Collingwood to explain how the non-reductivist's questions have to be reformulated in order to do justice to the concept of mind.

Collingwood looked to history rather than psychology as the form of inquiry whose subject matter is mind. Psychology, for Collingwood is a *natural* science, and, as such, not a good place to start if one wants to study the mind. Where you finally arrive is often determined by where you begin, and it is Collingwood's view that an examination of the concept of mind cannot begin from a reflection on a discipline, like psychology, whose methods are closer to those of the experimental sciences. I hope this book will be of some help to those undergraduate students who are interested in the philosophy of mind, who do not want to subscribe to some form of transcendentalism or be accused of being surreptitiously committed to it, but who nonetheless cannot identify with any of the non-reductivist positions currently on offer in their philosophy of mind module guide. I might, after all, have persevered with the philosophy of mind, if there had been a non-reductivist position with which I could comfortably have identified. It was, however, with some hesitation that I set out engaging Collingwood with current debates in the philosophy of mind. I could not, *and still cannot*, shake off the feeling of inadequacy that arises from the fact that I am trespassing on someone else's territory and that I cannot possibly do justice to the complexities of the field. For this very reason the book almost did not see the light of day. It should have been written in 2008 as a result of an Arts and Humanities Research fellowship, and although a draft was produced, which was later condensed into a couple of chapters of the present book, at the time I could not quite gather the courage required to point out that the emperor has no clothes, and that, paradoxically, much contemporary philosophy of mind effectively ignores the concept of mind itself.

In spite of these lingering doubts and hesitations I finally gathered the courage to relate Collingwood directly to these contemporary debates since I concluded that the problem did not simply lie with my limited ability to do justice to the complexities of the answers given to the question of the place of mind in nature (something which is of course true) but also, and crucially, with the question itself, and the presuppositions which give rise to it. If there is one thing that Collingwood teaches us, it is that examining the questions we ask is often more important than debating the answers that are given in answer to those questions. If it were not for this thought, I would probably never have written a book premised on the argument that the question of the place of mind in nature is the wrong question to ask.

I have tried to write in an accessible style that does not presuppose much background knowledge of Collingwood. I hope this was not a mistake since (and on this particular point, although not on very much else), I agree with John Heil that if one writes clearly and simply one incurs the risk of being understood.

Many of the book's themes have been explored in a number of articles or chapters, in particular 'Two dogmas of contemporary philosophy of action' (*Journal of the Philosophy of History* 2007 [1]: 11–26); 'The gap is semantic, not epistemological' (*Ratio* 2007, XX[2]2: 168–78); 'Davidson and the autonomy of the human sciences' (in Jeff Malpas [ed.] *Dialogues with Davidson: New Perspectives on His Philosophy*, 2011, MIT Press, pp. 283–96); 'Reasons and causes: The philosophical battle and the metaphilosophical war' (*Australasian Journal of Philosophy* 2012, 90[2]: 207–21); 'Unlikely bedfellows: Collingwood, Carnap and the internal/external distinction' (*British Journal for the History of Philosophy* 2015, 23[4]: 802–17); 'Collingwood's idealist metaontology: Between therapy and armchair science' (in D'Oro G. and Overgaard S. [eds] *The Cambridge Companion to Philosophical Methodology*, CUP 2017) 'The touch of King Midas: Collingwood on why actions are not events' (*Philosophical Explorations*, 2018, 21[1]: 1–10); 'Why explanatory pluralism does not entail relativism' (in Dharamsi, K., D'Oro G. and Leach S. [eds] *Collingwood on Philosophical Methodology*, Palgrave 2018); 'Non-reductivism and the metaphilosophy of mind' with Paul Giladi and Alexis Papazoglou (*Inquiry* 2019, 62[5]: 477–503); 'Beyond narrativism: the historical past and why it can be known' with Jonas Ahlskog (*Collingwood and British Idealism Studies* 2021, 27[1]: 5–33); 'Imagination and Revision' with Jonas Ahlskog (in *The Routledge Companion to History and Theory*, C. M. van den Akker [ed.], Routledge 2021). However, with the exception of Chapter 8, which reproduces large sections of 'In defence of a humanistically oriented historiography: the nature/culture distinction at the time of the Anthropocene' (in Matti-Kuukkanen J. [ed.], *Philosophy of History: Twenty-First-Century*

Perspectives. Bloomsbury 2020, pp. 216–36) and reprinted with permission of the publisher, the book has been conceived as a fresh and independent contribution.

I owe a debt of gratitude to many people and institutions. I should thank first of all Rex Martin and David Boucher for their encouragement when I first started focusing my research on Collingwood, the Centre for Collingwood Studies and British Idealism in Cardiff and later, the Centre for Idealism and the New Liberalism at Hull for providing numerous opportunities to present papers in the magical surroundings of Gregynog Hall. My thanks also go to James Connelly for many conversations over the years and to more recent collaborators, Jonas Ahlskog and Jouni-Matti Kuukkanen, who have rekindled my interest in philosophy of history. The contents of the book have been presented at many conferences and staff seminars, and it is often the questions and objections raised by the audiences that have spurred me on to expose the presuppositions on which many of the misunderstandings of Collingwood's conception of the role of philosophical analysis and the nature of his critique of scientism are based. If I succeeded in presenting the ideas in an accessible way then I owe this to several generations of third-year philosophy students at Keele, who have pushed me to make clear the relevance of what Collingwood says to what they studied elsewhere in the course. My thanks also go to the series editor, Constantine Sandis, for creating the opportunity to write this kind of book. Last, but not least, I should thank my long-suffering partner, Mark, and my daughter, Ceri, who, since a very young age, displayed a very keen sense of what kind of answers would be good enough to satisfy her curiosity.

1

The struggle against scientism

One would not normally expect a quantum physicist to be able to speak intelligently about the causes of the First World War, just as one would not expect an Egyptologist to speak intelligently about the nature of quarks. If you want to know about quarks ask a physicist, and if you want to know about the First World War ask a historian instead. It would seem to be common sense that the methods that a palaeontologist uses to study the fossilized remains of long extinct animal species, or an astronomer uses to investigate the death of a star, are not ideally suited to identify the causes of the First World War or the significance of Caesar's crossing of the Rubicon. They are not suited to this task because they are not meant to answer the kind of questions that historians typically ask. The point is not that the methods of the palaeontologist or that of the astronomer are somewhat lacking because they are unable to answer the questions posed by historians, but that they are meant to answer different kinds of questions.

Yet, on a particular model of the relationship holding between forms of knowledge – which goes under the name of the layered view of the sciences – there are certain ways of getting to know the world that yield superior explanations, capture more accurately what there really is, have greater predictive power and should ideally be applied across the board. On this view, the science which has been most successful in explaining and predicting – this is usually taken to be physics – should take over the task of answering all questions, including those which are not normally thought of as being questions that could be answered by the adoption of its methods. This of course is a rather simplistic way of putting things but it captures what is normally meant by the term scientism, i.e. the illegitimate extension of the methods of natural science into the domain of inquiry of the humanities. Much of Collingwood's later work is devoted to providing a defence of the autonomy of historical explanations, of the view that historical explanations are humanistic explanations which address and answer different kinds of questions from those asked and answered by physicists. The historical past, he claimed, cannot be understood by the methods of science any more than the natural past can be known by the methods of the humanities. But Collingwood did not simply provide an argument against scientism as it is normally (and narrowly) construed, that is, as the illegitimate encroachment of the methods of natural science onto the territory of the humanities. He also provided an argument against scientism construed more broadly, as the trespassing of *any* form of knowledge onto the territory of another. On this broader construal of scientism, the attempt to reduce all knowledge to historical knowledge is as insidious as the better-known argument for the reduction of all knowledge to scientific knowledge. This book presents Collingwood as providing an argument against scientism both narrowly and broadly construed, as defending the autonomy of scientific knowledge as much as that of humanistic understanding. It argues that Collingwood's critique of scientism narrowly construed – the attempt to impose the methods of science onto those of the humanities – does not aim to bring about an epistemic role reversal and to bestow onto history the title to which science aspires, namely to be a 'first science' in the epistemological sense. What should be acknowledged instead is that history and science ask different kinds of questions, which seek to satisfy different kinds of curiosities and that, for this very reason, do not compete with one another, since explanatory answers can compete with one another only if they are in fact addressing one and the same question. The task of philosophy is precisely that of bringing about the realization that physics, as the most basic of all natural sciences, and history, as exemplifying humanistic understanding, are not in conflict because the humanities and the natural sciences ask and answer different kinds of questions.

This, I argue, is why Collingwood matters. He matters because he challenged scientism both narrowly construed, as the trespassing of science onto the territory of the humanities, and broadly construed, as the attempt of any form of knowledge to impose its methods across the epistemic spectrum.

The key claim of this book, namely that Collingwood matters because he provides an argument against scientism both narrowly and broadly construed, goes against the grain of a reading of Collingwood that has been, and still is, rather prevalent. According to this reading Collingwood's defence of the autonomy of humanistic understanding, his argument against scientism in the narrow sense was motivated by the desire to bring about a sort of epistemological coup aimed at reversing the power relations between science and history, whilst leaving the general structures of domination intact. On this reading, which is still widespread, Collingwood is a sort of historical fundamentalist or radical historicist who aims to displace science from the position of epistemic privilege it has acquired in modernity and, having dethroned it, now attempts to install history in its place.

There is an extensive body of literature on Collingwood's alleged commitment to what I have called historical fundamentalism. The view that Collingwood is a radical historicist has a long and prestigious pedigree. It has been defended by Donagan (1962 and 1972), Rotenstreich (1972), Toulmin (1972) and more recently by Bernard Williams (2006c) and Adrian Moore (2012), to mention only a few relevant authors.[1] This alleged commitment to radical historicism is often, although not exclusively, discussed in the context of an account of the development of his thought, according to which the late work *An Essay on Metaphysics* marked a radical break from his earlier writings. The interpretative claim that often goes under the name of the radical conversion hypothesis tends to overlook the continuities between Collingwood's earlier metaphilosophical treatise

---

[1] For a discussion of the literature on the radical conversion hypothesis, see Browning (2004, chapter 1).

An Essay on Philosophical Method (1933) and *An Essay on Metaphysics* (1940). Both treatises share the same view of the task of philosophical analysis as that of achieving conceptual clarity and both outline a conception of philosophy as a logical inquiry whose task is to make explicit what is implicitly known, rather than as a genetic inquiry into how knowledge originates under certain socio-historical conditions; they are concerned with the context of justification, not the context of discovery. The historicist reading has unfortunately obscured the nature of Collingwood's critique of scientism and detracted from his defence of humanistic understanding, a defence which stands out precisely because it does not advocate an inverted scientism. The historicist reading has not gone entirely unchallenged. The idea of a radical break and a later historicist turn has been subjected to criticism by Rex Martin (1989), James Connelly (1990 and 2003), Tariq Modood (1989), Adrian Oldfield (1995), myself (2010 and 2018b) amongst others. I have also defended the continuity between *An Essay on Philosophical Method* and *An Essay on Metaphysics* in *Collingwood and the Metaphysics of Experience* (D'Oro 2002). I will not revisit this interpretative controversy here. This book presents Collingwood as an explanatory pluralist whose goal was to articulate an argument against scientism, and shows how his conception of metaphysics as the study of presuppositions informs his unique conception of the relation between different forms of knowledge, a conception which explains why humanistic understanding and scientific knowledge do not compete.

If the standard interpretation were correct, then Collingwood would not be merely contesting scientism in the narrow sense; he would also be undermining science in the name of a commitment to a form of scientism in the broader sense of the term. This is not the way this book presents either what Collingwood says, or why what he says matters. Collingwood was not an enemy of science, and to confuse his argument against scientism (narrowly construed) with an attempt to historicize scientific knowledge is a mistake. He matters precisely because, instead of turning the epistemic power relations between scientific knowledge and humanistic understanding upside down, he seeks to show that both forms of knowing are equally important, and that it is a mistake to judge either one of them by the standards of the other. His defence of the autonomy of historical in relation to scientific knowledge shows that in philosophy, just as in politics, it is not enough to depose the dictator in order to get rid of the dictatorship.

The danger of scientism lurks whenever there are concepts that are contested by different forms of knowing. The concept of mind is one such concept because it is claimed by both science and the humanities. Neurophysiologists who investigate activity in the brain claim to be explaining the mind. Egyptologists who explain the ritual of mummification by referring to the ancient Egyptians' cult of the afterlife see themselves as explaining the mindset of this ancient people. So who is right: the neurophysiologist who describes the causal processes of the brain or the historian who makes sense of the ancient Egyptians' ritual of embalming their dead by invoking the cult of the afterlife? Questions such as this one erroneously assume that the neurophysiologist and the historian are talking about the same thing, and that since they are talking about the same thing, their explanations must be in competition with one another, unless one can be shown to be reducible to the other, that is, unless it could be shown that speaking about the Egyptians' cult of the afterlife is reducible to talk about neurons. In fact, these explanations do not conflict because they home in on a completely different explanandum. It is the task of philosophy to disambiguate the explananda of the neurophysiologist (qua natural scientist) and of the historian (qua humanistic inquirer). In showing that there is no conflict between neurophysiological explanations and humanistic explanations, philosophy deflates the conflict between science and the humanities. The task of philosophy precisely is to bring about the realization that this kind of conflict arises because of the failure to disambiguate the explananda of different forms of knowledge.

Some might think that there is indeed a conflict between humanistic and scientific explanations, and that the conflict should be solved, not dissolved by showing that it is only an apparent conflict. They might also think that if the task of philosophy is not to look for a solution to the conflict between different explanatory frameworks, there is not much, or at least not much of any importance, for philosophy to do. But this would be an erroneous inference. When it comes to contested concepts failure to make the relevant distinctions can get us into a great deal of trouble, and not just *philosophical* trouble. Consider, for example, the concept of 'responsibility' and the case of Alec Baldwin, the actor who accidentally shot dead a cinematographer and injured a director by firing a prop gun on set of the film *Rust*. He clearly was *causally* responsible for the death of the cinematographer who he killed by firing the gun and for injuring the director. But whether he was *morally* responsible for the cinematographer's death will depend on what information he was given when handed over the prop gun, whether he knew the gun to be loaded or to be safe. If no distinction were made between *causal* and *moral* responsibility, there would be no need to conduct a review of safety regulations on the film set to determine whether Alec Baldwin had been careless or not, since the matter of whether he was causally responsible for the killing is not what is in dispute. Indeed, without such a distinction the question as to whether he was morally culpable would not arise. Only once the concept of 'responsibility' is duly disambiguated, can the question 'Is Alec Baldwin *morally* as well as *causally* responsible?' arise. These notions of responsibility, qua causal and qua moral, belong to different spheres of competency. It is the task of forensics to ascertain whether the gun that delivered the fatal bullet was the one fired by Alec Baldwin, but it is not the task of forensics to establish whether Alec Baldwin was morally culpable for the killing. Philosophy enables us to achieve conceptual clarity concerning the application of concepts, and the spheres of knowledge to which they belong. But it would be a mistake to think that achieving conceptual clarity is a pedantic exercise that does not have important implications in real life. If there were no distinction between kinds of responsibility, there would be no possible basis for the argument that Alec Baldwin should not be served a prison sentence. Redefining the fundamental task of metaphysics as that of achieving conceptual clarity rather than that of acquiring knowledge of the fundamental structures of reality does not entail that philosophy does not have important things to do.

What is distinctive about Collingwood's attempt to disambiguate contested concepts, concepts which are claimed by different spheres of knowledge, is that he denies that any one of the senses with which they are associated is the true or real sense, whereas the others are not. Discussing the concept of cause, he claims that this concept is supple, that it has different meanings in different explanatory contexts. For example (not Collingwood's own), a coroner and a political journalist are both interested in the causes of JFK's death. But they will give very different explanations in answer to the question concerning the cause of his death. On Collingwood's conception of philosophical analysis, whether one selects the notion of causation embedded in the coroner's explanation or that embedded in the explanation of the political journalist will depend on what it is one is trying to explain. It is not the case that the explanation of the coroner captures the 'real causes' and that of the political journalist does not. It is the philosophical tendency to identify one sense of causation as real – normally the notion of causation that is at work in the explanations provided by physics – that gives rise to the problems of causal overdetermination and explanatory exclusion that daunt much contemporary metaphysics. For if only one of the contested senses of causation is real, then one explanation must be true and the other false. It cannot both be the case, for example, that JFK died of a brain haemorrhage, as a coroner might conclude after her examination, and that his death was caused by a political conspiracy, as an investigative journalist might claim. It is precisely the philosophical tendency to identify one sense of causation as real, and the associated form of explanation as epistemically privileged, that lies at the heart of philosophical disputes in the philosophy of mind and metaphysics.

To bring home the importance of disambiguating contested concepts, compare the concept of cause to that of another ambiguous and potentially contested concept: the concept of parent. The concept of parent has two meanings. It can mean *biological* parent, when used to denote the genetic ancestry of an individual. But an *adoptive* parent is also a parent. When used in conjunction with the adjective 'adoptive' parent means a kind of primary carer. The two meanings of 'parent', i.e. genetic ancestor and carer, often coincide since those who care for their children also tend to be their biological parents, but they are not the same concept. The concept 'parent' is therefore ambiguous with either of its meanings potentially claimed as the true or real one. We can imagine a child accusing their biological parents of not being 'real' parents on the grounds that they neglect their caring duties. Equally one can imagine a child who recently discovered a genetic ancestry kept hidden from them accusing their adoptive parents of not being their 'real' parents. The dispute (if it were to arise) between those who claim that biological parents are the real parents, and those who claim that a true parent is a carer, is one of those cases where our thoughts get into tangles. Collingwood speaks of philosophy as undoing these tangles by putting our questions and answers in logical order, as we shall see in the next chapter when discussing his account of presuppositions. What he would be likely to say is that choosing one concept of parent or the other (biological ancestor or carer) depends on the context. When optometrists carrying out an eye examination ask their patients 'is there any history of glaucoma in the family?' they are asking whether there are instances of this condition in the *biological* parents and grandparents of the person undergoing an eye examination. They are concerned with biological parenthood. But the reason why they are invoking the concept of biological ancestor rather than that of carer is *not* because they think that the *biological* parents are the real parents and the *adoptive* parents are not, but because they are concerned with a particular kind of natural/genetic history.

Analogously, the reason why the physicist, the coroner and the investigative journalist are selecting a particular notion of cause, for Collingwood, has nothing to do with it being real in some absolute sense. The concept of causation is selected in the light of its fitness to answer the questions one is seeking an answer to. Just as it would be no use to an optometrist to know whether there is any history of glaucoma in relation to a patient's adoptive parents, so suggesting that JFK died of a brain haemorrhage does not answer the question that the investigative journalist wants answered, namely who had motive to kill him. Understanding how contested concepts operate in different explanatory contexts eases the conflict between different kinds of explanations. It is the assumption that one sense of the term 'cause', just as one sense of the term 'parent', captures the true or real concept that generates the impulse either to eliminate what is deemed to be the least basic explanation or reduce it to the most basic one by privileging one conception of causation. An important characteristic of Collingwood's handling of contested concepts is that he dismissed the question as to which concept is real as nonsensical, a point which, as we shall see in the next chapter, he makes by saying that there is no sense in asking whether the presuppositions that govern certain forms of inquiry are true or false.

Collingwood dedicated a great deal of his philosophical career to disentangling contested concepts. One such concept was that of the past. Like the concept of 'parent' the concept of the past is ambiguous and is claimed by natural science as well as the humanities. By 'the past' one can mean the evolutionary past of a biological species. In this case the past is the object of investigation of natural science. By 'the past' one can also mean what is studied by historians of ancient civilizations. In this case the past refers to different cultures and tends to be the object of investigation of history understood as humanistic discipline. A humanistic concern with the past is very different from a scientific concern. The methods adopted by a palaeontologist who studies the fossilized remains of extinct species with a view to mapping their evolutionary development is very different from that of an historian who studies the Egyptian civilization and their cult of the afterlife. For a long time the idea of a distinctively *historical* past had not been recognized. The idea of history as an autonomous form of inquiry with a unique subject matter emerged only as the concept of the past was disambiguated to allow for the distinction between the natural past, the past as known by the methods of science, and the historical past, the past known by investigating the cultural context, the 'mindset' of past historical agents. The idea of history as a form of knowing distinct from scientific knowledge, for Collingwood, requires us to disambiguate the historical from the natural past. The concept of the past is therefore one which is claimed by both natural science and the humanities. Just as the concept of 'parent' has different meanings depending on whether it is qualified by the adjectives 'biological' or 'adoptive', so the concept of the past has radically different meanings if it is qualified by the adjectives 'natural'/'evolutionary' or 'historical'. Evolutionary history and the history of ancient civilizations are both histories, but only in the sense in which both a bean burger and a beef burger are kinds of burger. The beef burger and the bean burger have in common the fact they are kinds of patties or fritters. Likewise evolutionary history and what tends to be called simply 'history' have in common the fact that the objects that they study lie in the past, but the methods by which they come to know what lies in the past are as different as the ingredients contained in the beef and the bean burger. Even when they apparently seem to be homing in onto one and the same thing, they never capture the same explanandum. When evolutionary history focuses on the human Past, it focuses on the concept of human as a biological being. It is concerned with discovering the genetic past of humans, whether, for example, there is Neanderthal DNA in modern humans. When history as a humanistic discipline focuses on past civilizations, it is concerned with humans insofar as they are the kind of beings who developed legal systems and civilizations, forged treatises and alliances which they took to be binding, but which they occasionally transgressed. The humanistic-oriented historian is concerned with norms of conduct which are likely to vary from time to time, not with timeless natural laws which apply across all times and places. Forensic scientists, for example, can use DNA information to retrodict the eye colour of a Neanderthal individual with the same techniques that they use to predict the eye colour of a present-day criminal by saliva samples left at a crime scene. Humanistic-oriented historians, by contrast, cannot assume that past agents were responsive to the same legal norms as the historians' own contemporaries.

When the distinction between natural laws and norms is overlooked, the past becomes a contested concept. Much of the literature which has sprung from the concept of the Anthropocene, as we shall see in

Chapter 8, claims that the history of civilizations, far from being a distinctive kind of history that focuses on a unique kind of *historical* past, is just a chapter in, or small time fragment of, the natural history of the planet. The history of past civilizations, on this view, is not a distinctive kind of inquiry that is concerned with a certain kind of agent, one who is responsive to norms rather than subject to laws. There is only one kind of past, the natural past, and one kind of agent: historical agents are no different in kind from agents in chemical reactions whose behaviour is understood not as responsive to norms but as subject to scientific laws. In this context the task of disambiguating the concept of the past is therefore important to make sense of the different interests that the humanistically oriented historian and the evolutionary historian have in times gone by. What seems to be particularly difficult in the case of contested concepts, concepts which are claimed as territory by different ways of knowing, is that there is no specific class of things by reference to which such concepts can be told apart. There is no determinate class of actions which instantiate the concept of moral responsibility in contrast to that of causal responsibility: a shooting, for example, could be a case of murder as well as of accidental killing. And there are no two such things as the biological humans who lived at the time of the Egyptians and the Egyptians in the sense of the ancient civilization which developed an elaborate cult of the afterlife which found expression in the erection of the pyramids and the mummification of the dead. The concepts of the historical and the natural past are nonetheless distinct concepts; and distinguishing them is precisely the task of philosophical analysis. Amongst the contested concepts which Collingwood seeks to clarify are concepts such as those of 'reasons', 'cause' and 'action' which, like the concept of 'parent', 'responsibility', 'past' can have different meanings. We say things like 'the reason why the river flooded was unusually high rainfall'. We also say that political ambition was the reason for Caesar's crossing of the Rubicon. The term 'reasons' here is used in different ways to mean, on the one hand, an antecedent condition, the rainfall and, on the other, a motive. Failing to disambiguate these different meanings is analogous to the failure to distinguish the meaning of responsibility in the causal and moral sense. Philosophy is a kind of trouble shooter that is called in when our concepts go awry. Its most important role is to monitor those concepts that are contested across the sciences and the humanities and thus to establish what kind of questions can be answered by the one and what kind of questions can be answered by the other.

Collingwood's argument against scientism and his defence of the autonomy of humanistic understanding is based on his views of the role and character of philosophical analysis. Chapter 2 (Philosophy as disentanglement) sets out to explain what it is that philosophy does. Philosophy undoes conceptual knots. These conceptual tangles occur if questions and answers are misaligned, something which tends to happen when explanations of one kind are assumed to be answering questions of a different kind. Philosophy undoes these tangles by aligning explanatory answers to their questions, and questions to the presuppositions which give rise to them. In contrast to the dominant conception of metaphysics as the study of the ultimate structures of reality, Collingwood sees the fundamental role of conceptual analysis in metaphysics to be that of uncovering the presuppositions that inform different forms of knowledge. All knowledge, he claims, rests on some presupposition or other, and there is no such thing as presuppositionless knowledge or knowledge of pure being. In saying this he is not endorsing a form of epistemic humility according to which pure being is inaccessible to finite minds. He is making the rather different claim that talk of presuppositionless knowledge, if taken literally, is a misnomer because presuppositionless knowledge is not a kind of knowledge at all; it is not the sort of knowledge that could only be enjoyed, for example, by a being with an infinite mind. Since there is no such thing as presuppositionless knowledge of pure being, the presuppositions which govern forms of knowledge are not true or false of an inquiry-independent reality or pure being. Indeed to ask whether the fundamental presuppositions which govern forms of knowledge are true or false is to ask a nonsensical question because true or false claims arise within forms of inquiry, once certain criteria about what it means to explain something are presupposed. Since the notion of pure being plays no role in Collingwood's metaphysics, the choice between different kinds of explanations (and the presuppositions on which they rest) is made not by invoking the notion of pure being but that of fitness for purpose: one chooses the explanation which satisfies one's curiosity and answers the kind of question one wants answered. Collingwood's metaphysics of presuppositions therefore supports a form of explanatory pluralism which is committed to the claim that explanation is contextual and varies in accordance with the goals of inquiry, not a form of epistemic relativism which suggests that knowledge claims are relative to the subject (however narrowly or broadly the subject is construed).

As an explanatory pluralist Collingwood is also, clearly, a non-reductivist. His non-reductivism is however very different from the best known and most successful forms of non-reductivism in twentieth-century analytic philosophy of mind. Most forms of non-reductivism in contemporary philosophy of mind are not forms of explanatory pluralism in Collingwood's sense because they operate with a homogeneous concept of causation and thus with a unitary notion of what it means to explain something. Chapter 3 (Causal exclusion and the elephant in the room) explores the distinctive nature of Collingwood's defence of the autonomy of the mental, a defence which is based on the claim that explanation must be fit for purpose and that choosing which concept of causation (which kind of explanation to adopt) depends on one's explanatory goals. In contrast with Collingwood's explanatory pluralism, twentieth-century forms of non-reductivism operate with a monolithic concept of causation which does not acknowledge that different forms of inquiry operate with different kinds of explanation. They also operate with a layered/hierarchical model of the relation between the sciences. In this layered model, physics, as the most basic science, takes over from metaphysics, as traditionally conceived, the title of the science of pure being (of being as such). Explanations in physics, unlike the explanations in the special sciences, chemistry, biology, psychology and so on are deemed to capture metaphysically real relations. Forms of non-reductivism which operate with a unitary notion of causation and a layered model of the sciences encounter the problem of causal exclusion. They see the task of philosophy, in its role as the underlabourer of science, to be that of accounting for how one might reconcile the explanations in the upper layers (chemistry, biology, psychology) with those of physics and what adjustments may have to be made to avoid conflict between them. Contemporary non-reductivism blatantly fails to address the elephant in the room, i.e. the consideration that the concept of mind is a normative or, as Collingwood puts it, a criteriological concept (Collingwood 1938: 171, note to p. 164) and that 'mentalistic' explanations are not simply nomological explanations which invoke psychological, rather than physical, chemical or biological laws, but altogether different kinds of sense-making explanations which invoke a completely different notion of causation and answer radically different kinds of questions. Unlike most forms of contemporary non-reductivism in the philosophy of mind, Collingwood's defence of the methodological autonomy of the mental rests on a commitment to the thesis of the disunity of science, according to which humanistic explanations of actions have a different logical form from nomological explanations of events. Humanistic explanations do not merely invoke different concepts (the concepts of beliefs or desires rather than those of atoms or molecules). They have a completely different understanding of what it means for one thing to cause another.

It is when one seeks to interpret the actions of past agents that one realizes that explanations which invoke general laws, whether those of physics or psychology, are unsuited to the task at hand, since the actions of past historical agents are unintelligible when considered in abstraction from the norms of conduct to which they held themselves accountable. It is therefore to history, not to psychology, that Collingwood turns to articulate a defence of the autonomy of the mental. His explanatory pluralism exposes the way in which the word 'science' has come to be used, viz. as a loose equivalent for 'natural science', as symptomatic of the position of privilege which scientific explanations enjoy in the layered/hierarchical model of the sciences.

Collingwood aims to reinstate the use of 'science' in the original Latin sense of *scientia*, as a form of knowledge with a distinctive method and subject matter. History is a form of knowledge in the Latin sense of the term *scientia* (cf. Collingwood 1940: 4), not in the contemporary sense, which assimilates science to natural science, just as drink has become synonymous with alcoholic drink. It is the true 'science' of the mind because it is in history that one finds humanistic explanations with a distinctive logical form which deploy a sense of causation that differs from the causal explanations at work in physics and other natural sciences.

Unlike contemporary forms of non-reductivism in the philosophy of mind Collingwood's explanatory pluralism does not take the explanations of physics to be ontologically basic and epistemically privileged. As a result, his non-reductivism does not face the problem of causal exclusion and does not need to answer the question of the place of mind in nature, a question that arises for forms of non-reductivism which operate with a homogeneous notion of causation and a layered view of the sciences. Collingwood's conception of philosophy as a form of presuppositional analysis involves a form of non-reductivism which is genuinely pluralistic because it is aimed at uncovering the chains of questions and answers characteristic of different forms of inquiry. Rather than seeking to solve the problem of causal exclusion and answer the question of the place of mind in nature he urges a re-examination of the fundamental questions that a philosophy of mind should be addressing.

A clear implication of Collingwood's explanatory pluralism is that there are some questions that science should not try to answer. It should not, for example, try to answer the question of why Paul went to town if addressing this question requires explaining what the *point* of Paul's trip is (for example, to pay a visit to the fishmonger). The fact that there is no scientific answer to questions of this kind is not, however, a deficiency of the scientific method per se, precisely because this is not the kind of question that science *aims to* address. It would therefore be inappropriate to view the 'inability' of science to answer the question of the humanities as a limit on the reach or extent of scientific knowledge. The error rather lies in the expectation that science should be able to answer all questions. Yet, more often than not, the claim that science should not try to answer all questions is received with suspicion, as an inappropriate attempt to limit the reach of scientific knowledge and open the door to the existence of spooky transcendent entities. Chapter 4 (The 'limits' of science) examines two assumptions that tend to govern much contemporary philosophy in relation to the issue of the limits of science. The first is that what lies beyond the capacities of science to explain is mysterious in a suspicious kind of way. The idea of an insoluble mystery (as opposed to a soluble one) is often understood in relation to what is in principle beyond, in contrast to what is in principle within, the power of science to solve. This way of thinking about the nature of insoluble mysteries is the legacy of logical positivism, according to which all genuine problems and disputes can in principle be solved empirically. Those problems or disputes that cannot be settled, at least in principle, if not in practice, by adopting the methods of science (disputes, for example, about whether God does or does not exist, or whether entities such as tables and chairs are real or ideal) are pseudo-mysteries or problems that one should dismiss rather than try to solve. Collingwood rejects this way of characterizing what is mysterious in relation to what is and isn't within the power of science to explain. Murder mysteries, for example, are not pseudo-mysteries, even if they cannot be solved by a physicist. Of course the tools of science can be mobilized to assist Mrs Marple in identifying the guilty party, by providing her with forensic evidence, but forensic science cannot answer the question as to who had motive to kill, as there are no motives in physics. But it does not follow from the fact that physics can offer no solution to murder mysteries that they pose unanswerable and suspicious pseudo-questions; they are just not the kind of mysteries that are within the remit of physics to solve. Collingwood would agree with the sort of consideration that A. J. Ayer (1934; 1936) made in the context of his critique of traditional metaphysical disputes, namely that a dispute is genuine if there are criteria appeal to which would enable us to establish what a true or false answer to a question is. He would however disagree with the logical positivist's claim that there is only one such criterion, namely the principle of verification as the logical positivists conceived it. Just as the criteria required to settle whether answers to mathematical questions are true or false are not the same as the criteria required to settle empirical disputes, so for Collingwood, the criteria to which one appeals to establish who had motive to eliminate Sergei Skripal are not the same as those which are invoked to decide between competing theories in physics. The question that the political journalist investigating the poisoning of Sergei Skripal is trying to answer (who had motive to eliminate him?) is not an unanswerable metaphysical question. There are genuine mysteries that are not within the remit of physics to solve. The fact that there are mysteries which physics cannot solve does not make the questions of the political journalist unanswerable, like the questions of traditional metaphysics in Ayer's view. Nor does it point to a deficiency of the method of physics since murder mysteries are not the sort of mysteries that physics should be tasked to solve.

There is another key assumption that underpins the discussion of the limits of science in contemporary philosophy of mind. This assumption is that consciousness is the most mysterious of all things, the last stop on the journey of scientific knowledge. The reason why consciousness is normally taken to pose a hard if not intractable problem from a scientific perspective is that conscious states have a distinctive first personal mode of access which creates an insurmountable explanatory gap. Much philosophy of mind accepts the Cartesian distinction between inner mental states and outward bodily movements and construes the distinction between the mind and the body as a distinction between the inner and the outer. While Collingwood has been often criticized for recreating this inner/outer distinction, in reality he views the nature of the obstacle that impedes the naturalization of the mind in a very different way. He agrees that there is an explanatory gap between the concepts of mind and body, actions and events. But the reason why actions remain beyond the power of science to explain is not because conscious states, being inner, rather than outer, are accessed in a different way from bodily movements, but rather because to identify something as an action requires a distinctive form of explanation, one that rationalizes it by invoking a different sense of causation. The mind body gap, for Collingwood, is semantic, not epistemological: we mean different things when we say that she raised her hand *because* she wanted to ask a question and when we say the water froze *because* the temperature dropped. Actions and events are sui generis, and involve irreducible categories. The concept of action is the correlative of rationalizing explanations while the concept of event is the correlative of a nomological explanation. Rather than accepting the distinction between the inner and the outer which has governed the discussion of the limits of science in philosophy of mind, he urges us to rethink the question posed by the mind-body problem as a question about the distinctive concerns of the human and natural sciences and the methodologies needed to answer their distinctive questions.

It is in history, for Collingwood, not in psychology that one finds the sort of questions which are genuinely representative of humanistic concerns. Chapter 5 (History as the study of mind) undertakes to explain why Collingwood believes that history, not psychology, is the study of mind. History, as Collingwood understands it, should not be confused with the academic discipline taught in university departments. It is rather a form of knowledge, a mode of inquiry which homes in on a specific explanandum: action. Its subject matter partially overlaps with what is taught and studied in university departments but it is not the same. Practising historians use a variety of explanations which deploy different senses of 'cause'. When talking about how Pompei came to an end, they explain its destruction in the way in which a scientist explains natural phenomena in the past. Pompei came to an end because of Vesuvius' explosion, which covered it in ashes, just as the dinosaurs became extinct as a result of the impact of a meteorite which covered the Earth in dust. One would certainly not expect practising historians to explain the end of Pompei in any other way. But there is also a distinctive way of looking at the past, one that requires explaining it in a very different way from that in which an evolutionary biologist explains the extinction of the dinosaurs or an astronomer explains the death of a star in the distant past. When a Roman historian claims that Caesar's crossing of the Rubicon was historically significant because it marked the beginning of the end of the Roman republic, they understand what Caesar was doing as breaching a legal norm. They explain it in the way in which it would have been understood by a contemporary of Caesar who recognized that the Rubicon marked a border and that crossing it with an army signalled an aggressive intention. The past, for Collingwood, is an ambiguous term which can be brought either under the description of action and investigated by humanistically oriented historians or under the description of event and investigated by the methods of science. When it is brought under the description of action, it is studied in relation to the cultural context of past agents, and understood in the way in which one understands contemporary agents, namely by interpreting their actions in the light of contemporary norms of behaviour. When the rules of engagement are shared by the historian and the agents whose behaviour she seeks to understand, the norms which govern the conduct of agents do their work quietly in the background and can easily be taken for granted, creating the illusion that the actions of other agents may be explained by invoking mere empirical regularities, and understood through the empirical method of observation and inductive generalization. It is when we turn our gaze to past agents that the presuppositions which enable us to understand other minds become evident: since the norms to which past agents are responsive are less likely to be shared by the historian, the actions of past agents will appear unintelligible if the changes in the rules of engagement are not acknowledged. What distinguishes history from science is not that history is concerned with understanding the past whilst science is concerned with predicting the future. The difference lies in the ways in which they approach their subject matter and establish explanatory connections. The action of Caesar is explained in relation to a legal norm which he transgressed, not subsumed under a natural law which was falsified when he crossed the Rubicon. Norms are not universal laws: they can be transgressed without being falsified. To understand agency, whether past or present, is to understand the norms to which historical agents are responsive. When one attempts to understand past agents within a purely extensional context (that of bodies and their movements), the result is not piecemeal misunderstanding of *this* or *that* action, but a systematic conflation of the category of action with that of event and of the subject matter of history with that of science.

Collingwood's claim that it is nonsensical to ask whether the (absolute) presuppositions which govern forms of inquiry are either true or false of an inquiry independent reality may raise some eyebrows and give rise to the suspicion that he was ultimately sceptical about the possibility of obtaining objective knowledge. This is far from the truth. Nowhere is his commitment to the possibility of acquiring objective knowledge more evident than in his philosophy of history where he defends the view that the past can be known, at least in principle, as it always was. His philosophy of history challenges the revisionist conception of historical knowledge that has governed the philosophy of history since the narrativist turn. The consensus that has governed much philosophy of history after Collingwood's death is that there is not one past, but many pasts. This revisionist conception of the nature of historical knowledge is largely the result of a commitment to 'presentism', the view that the past should be understood through the categories of the present. This is a view that clearly goes against the grain of Collingwood's conception of historical understanding, according to which to be understood historically, the past must be understood through the categories of past agents, not those of the interpreter. Chapter 6 (The past as it always was) examines some of the assumptions that underpin the revisionist consensus that has governed philosophy of history after Collingwood's death. The first is that the categories of the historian are a skin so tight it cannot be shed. According to Collingwood, what underpins the idea that the past cannot be understood from the point of view of the agent is the mistaken assumption that the propositional content of thought cannot be isolated from the context of its occurrence. If this doctrine were accepted, he claims, it would be impossible to understand anyone, let alone agree or disagree with them, because no one occupies the same spatio-temporal coordinates. He blames the view that it is impossible to entertain the same thoughts of past agents on a failure to recognize that the criteria for the identity of thought are not the same as those which apply to feelings and sensations, which, unlike thought, have a specific location in space and time. The second assumption that has tended to dominate the philosophy of history in the latter half of the twentieth century is the view that defending the autonomy of historical knowledge requires accepting the idea that there is an important asymmetry between scientific and historical knowledge. Historical claims differ from scientific hypotheses because they are constructions which come into being as the events of the past are connected in a particular order and manner through historical narratives. While claims about the occurrence of the events which historical narratives weave together are verifiable (there is a fact of the matter about whether or not Caesar crossed the Rubicon), there is no fact of the matter that can verify or falsify historical narratives precisely because, unlike scientific hypotheses, they are narrative constructions. Collingwood does agree that historical knowledge is autonomous and irreducible to scientific knowledge, but he rejects this asymmetry between scientific and historical knowledge and would deny that verifiability is the preserve of scientific knowledge. There are verifiably true and false historical claims, just as there are verifiably true and false scientific claims. His view is not that history differs from science because it is more like fiction, but rather that the evidence which verifies historical claims is of a different kind from that which verifies scientific claims because history and science operate with different senses of causation to which there correspond different criteria of verification. A third assumption is that revisionism is the inevitable corollary of the rejection of an empiricist conception of history according to which the facts speak for themselves without the need for interpretation or conceptual mediation. History, it is claimed, is not mere chronicle; the step from chronicle to history requires interpretation and conceptual mediation. Turning uninterpreted facts of the matter into narratives that make sense of the past requires bringing the categories of the historian to bear upon those facts. Collingwood agrees with the claim that history is more than mere chronicle, but rejects the implication that the categorial mediation that is needed to turn chronicles into histories is the conceptual mediation of the historian. The values and concepts through which the past is understood are not poured over them like a thin coating over a cake; they are already baked into the facts and congealed into the texture of the cake like the eggs, sugar, butter and flower of which it is made: the significance of Archduke's Ferdinand assassination, for example, cannot be extricated from the context of the treatises and alliances in place at the time; without them it could not have become a trigger for the Great War: one cannot remove the context of the treatises and alliances and leave intact the significance of the assassination. To claim that the context that is relevant to understanding the past historically is that of the agents is not to defend the notion that the facts speak for themselves: *knowing the past as it was for the historical agents is not the same as knowing it in itself, independently of any categorial mediation.* Understanding the past historically, for Collingwood, requires suspending disbelief in the way in which one does when watching a period play. When the audience of a period play suspends disbelief they take up the view from elsewhere, not the view from nowhere. If revisionism is motivated by the fear that denying that the past must be reinterpreted anew from the perspective of the present entails a commitment to the view from nowhere, to some mythical notion of the past as it is in-itself, such fears are ungrounded.

An important presupposition of historical inquiry, for Collingwood, is that the past should be seen from the perspective of historical agents, in terms of *their* conception of reality. This assumption which, according to Collingwood, governs historical inquiry is often taken to imply the additional claim that reality can *only* be known historically. But this inference is unwarranted: it is one thing to say that all knowledge is governed by presuppositions and it is another to say that all knowledge is historical knowledge. The latter claim, viz. that all knowledge is historical knowledge, denies the autonomy of scientific knowledge from historical knowledge and leads to a form of inverted scientism. Chapter 7 (Beyond scientism and historicism) argues that the widespread reading of Collingwood as a sort of historical fundamentalist who seeks to reverse the epistemic power relations between science and history is based on a conflation of the claim that all knowledge rests on presuppositions with the claim that all knowledge is historical knowledge. Scientific knowledge rests on the presupposition of the uniformity of nature, on the assumption that the laws of nature do not change, and that what science investigates is a reality that is independent of the changing historical representations of it. To say *this*, however, is not to say that scientific knowledge is knowledge of pure being whilst historical knowledge is knowledge of reality as it is for x, y and z. It is rather to spell out the presuppositions which govern natural science and history respectively. Historical knowledge rests on the presupposition that agents are responsive to norms and that past agents must be understood in relation to *their* aesthetic, epistemic and other norms. To say *this* is, however, not to say that all knowledge is historical knowledge, i.e. that all knowledge is governed by this presupposition since scientific knowledge clearly is not. Collingwood's conception of philosophy as a form of presuppositional analysis is not a form of historical fundamentalism which denies science its autonomy in the way that traditional forms of scientism deny history is an autonomous form of inquiry; he argues for a rebalancing rather than a reversal of the epistemic power relations between science and history. Turning the power relations upside down would simply lead to yet another form of scientism, in reverse gear.

One of the concepts that philosophical analysis tries to disambiguate is the concept of the past. Had Collingwood been alive today he would have been very critical of recent attempts to undo the distinction between the historical and the natural past. Chapter 8 (The historical past and the nature/culture distinction at the time of the Anthropocene) engages Collingwood's conception of history with a new form of naturalism which claims that the distinction between the historical and the natural past does not serve us well and should be abandoned since it supposedly rests on unacceptable anthropocentric assumptions. The distinction between the historical and the natural past, so it is argued, presupposes that human beings, qua historical beings, can be treated as if they were transcendent beings, which stand outside of nature. These attempts to overthrow the distinction between the historical and the natural past singularly fail to grasp that the distinction between the natural and the historical past, as Collingwood draws it, is not an ontological distinction between natural and not-natural beings, but between the explananda of different forms of knowing: science and history. Rejecting the notion of a specifically historical past ipso facto undermines the idea of a possible historical future, one that can be shaped by rethinking the norms which govern historical beings rather than simply anticipated in the manner in which a weather forecast anticipates the arrival of a cyclone.

Collingwood's metaphysics of absolute presuppositions provides us with a means of tackling one of the most important questions that has faced us since the rise of modern science, namely whether the progress of natural science will spell the demise of humanistic explanations of actions as proto-scientific explanations which will ultimately be replaced by more sophisticated scientific explanations with greater predictive power. Collingwood denies that humanistic explanations will wither away with the progress of natural science. Chapter 9 (The manifest and the scientific images) shows that his metaphysics of absolute presuppositions provides a very different model for understanding the relation between what Sellars called the manifest and the scientific image of reality (Sellars 1963). Collingwood rejects the predominant view that the relation between the manifest and the scientific image should be understood in terms of the relation between what is more and what is less fundamental and that philosophy should be tasked either with determining what the most fundamental components of reality are, or of determining how what is less fundamental is entailed by what is more fundamental. On the predominant view reality is like a cake, which is soft, moist and tastes sweet; the task of conceptual analysis in metaphysics is to determine what the fundamental ingredients of reality (qua cake) are and how these ingredients (butter, sugar flour, eggs) are responsible in combination for the cake's texture and taste. For Collingwood, by contrast, the task of philosophical analysis is to enable us to make conceptual distinctions, to distinguish between kinds of inferences and the knowledge claims which they make possible. When the task of philosophy is so understood, philosophy does not conflict with science because its role is not to deliver knowledge of reality, but of the presupposition on which knowledge of reality is based. Nor is philosophy the preserve of academic philosophers; it is ubiquitous and can be found everywhere, in reflective individuals who can make conceptual distinctions which do not correspond to determinate empirical classifications.

I should not close this chapter without pre-empting three possible objections. First, this book often makes use of the generic terms 'science' and 'scientific knowledge' in a way that some readers may find objectionable because it does not differentiate sufficiently between different kinds of natural sciences and their methodologies. One might even think there is an irony in the fact that an argument for explanatory pluralism should speak of 'natural science' in the singular. The generic use of terms like 'science' and 'scientific knowledge' should not be construed as a commitment to the view that there are no differences between the natural sciences, between the questions they ask and the methods by which they answer them. It is simply not the purpose of this book to provide that nuanced account. The main goal of this book is to provide a defence of humanistic understanding; the primary distinction on which it focuses, therefore, is that between humanistic understanding and scientific knowledge. Second, those who think of Collingwood as a radical historicist (as many still do) may find the project of confronting and comparing Collingwood's ideas with contemporary debates to be anachronistic and a rather unCollingwoodian thing to do. I beg to disagree. Collingwood certainly thought that when interpreting either actions or texts from the past one should understand them in *their* own terms. But to say *this* is not the same as endorsing a form of radical historicism which undermines the possibility of any critical engagement with them. It is just that unless one is in the business of erecting straw men, the task of understanding must come first. Awareness of the historical context in which certain claims are made does not entail the kind of relativism which prevents critical engagement. And this critical engagement can work both ways: once the past is understood historically, it can be critiqued from the perspective of the present. Likewise, the views of past philosophers can be used to engage critically with philosophers who were still to come, as indeed this book undertakes to do. Unless one thinks of Collingwood as a radical historicist, there is no inconsistency in mobilizing and developing his views, in asking whether he was right or wrong and what he would or could have said about the debates which have subsequently taken place in the philosophy of mind, and in the philosophy of history, had he been alive in the latter half of the twentieth century. Unless one interprets Collingwood as a historical relativist, there is no irony in relating him productively to contemporary debates to offer a perspective that was lost as the conception of the role of philosophical analysis changed. A third objection that might be raised is that there are many reasons why Collingwood matters that are not discussed in this book. There is no discussion, for example, of why Collingwood matters to aesthetics. Insofar as the main concern of this book is the relation between scientific knowledge and humanistic understanding, its focus is firmly on Collingwood's defence of a humanistically oriented historiography and the conception of the nature of philosophical reflection that enabled him to articulate an argument against scientism without committing the opposite error of denying that scientific knowledge is sui generis and autonomous with respect to historical knowledge. It was simply not the purpose of this book to provide an exhaustive list of the reasons why Collingwood's thought remains important. Its selectivity should not be interpreted as claiming that his defence of the autonomy of humanistic understanding is the only reason why he matters.

2

Philosophy as disentanglement

Disambiguating the concept of cause

Philosophical analysis, Collingwood claims, enables us to achieve conceptual clarity by disambiguating concepts which do not capture different classes of objects. This conception of the task of philosophical analysis, as the distinguishing of concepts which coincide in their instances, is a persistent feature of Collingwood's metaphilosophy. It was first developed in the Lectures on Moral Philosophy (Collingwood 1929 and 1932) which were later integrated in Collingwood's first mature metaphilosophical treatise, *An Essay on Philosophical Method* (1933). The concept which *An Essay on Philosophical Method* selects for disambiguation is the concept of the good; this is unsurprising given that the essay developed out of Collingwood's earlier reflections on moral philosophy. The concept of the good is an ambiguous concept because it can mean the good in the hedonistic sense of what is pleasant, the good in the consequentialist sense of what is expedient, and the good in the deontological sense of what is right (Collingwood 1933: 41 ff.). The distinction between these three senses of the good is not an empirical classification, like the classification of animals into vertebrates and invertebrates because these different conceptions of the good may be exemplified by one and the same action, as in Kant's example of the shopkeeper who returns the correct change to a customer because he believes that honesty is a good policy. The action that the shopkeeper performs is indistinguishable from the action he would have performed had he been acting out of duty rather than from prudential considerations. The distinction between the different senses of the good does not sort actions into separate empirical classes, such as the class of hedonistic, the class of expedient and the class of deontological actions; it is a philosophical distinction between the different meanings or senses of the term 'good'.

While the focus of *An Essay on Philosophical Method* was on the concept of good, *An Essay on Metaphysics* seeks to clarify the different meanings that the concept of cause has in different explanatory contexts. In one sense the concept of cause signifies an event 'by producing or preventing which we can produce of prevent that whose cause it is said to be' (Collingwood 1940: 296–7). So understood, causes can be regarded as handles for either bringing about a desired effect or preventing an undesired one from happening. The term 'cause' is used in this sense in claims such as '… the cause of books going mouldy is their being in a damp room; the cause of a man's sweating is a dose of aspirin … the cause of seedlings dying is that nobody watered them' (Collingwood 1940: 299). This (handle) conception of causation belongs to a particular explanatory context, that of the practical sciences of nature, sciences such as engineering and medicine, whose goal is to alter the environment to serve human ends by, for example, deviating the course of a river to enhance agricultural production, or prescribing medical remedies to prevent illness and alleviate suffering. The sense of causation that belongs to the practical sciences of nature differs from the meaning this term has in the theoretical sciences of nature, such as physics or astronomy where no intervention is possible or is intended and the cause is an event that unconditionally brings about its effect. The relevant contrast that Collingwood seeks to establish between explanations in the practical and theoretical sciences of nature, and their corresponding sense of causation, is one between a conception of causation that allows for intervention and one that does not. The concept of 'cause' is therefore heterogeneous as it varies according to explanatory context. Selecting one concept of causation instead of another requires ensuring that the kind of explanatory answers one gives address the kind of question which is being asked:

If my car fails to climb up a steep hill, and I wonder why, I shall not consider my problem solved by a passer-by who tells me that the top of the hill is farther away from the earth's center than its bottom, and that consequently more power is needed to take the car uphill than to take her along the level ... All this is quite true; what the passer-by has described is one of the conditions which together form ... what I call the cause in sense III ... But suppose an AA man comes along, opens the bonnet, holds up a loose high-tension lead and says: 'Look here sir, you're running on three cylinders'. My problem is now solved ... If I had been a person who could flatten out hills by stamping on them the passer-by would have been right in calling to the hill as the cause of the stoppage; not because the hill was a hill, but because I was able to flatten it out.

(Collingwood 1940: 302–3)

Whether one selects the concept of causation that belongs to the practical or the theoretical sciences of nature depends on whether the questions one asks can be answered by making an intervention or providing a description. On the surface the theoretical physicist and the AA man appear to be providing different answers to the same question, namely, 'why did the car stop?' In fact, their answers are not merely different answers; they are different *kinds* of answers, directed at different questions which resemble each other grammatically, but which arise as a result of the endorsement of different assumptions concerning what it means to explain something causally. To understand this one must take a closer look at Collingwood's account of the relation holding between answers, questions and presuppositions.

All explanations, for Collingwood, are answers to questions. And all questions rest on presuppositions. For example, the question 'has he stopped beating his wife yet?' rests on the assumption that he was beating his wife; in order to ask 'has he stopped beating his wife yet?' one has to presuppose that he had been beating his wife (Collingwood 1940: 296). There is a relation of logical entailment between presuppositions and the questions to which they give rise. The question 'has he stopped beating his wife yet?' for example, is not entailed by the presupposition 'there are fish in the sea'.

The claim that there is a relation of entailment holding between questions and the presuppositions which give rise to them has far-reaching implications. If presuppositions can give rise to certain questions only, and not others, then presuppositions indirectly determine the *kind* of propositions that can qualify as potential answers to the questions they give rise to. The question posed by the driver, for example, presupposes that reality is something that can be moulded and that a cause is an event by producing or preventing which one can produce or prevent that whose cause it is said to be. The explanation of the physicist could not count as an answer to the question posed by the driver because it answers a different question, one that arises as a result of a different presupposition concerning what it means for one event to be a cause of another. For something to count as an answer to a question, rather than as a stand-alone statement, it must address the specific question that was asked. And to address *that* question it must be sensitive to what the question is asking, to the presuppositions that gave rise to the question. It is because the answer given by the physicist and the question posed by the driver belong to different complexes of questions and answers that the explanation of the physicist is not fit to satisfy the curiosity of the driver.

The philosopher is a logical detective whose task is to render explicit which presuppositions give rise to what questions and the entailment relations holding between presuppositions, the questions to which they give rise, and the statements which can legitimately count as answering those questions:

> In unscientific thinking our thoughts are coagulated into knots and tangles; we fish up a thought out of our minds like an anchor foul of its own cable, hanging upside-down and draped in seaweed with shellfish sticking to it and dump the whole thing on deck quite pleased with ourselves for having got it up at all. Thinking scientifically means disentangling all this mess, and reducing a knot of thoughts in which everything sticks together anyhow to a system or series of thoughts in which thinking the thoughts is at the same time thinking the connexions between them.
>
> (Collingwood 1940: 22–3)

Answering the question 'why did the car stop?' as posed by someone who is interested in fixing his vehicle in order to reach a destination requires selecting an explanation that invokes the handle conception of causation at work in the practical sciences of nature. To reply to the driver's question in the way in which the physicist does is to provide not merely a different answer from the one that the AA mechanic proffers, but an altogether different *kind* of answer, one that addresses a different question, satisfies a different kind of curiosity, and does not count as an answer to the driver's question. Philosophy realigns questions and answers by identifying and pursuing the entailments holding between explanatory answers, questions and the presuppositions which give rise to them.

Choosing between different kinds of explanations, i.e. explanations which invoke *different senses of causation*, is not the same as choosing between different explanations which invoke the *same sense of causation*. Suppose that not one but two AA mechanics came along. The first claimed that the car stopped because it was running on three cylinders; the second claimed the car stopped because it had run out of petrol. To choose between explanations of the same kind one needs to check the facts and, on that basis, determine which explanation best accounts for the facts. One does not choose between explanations of different kinds (explanations which invoke different senses of causation) in the same way in which one chooses between different explanations of the same kind (explanations which invoke the same sense of causation). The choice between one kind of explanation and another is determined by whether the sense of causation that is invoked is fit to answer the question that is being asked. The explanation given by the AA mechanic is selected not because the sense of causation it invokes is real or true of an inquiry-independent reality, but because it addresses the problem the driver wants solved: how to fix his vehicle in order to reach his destination. Explanations invoking the same sense of causation can genuinely be said to conflict. For example, the explanation that the car stopped because it was running on three cylinders, or because it had run out of petrol are *potentially* competing explanations because they invoke the same sense of causation and provide *different* answers to the *same* question. But explanations involving different conceptions of causation (such as those of the physicist and the AA mechanic) are not even *potentially* conflicting explanations because they answer different questions. They are not simply *different* answers, they are different *kinds* of answers.

Collingwood's approach to contested concepts, such as that of causation, is not to ask which one of them is *real* and which one is not, but rather to show that these concepts feature in explanations which have different explanatory purposes and a different logical form that matches the investigative goals of different forms of inquiry. It is only once one settles on a particular conception of causation, or a set of explanatory purposes, that one can ask (and answer) these kinds of 'really' questions. There is a true or false answer to the question as to whether Covid 'really' is a virus, just as there is a true or false answer to the question as to whether the car 'really' stopped because it had a flat battery. But there is no true or false answer to the question as to whether there 'really' are causes as they feature in explanations in the practical or theoretical sciences of nature, i.e. whether the explanatory connections that they enable us to establish have an inquiry-independent status:

> Thus if you were talking to a pathologist about a certain disease and asked him 'What is the cause of the event E which you say sometimes happens in this disease?' he will reply 'The cause of E is C'; and if he were in a communicative mood he might go on to say 'That was established by So-and-so, in a piece of research that is now regarded as classical.' You might go on to ask: 'I suppose before So-and-so found out what the cause of E was, he was quite sure it had a cause?' The answer would be 'Quite sure of course.' If you now say 'Why?' he will probably answer 'Because everything that happens has a cause.' If you are importunate enough to ask 'But how do you know that everything that happens has a cause? He will probably blow up right in your face because you have put your finger on one of his absolute presuppositions, and people are apt to be ticklish in their absolute presuppositions. But if he keeps his

temper and gives you a civil answer, it will be to the following effect. That is a thing we take for granted in my job. We do not question it. We do not try to verify it. It isn't a thing anybody has discovered, like microbes or the circulation of blood. It is a thing we just take for granted.'

(Collingwood 1940: 31)

The conceptions of causation at work in the sort of explanations one comes across in the practical and theoretical sciences of nature are what Collingwood calls 'absolute' presuppositions. What makes these presuppositions absolute is that they cannot be waived without renouncing the conception of reality that makes a particular form of inquiry possible. It is not possible, for example, to be a practising physician without presupposing that the natural course of illness can be either stopped or delayed to improve a patient's health. A doctor could not renounce a commitment to what we called the handle conception of causation without renouncing the practice of medicine. Not all presuppositions are the same. Some presuppositions are less fundamental than others or, as Collingwood puts it, are relative, rather than absolute ones. It is conceivable, for example, that we may one day revise our understanding of the causes of cancer and discover that it is an infectious disease. Presuppositions within pathology are constantly being refined or revised and such refinements lead to progress in medicine. But what cannot be revised is the view that nature can be tampered with to improve human health, unless of course one is no longer in the business of healing.

Mapping the relations of entailment holding between explanations given in answers to questions, and the presuppositions which are entailed by these questions, enables Collingwood to disambiguate the concept of causality in such a way as to support a form of explanatory pluralism in which the context of inquiry dictates what concept of causation and thus what *kind* of explanation (not what specific explanation) one should select. Aristotle once said that it would be as foolish to ask for probable demonstrations from a mathematician as it would be to expect precision in matters of ethics, that it is the mark of an educated man not to demand more precision than the subject matter permits or requires (Aristotle 2002: book 1.3, 1094b25). Paraphrasing Aristotle, one might say that for Collingwood it is the mark of an educated person (one who has learned to make relevant conceptual distinctions) to be able to judge which of the contested meanings of a concept should be called for in a given explanatory context. Just as, for Aristotle, it would be foolish to expect mathematical precision in matters of ethics, so for Collingwood, it would be just as foolish to call in a theoretical physicist to explain that the ceiling plaster in your decrepit Victorian house fell to the floor because of gravitational force rather than to consider calling in a builder to fix the collapsed ceiling plaster (assuming, of course, that your goal was to get your house in better shape). And, if you were to conclude from the fact that the explanation of the builder ('it was the damp') and that of the physicist ('it is gravity') differ, that one of them must be right and the other must be wrong, presuppositional analysis would show that appearances notwithstanding there is no conflict between them because they answer different questions that arise because of different presuppositions and serve different explanatory goals. They are not only different answers, but different *kinds* of answer. The task of presuppositional analysis, then, is that of disambiguating concepts that are claimed or employed by different forms of knowledge and disentangling the conceptual knots in which one gets caught when one fails to align the right kind of causal/becausal answer with the right kind of 'why' question.

Humanistic and scientific explanations

The greatest conceptual mayhem, for Collingwood, occurs at the intersection of natural science and the humanities. For there is yet a different sense of causation that is operative in humanistic explanations, one that differs from the sense of causation in both the practical and the theoretical sciences of nature. Humanistic explanations explain by rendering intelligible behaviour that would otherwise seem puzzling.

They do so by rationalizing it. In *The Idea of History*, Collingwood gives the example of an ancient tribe which takes a very tortuous and dangerous path to reach a certain destination rather than a much shorter and less perilous route. Understanding what seems to be inexplicable behaviour here involves finding a practical argument that rationalizes the decision to take the longer and more arduous route in the eyes of the agents (Collingwood 1946: 317). This kind of explanation has two elements: the *causa ut* (a goal) and the *causa quod* (a belief concerning a particular state of affairs) (Collingwood 1940: 292). In a humanistic explanation the *causa quod* and the *causa ut* play the role of premises in a practical argument that explains the action by showing that it is rationally entailed by the premises. In a humanistic explanation, in other words, the action is not explained by invoking antecedent conditions (mental states such as *believings* or *desirings*) and a general psychological law, in the way in which one would explain, for example, that the water froze because the temperature dropped below 0°C (antecedent condition) and every time the water drops below 0°C water freezes (general empirical law). Humanistic explanations are sense-making explanations. Making sense requires providing justification of a sort for the action by rationalizing it, rather than merely showing that the action is what normally ensues when certain antecedent conditions hold. To explain an action by invoking a practical argument is to justify it in the sense of showing it to be the right thing to do given the premises (the *causa ut* and the *causa quod*). Humanistic explanations do not justify action in the stronger sense that the practical argument which makes sense of the action needs to have true premises. Nor does rationalizing the action require the interpreter to believe what the agent believes to be true (for example, that there exist evil spirits inhabiting the mountains). We shall look in more detail at the nature of humanistic explanations and how they differ from scientific explanations in the following chapters. For the moment we just want to take stock of the fact that there is a distinctive sense of causation that is required to distinguish the *explanandum* of humanistic explanations (actions) from that of the sciences of nature (events) and to delineate the subject matter of what Collingwood takes to be the paradigmatic example of a humanistic discipline: history. The subject matter of humanistic explanation is distinct from that of the natural sciences, not because they investigate different classes of things, but because they home in on a different *explanandum*. Hence, just as explanations in the practical sciences of nature do not conflict with explanations in the theoretical sciences of nature (there is, as we have seen, no conflict between the explanation of the car mechanic and that of the physicist), there is no conflict between humanistic and scientific explanations. Consider, for example, the case of the Russian ex-spy Sergei Skripal who collapsed in Salisbury outside a supermarket (clearly not Collingwood's example). What happened? If the fact to be explained is a physiological one, the answer will be that Skripal's symptoms were caused by exposure to the nerve agent Novichok. If, on the other hand, the fact to be explained is of a political nature, then knowing that it was nerve agent smeared on the handle of his front door that was responsible for his collapse, and that the nerve agent was Novichok, will enable an investigative journalist to restrict the list of suspects to those who have access to this rare and lethal chemical compound, but it will contribute little or nothing to understanding the political motives behind it. If the relevant fact to be explained is of a political nature, it will not satisfy the curiosity of those who want to know what happened in Salisbury to be told in reply that Sergei Skripal had come into contact with the nerve agent Novichok, which had been smeared on the handle of his front door, and that certain symptoms normally manifest themselves when someone comes in contact with Novichok, just as it will not satisfy the curiosity of the driver at the side the road to know that the top of the hill is further removed from centre of the earth than the bottom of the hill. The explanations of the pathologist and of the investigative journalist do not conflict, because they have different explananda, and answer different kinds of questions by providing different kind of evidence in support of their respective explanations; when choosing between them, one cannot do so by claiming that the forensic evidence which established that Novichok was smeared on the handle of Skripal's front door was 'better' than the evidence of the investigative journalist who revealed that the perpetrators were working for the Russian secret services. Whether the explanations of the pathologist and the investigative journalist were rigorously carried out will depend on the evidential standards of investigative journalism and forensic investigation. The forensic scientist and the investigative journalist explain what happened in Salisbury in different ways, but their explanations do not compete, just as there is no competition between the answers of the AA mechanic and that of the theoretical physicist to the question 'why did the car stop?' We are here dealing not with different answers, which might legitimately compete, but with different kinds of answers. It would be unreasonable to expect the forensic scientist to be able determine the motive for the poisoning of Sergei Skripal by examining the nature of the substance smeared on the handle of his front door, just as it would be unreasonable to expect the investigative journalist to know all about the toxicological properties of Novichok. The conflict between humanistic and scientific explanations is therefore dissolved in the same way in which the problem of causal exclusion between the practical and the theoretical sciences of nature is dissolved, namely by disambiguating their respective *explananda*. There is a famous example in Anscombe's *Intentions* (1957) where a man pumps water into a house by moving his arm. The action could be described as replenishing the water supply, or as poisoning the inhabitants (since the water contained poison). There is no suggestion that there are two persons, one who is replenishing the water supply and another one who is poisoning the inhabitants of the house; there is one person whose behaviour is brought under different descriptions. Equally, for Collingwood, there is only one car that came to a halt, but there are however two *explananda* that correspond to the different senses of causation invoked by the theoretical and the practical sciences of nature respectively; so too there is only one poisoning that happened in Salisbury, but two explananda that correspond to the investigative goals of forensic science and political journalism. The philosopher is called in to adjudicate disputes which arise not when explanations which invoke the same concept of causation conflict (these conflicts are an in-house matter for the practitioners of the first order discipline within which they arise), but when explanations which invoke different senses of causation come into contact and conflict with one another. If two forensic investigators were disagreeing about whether the nerve agent smeared on the handle of Skripal's door was indeed Novichok, the dispute would lead to further tests and possibly further consultation with other forensic experts; if two physicians were to disagree about how to treat a person who came into contact with nerve agent, past cases would be referred to and other physicians consulted; if two car mechanics explained why a car stopped in different ways, one by suggesting that it had a flat battery, the other by saying that it had run out of petrol, the explanations would have to be checked against the facts (Is the tank empty? Does the battery need recharging?). These disputes would not be settled by calling in a philosopher to adjudicate which forensic scientist is right or which physician has reached the right conclusion or which mechanic has correctly identified the problem with the car. Rather, the philosopher comes on the scene when a different kind of puzzle arises, when concepts which are invoked or contested by different forms of inquiry come into contact and clash with one another.

These clashes typically arise because there are no separate empirical classes of things that constitute the subject matter of one form of inquiry rather than another: delineating these subject matters specifically requires us to make a philosophical distinction between concepts (such as the different senses of causation) that coincide in their instances and *appear* to be explaining the same kind of thing. Just as the conceptions of the good as what is expedient, and the conception of the good as what is right, do not capture distinct empirical classes of actions (the action of the shopkeeper who gives the correct change to his customers because honesty pays off is not discernibly different from the same action performed because he recognizes that is the right thing to do), there are no separate empirical classes of things that are captured by different kinds of explanations. This 'overlap in classes', as Collingwood describes it in an *An Essay on Philosophical Method* (Collingwood 1933: 26ff), causes conceptual havoc. This is when and why presuppositional analysis is needed.

Confining science to its own explanandum

Presuppositional analysis exposes the relations of entailment holding between propositional answers to questions and the presuppositions that give rise to the questions they seek to answer. As we have seen, the theoretical physicist's suggestion that the car stopped because the centre of the earth is further removed from the top of the hill than the bottom of the hill cannot count as a propositional answer to the question of the person who is concerned with reaching his destination on time and wants to identify the kind of intervention required to fix his vehicle. To identify the explanandum of the practical sciences of nature requires deploying a conception of causation as a sort of handle. There is therefore a reciprocal relation between the form of the explanation and what it is one explains, the explanandum, between method and subject matter. Let us call this the Reciprocity Thesis.

Committing to the Reciprocity Thesis requires rethinking the predominant conception of the relation between the sciences. On the predominant conception of the relation between the sciences forms of knowledge are arranged hierarchically. On this layered/hierarchical model, physics occupies the bottom layer and becomes *the* science *par excellence*. The explanations of physics are thought to be both ontologically and epistemically privileged. They are ontologically privileged because the explanations of physics alone are taken to capture real causal relations that hold among events independently of how they are described in any given context of inquiry; they are epistemically privileged because they are taken to be the explanations with the greatest predictive power. The explanations of chemistry, biology psychology and so on are said to supervene upon those of physics, just as the secondary qualities of objects supervene upon their primary properties.

Commitment to the Reciprocity thesis requires us to reject the epistemic and ontological primacy that the method of physics enjoys in the layered model of the sciences. In Collingwood's conception of metaphysics as presuppositional analysis, physics is not ontologically privileged because determining which kind of explanation is appropriate is not a question of establishing which absolute presupposition is real or true of an inquiry-independent reality but of identifying which explanation is fit for purpose. What counts as an answer to a question depends on what the question is asking, and this, in turn, depends on the presuppositions which are entailed by the asking of the question. Given the entailment relation between answers, questions and presuppositions there is no form of explanation that captures an explanandum independently of a given set of investigative goals: there is no explanandum from nowhere. Physics is not epistemically privileged either; there are, as we have seen, explanatory contexts in which the explanations of physics will not do, such as the context of the driver who expects the kind of interventionist explanation that deploys the sense of causation that belongs to the practical, not the theoretical, sciences of nature. On the layered model of the relation between the sciences the question to be asked is: 'which form of explanation is better simpliciter?' On the model implied by Collingwood's conception of the role of philosophical analysis the question to be asked is rather: 'which form of explanation is *better at* solving the problem in hand?'

The Reciprocity thesis limits the claims of physics not to the phenomenal realm, as Kant would say, but to its own explanandum (D'Oro, Giladi and Papazoglou 2019). Just as the humanities ask (and answer) a certain kind of question, so physical theories are answers to the questions asked by physicists, questions that arise from the presuppositions that underpin physics as a distinctive form of knowledge, with its own method and domain of inquiry. Physics is therefore not *the* form of knowledge. It is *a* form of knowledge whose explanations do not and cannot answer the questions posed in other domains.

The view that science can answer all possible meaningful questions and that scientific knowledge is the archetype for all knowledge, Collingwood claims, is so entrenched as to be sedimented in language where, as we saw in the previous chapter, the term 'science' has lost the connotation of the Latin term *scientia*, which once signified any body of knowledge with a distinctive method and subject matter and has become synonymous with 'natural science' (Collingwood 1940: 4). Presuppositional analysis shows that natural science answers a certain kind of why-question, but is unable to address others, which are best answered by other forms of knowledge through the application of different methods.

Collingwood's disambiguation of the concept of causation therefore leads to an argument against scientism understood as the idea that science can answer all questions, that it is the only form of genuine knowledge. But his argument against scientism is not an argument against science itself. It is an argument against a rival *philosophical* conception of the relation in which physics stands to other forms of knowledge. Presuppositional analysis does not seek to undermine scientific claims, such as claims about atoms, molecules or quarks, or claims about the circulation of the blood. It takes issue *not* with scientific claims, *but* rather with second order *philosophical* views concerning the relation between physics and the rest of the sciences according to which physics enjoys a position of ontological and epistemic priority vis-à-vis other forms of knowing.

Scientism, narrow and broad

Scientism is normally understood in a narrow sense as a claim concerning the inappropriate trespassing of science onto the territory of the humanities. But there is a broader understanding of this term according to which scientism consists in the trespassing of any form of knowledge and its characteristic methods onto the subject matter of another. Collingwood is well known for his defence of the autonomy of humanistic understanding, and thus, for his attack on scientism in the narrow sense. His argument for the autonomy of historical explanation vis-à-vis scientific explanation was once regarded as one of the most important attempts to articulate a defence of humanistic explanations against the claim for methodological unity in the sciences. What is often not realized, on the other hand, is that his argument against scientism in the narrow sense is based on an argument against scientism in the broad sense, i.e. against the encroachment of any form of knowledge onto the territory of another. Presuppositional analysis, as we have seen, shows that different forms of knowledge have their own distinctive presuppositions and subject matters. In defending the disciplinary autonomy of history against the encroachment of scientific method, presuppositional analysis also furnishes ipso facto a defence of the disciplinary autonomy of science against the potential encroachment from the side of the humanities. We shall revisit the distinctive presuppositions of history and natural science later in Chapter 7. For the moment let us simply note that Collingwood's metaphysics of absolute presuppositions offers a defence of the autonomy of humanistic explanations that does not threaten the sui generis nature of scientific investigation. As an explanatory pluralist Collingwood would have considered the attempt to reduce scientific knowledge to historical understanding to be as insidious as the attempt to reduce humanistic understanding to scientific knowledge, and would have regarded this as the same error in reverse, as it were. Presuppositional analysis defends the claim that all forms of knowledge rest on presuppositions, which differ according to their explanatory goals, rather than the claim that all knowledge (including scientific knowledge) is historical knowledge because all presuppositions are believed to be true at some time or other by certain people. Yet, as we shall see in the next section, presuppositional analysis is often (erroneously) assumed to support an argument for epistemic relativism rather than being recognized as an argument for explanatory pluralism.

Explanatory pluralism in place of epistemic relativism

Explanatory pluralism is the view that the standards of evidence invoked to determine what is true or false are 'relative' to the goals of inquiry, i.e. to one's explanandum. Epistemic relativism is the view that truth and falsity are relative to standards of evidence adopted or assented to by certain people at certain times. The former is often thought to entail the latter and, as a result, the sort of explanatory pluralism that presuppositional analysis makes possible is not clearly distinguished from epistemic relativism. Collingwood, so it is argued, claims that acquiring knowledge requires answering questions, and that questions rest on presuppositions. Presuppositions are propositions that people believe to be true. Thus, Collingwood's metaphysics of absolute presuppositions, so the arguments goes, identifies philosophy with a historical inquiry into fundamental beliefs that dominated at certain periods of time. In other words, Collingwood is a historical relativist or historicist. But reading Collingwood in this way explicitly goes against his claim that presuppositions are not propositions. Propositions are answers to questions which arise because of some presuppositions that already obtain. Presuppositions do not give rise to questions in virtue of being either true or false or of being believed to be true or false since they have no truth values: we should not ask, as we have seen, which sense of causation is true and which is false, for this question has no intelligible answer.

Explanatory pluralism and epistemic relativism make different claims, and commitment to the former does not entail commitment to the latter. Relativism claims that what is true or false is relative to what the subject believes (be this an individual or a collective) to be true or false; relativism makes what the subject believes the standard of truth and falsity. Explanatory pluralism claims instead that the notion of truth and falsity does not apply to presuppositions because presuppositions do their work neither in virtue of being true nor of being believed (to be true). It is not in virtue of being believed (to be true) by an inquirer or a group of inquirers that presuppositions have logical efficacy (the power to give rise to questions). Just as the conclusion 'Socrates is mortal' is entailed by the propositional content of the premises 'All men are mortal' and 'Socrates is a man', *not* by a person believing the premises of the argument to be true, so the ability of a presupposition to give rise to a question, namely its 'logical efficacy' (Collingwood 1940: 27), is not something a presupposition has in virtue of being believed (to be true).

Explanatory pluralism and relativism deflate the conflict between different forms of knowledge in a very different way. The moral relativist is committed to the meta-ethical claim that what it means for an action to be right or wrong is that it is believed to be right or wrong by the subject (be this the individual or the culture). Similarly, the epistemic relativist is committed to the metaphilosophical view that what we mean when we say that a claim is true or false is that it is believed to be either true or false by the relevant subject (be this the individual or the culture). For the relativist (be it the moral or the epistemic relativist) there can be no genuine disagreement between individuals or cultures who hold different epistemic or moral beliefs because the possibility of disagreement rests on there being a subject-independent fact of the matter. Since there is no such thing, there is no genuine disagreement between subjects who hold different beliefs, but just a difference of opinions. Presuppositional analysis does *not* deflate the apparent conflict between forms of knowledge, say, the theoretical and the practical sciences of nature, in characteristic relativist fashion, i.e. by saying that there is no contest between the explanations of the theoretical and the practical sciences of nature because the true notion of causation is relative to what the subject believes, say to the group beliefs of practical or theoretical scientists of nature. Presuppositional analysis states *not* that absolute presuppositions are relative to the subjects who believe them (to be true), but that the notion of truth and falsity has no applicability to absolute presuppositions. Presuppositional analysis dissolves the alleged conflict between explanations invoking different conceptions of causation not by arguing that truth is a notion that is relative to the subject, but by showing that the conflict between forms of knowledge arises as a result of a failure to see that different absolute presuppositions give rise to different questions and that answers to different questions are not in conflict. The conception of causation that is absolutely presupposed in a certain explanatory context is selected neither because it is true, nor because it is believed to be true, but because of its suitability to answer the question at hand. Relativity to explanatory goals is not the same as relativity to inquirers.

Epistemic pluralism (as conceived by Collingwood) and epistemic relativism are therefore different claims (pace Boghossian 2006) and the latter does not entail the former (D'Oro 2018b). It is an error to infer from the claim that relevance to the task at hand is the criterion for determining which notion of causation to invoke, that the particular conception of causation which is fit for purpose in any given case does its logical work in virtue of being believed to be true by those who select it. To say that the handle conception of causation should be presupposed in explanatory contexts that require an intervention (contexts such as that of medicine and engineering) is not the same as saying that practising doctors and engineers believe it to be true. Selection according to explanatory goals is not the same as selection according to the group beliefs of practical or theoretical scientists of nature but depends on whether the rules of engagement of a particular form of knowledge are fit to answer the questions one wants to be answered (as when, for example, one is booking a doctor's appointment, or taking one's car to the mechanic, rather than attending a physics class). Endorsing the view that fitness for purpose (rather than metaphysical truth) is the criterion to be deployed in selecting which form of explanation to deploy is not the same as committing to the quite different idea that the criterion of truth and falsity is subjective (rather than objective).

Nonetheless, presuppositional analysis is often understood as favouring an argument for a form of historical relativism[1] and Collingwood is still widely regarded as a historicist or historical relativist who claims that all knowledge (including scientific knowledge) is ultimately a form of historical knowledge because absolute presuppositions are beliefs held by some people at some time or other. Just as Leibniz's rationalism defended the view that all knowledge is ultimately analytic knowledge (because in order for a proposition to be true the predicate must, overly or covertly, be entailed in the subject), so on the historicist reading of Collingwood all knowledge is ultimately historical knowledge because all presuppositions are covert propositions that are believed to be true by some people at some point in time. This is something that Collingwood explicitly denies. He considers the view that 'all reality is historical ... to be an error' (Collingwood 1946: 209).

Collingwood agrees with the epistemic relativist that there is no metaphysical fact of the matter by reference to which one could, for example, establish which one of the various senses of causation is true of an inquiry-independent reality. But explanatory pluralism deflates the tension between forms of knowledge not by claiming the different senses of causation are relative to the beliefs of different user groups, but by disambiguating the kind of thing they aim to explain. To claim that different forms of knowledge have a different explanandum is to say something quite different from what the relativist says, namely that there cannot be any disagreement between forms of knowledge because the notion of truth is relative to what the subject believes to be true.

---

[1] Collingwood does make some explicitly historicist statements in *An Essay on Metaphysics*. He says, for example: 'To sum up. Metaphysics is the attempt to find out what absolute presuppositions have been made by this or that person or group of persons, on this or that occasion or group of occasions, in the course of this or that occasion or group of occasions, in the course of this or that piece of thinking. Arising out of this, it will consider (for example) whether absolute presuppositions are made singly or in groups, and if the latter, how the groups are organized; whether different absolute presuppositions are made by different individuals or races or nations or classes' (Collingwood 1940: 47) But this kind of statement is also incompatible with his often repeated claim that presuppositions have logical efficacy and that metaphysics is a logical inquiry which traces the entailment relations between questions and the presuppositions which give rise to them (Collingwood 1940: 30).

Sources of dissatisfaction

This conception of the role of philosophical analysis has not been widely shared. One reason why this conception of philosophical analysis may be regarded with some suspicion is that it denies that the question of truth or falsity applies to absolute presuppositions, and that it therefore undermines the possibility of making objective claims. At a time where post-truth discourse poses a threat to the very idea of objectivity some might well be wary of this claim. Defending presuppositional analysis from this objection provides an opportunity for explaining the nature of this claim in more detail and showing that it does not pose a threat to the idea that objective truth matters. Presuppositional analysis does indeed deny that the notion of truth and falsity applies to absolute presuppositions. These are, in a sense that will be clearly explained in due course, beyond verification. Presuppositions are beyond verification not in the sense that we are unable to verify them because we cannot jump outside of our historical skin; rather, the argument is that the demand they should be verified is nonsensical because they themselves enable the asking of questions to which true or false answers can be given. Take, for example, the sense of causation that characterizes explanations in the practical sciences of nature. Once this sense of causation is in place one can try and find out whether it is true that leaving books in a damp room will cause them to become mouldy, whether overwatering plants causes their roots to rot or whether vaccination reduces the spread of viruses. Or consider the principle of the uniformity of nature which Collingwood regards as an absolute presupposition of a certain kind of empirical inquiry. Hume was notoriously sceptical about our ability to provide a justification for this principle and, as a result, for specific inductive inferences, thereby casting doubt on large swathes of our empirical knowledge, i.e. on any claims which are not based on present observation. Inductive inferences, he argued, presuppose the principle of the uniformity of nature, but since this principle is neither a proposition about matters of fact nor one about relations of ideas, it is an illegitimate metaphysical proposition. Presuppositional analysis shows that the principle of the uniformity of nature is no ordinary proposition. The demand that it should be verified arises from a misunderstanding of its logical status: 'Any question involving the presupposition that an absolute presupposition is a proposition, such as the question "Is it true?" "What evidence is there for it?" "How can it be demonstrated?" "What right have we to presuppose it if it can't?", is a nonsense question' (Collingwood 1940: 33). To ask that it should be verified, as if it were an ordinary proposition, is to misunderstand its role, which is not to answer questions, but to give rise to questions to which true or false answers can be found. Without the principle, the question 'what normally happens when certain circumstances occur, e.g. when plants are overwatered or books placed in a damp room or people vaccinated?' would not arise. For the question arises only on the assumption that nature is uniform. The possibility of argument on the basis of empirical evidence rests on standards of evidence that must be presupposed. This is what it means to say that it makes no sense to extend the demand for verification to absolute presuppositions.

Collingwood's account of absolute presuppositions provides an interesting angle on the question of inductive scepticism. Inductive scepticism rejects the conditions of the possibility on which (empirical) knowledge rests. If one questions the principle one cannot justifiably claim, for example, *either* that an increase in vaccination will lead to a reduction in Covid related deaths, *or* that it will fail to do so, for one would have no means to provide empirical evidence for this claim. And if one *did* claim one way or the other whilst still rejecting the principle, one would be advancing a dogmatic statement, a statement that could not be evidenced in the way in which genuine inductive claims which rest on the principle of the uniformity of nature can. Perhaps one could choose not to make any inferences based on the principle of the uniformity of nature, just as a doctor who doubted whether the handle conception of causation is true would have to give up prescribing remedies in order not to be accused of some sort of intellectual hypocrisy. To make a contribution to knowledge one must absolutely presuppose what it means to establish certain explanatory connections.

These presuppositions are not generalizations of an empirical nature. Rather they are norms which govern certain epistemic inferences, norms without which there would be no knowledge, but only arbitrary assertions. From this perspective the threat to objectivity in any given form of inquiry does not come from the acceptance of the rules of engagement for that form of inquiry, but from the demand that those rules of engagement should be subjected to the same demand for verification as the verifiable claims which they make possible.

Another source of dissatisfaction with presuppositional analysis may arise from the consideration that if the role of philosophy is to disentangle conceptual knots by disambiguating contested concepts, then philosophy does not appear to contribute very much. In other words, patrolling the borders between the humanities and science by sorting out the relations of entailment between presuppositions, questions and answers seems too modest a role for philosophy to play. Philosophy, so this sort of objection goes, should not merely be in charge of determining whether a question should be answered by historians or natural scientists; it should be much more ambitious in its aims. The source of this dissatisfaction with presuppositional analysis comes from a traditional conception of metaphysics as a science of pure being whose task is to deliver knowledge of the fundamental structures of reality. What philosophy should do, according to this traditional view of metaphysics, is to give us knowledge, and knowledge of a very fundamental kind. Presuppositional analysis is certainly not ambitious in the sense in which traditional metaphysics can be said to be, since it is not concerned with knowledge acquisition at all. Knowledge, according to Collingwood, is something that is acquired within the sciences, once certain presuppositions are in place. It is chemistry, biology, history that expand our knowledge; if we want to extend our knowledge we should turn to the special sciences; in this regard we should ask the chemist, the biologist and the historian, not the philosopher. What philosophy does provide us is an understanding of the presuppositions on which our thought and knowledge in general rest. But while presuppositional analysis is not ambitious in the sense in which traditional metaphysics is ambitious, since the former denies that it is the task of philosophy to advance knowledge of the fundamental structures of reality, presuppositional analysis is not modest in the same sense in which the Lockean conception of philosophy as the underlabourer of science is modest. In the underlabourer conception physics replaces metaphysics as the science of pure being that is supposed to deliver presuppositionless knowledge of reality and philosophy takes on the much more *modest* role of establishing how and whether the manifest image of reality can be reconciled with the scientific image.

On the underlabourer conception, the task of philosophy is to determine which aspects of the manifest image of reality are compatible with scientific truths, and can therefore be retained without threatening scientific explanations and which aspects, on the other hand, are not, and are therefore to be excised. If a phenomenon that comes under the different descriptions of humanistic and scientific explanations presents the problem of explanatory exclusion, the options available to the underlabourer conception are either to reduce humanistic explanations to scientific ones or, failing that, to eliminate them. We shall return to the way in which the problem of explanatory exclusion is handled by the underlabourer conception in the next chapter. For the time being let us take note of the point that presuppositional analysis is neither ambitious, in the style of traditional metaphysics, nor modest, in accordance with the underlabourer conception. It is not ambitious because it claims that knowledge arises within forms of inquiry and there is no such thing as knowledge independent of context-sensitive standards of evidence. It is not modest because it does not hand over to physics the title of the science of pure being or the science of reality as such. Presuppositional analysis gives philosophy a much more robust role than the underlabourer's conception since it puts it in charge of determining the assumptions on which natural science (as one form of knowledge in the Latin sense of the term *scientia*) rests and thus the conception of reality that corresponds to this set of assumptions. In contrast to the underlabourer conception, presuppositional analysis does not begin with ontological truths which are handed over to it by the physicist, and subsequently try to establish what other truths are compatible with the more basic physical ones. Rather, philosophy seeks to uncover the *forms of inference or judgement which are implicit in the categorial descriptions of reality* of the physicist, just as it tries to uncover the presuppositions which inform the conception of reality of other forms of knowing. The reciprocity thesis (the claim that how we explain and what we explain are inexorably connected) challenges not only the predominant conception of the relation between the sciences, but also the predominant conception of the relation between philosophy and science, thereby rejecting the widespread view that philosophy should take on the role of science's underlabourer. The role of philosophy is instead that of uncovering the presuppositions of knowledge, including scientific knowledge.

A child's question

One of the basic lessons we can learn from Collingwood's account of presuppositional analysis is that scrutinizing questions is as important as assessing answers because the questions we ask betray the presuppositions which give rise to them. Questions are like footprints in the sand left by a person who is no longer on the beach: by following the footprints backwards you can retrace where the person who left them came from; analogously, by understanding the nature of the questions asked, one can detect the presuppositions which gave rise to them. The work of aligning questions with the presuppositions which give rise to them is a kind of logical detective work, but it is not the preserve of professional philosophers. When my daughter was nine a boy in her class died quite unexpectedly. It was a shock. My daughter asked, 'Why did Jack die?' I gave her the medical answer. 'Well', I said, clearing my throat, 'He developed a sore throat which was caused by a very common bacterium. This bacterium – something that happens in very rare cases – became very aggressive. He developed an infection which caused fluid to build around the heart and led to heart complications which eventually caused his death.' My daughter protested loudly, enraged by my failure to grasp *her* question: 'How can you be such an idiot! I do not want the cold fact story. I want the warm feeling story!' She knew that Jack died of heart failure and that this had been brought about by some event further down the chain of efficient causes (although, of course, she did not call them 'efficient causes'). She was not looking for that *kind* of answer. 'He was 9, he had not done anybody any harm, so why him?', she protested; that is what she wanted to know. She was asking me what the *point* of his death was. I tried to explain that, in this case, there was no answer to the *kind* of question she was asking that I could give her, and that is why I answered it the way I did, namely by giving her the medical story she was so clearly uninterested in. So I said: 'If there was a God, then your question could be answered by revealing his plan to us, but since I am not a believer, I do not think there is an answer to the kind of question you are asking; this is not because fathoming God's plans is hard, but because there are no motives to be fathomed in the natural course of events. This, is the only explanation I can give you because I do not believe in God and therefore I cannot give you the kind of answer you are looking for.' She accepted the answer that I could not give her the *kind* of answer she was after because this account of why I did not reply the way she was expecting me to acknowledged the sort of question she was asking, rather than providing an answer to a different kind of question, namely one of a medical nature. My enraged nine-year-old was looking for an explanation that invoked a humanistic sense of causation, where to find a cause is to uncover the point of what happens. She distinguished between different kinds of explanatory answers and was clearly unhappy when my because-answer did not address the kind of why-question she was asking. She did not tolerate what she took to be either a gross misunderstanding of her question or an attempt to change the subject by pretending that she had asked a different *kind* of question, one that *could* indeed be answered by invoking an efficient notion of causation. The *kind* of question that she identified as remaining unanswered by the medical story is the kind of question which is addressed by humanistic explanations, explanations which satisfy our thirst for meaning. When we seek to interpret the actions of others and ask why they acted as they did, what motives they had for so acting, we do not want their actions to be explained in the way in which an engineer answers questions about the working of the air-conditioning system or a car mechanic explains engine failure. Our curiosity is satisfied when the explanation enables us to see the point of their action and thereby makes it meaningful. Sometimes explanations invoking motives can be misapplied. We can say that the plant turns its leaves towards the window because 'it seeks the sun' or that the weather 'is punishing us'. When we say this sort of thing, we overextend humanistic explanations beyond their proper sphere of application. But equally, if we answer a request for a motive or reason by invoking a sense of 'because' which does not align with the kind of 'why-question' asked, we also trespass into a different explanatory territory. The boundaries between the conceptual territory to which different kinds of explanations apply will always be disputed. Religiously inclined persons may object that my daughter's question was appropriately posed and that she was not mistaken in asking for an explanation of her classmate's death that invoked some reason or motive. Whilst border disputes may be unavoidable and the borders between one territory and another may be redefined (we might one day discover to our complete dismay that rocks are agents whose plans we were just unable to fathom), the distinction between one kind of explanations and the other cannot be obliterated without assuming there is no possible context in which one might ask questions whose answers require making sense of things in the way in which my daughter would have liked to have made sense of her classmate's death.

3

Causal exclusion and the elephant in the room

Rationalizing explanations (of actions) and nomological explanations (of events)

Humanistic explanations, for Collingwood, are sense-making explanations which invoke a specific sense of causation and have a distinctive logical form (Dray 1957; 1958; 1963; 1980). They make sense of what happens by rationalizing it rather than showing that something happens as a matter of routine. Making sense of something is quite different from showing that it is something that happens in certain circumstances: one could know that something happens routinely, when certain circumstances apply, without understanding why it happens in a way that makes sense of it. One could know, for example, that a particular tribe performs a certain dance after prolonged periods of draughts and one could formulate a general empirical law according to which whenever the rainfall is low the tribe performs the dance, without thereby understanding the point of the dance. But if one knew that the tribe danced because they were pleading with the rain gods, one would know what the dance was for and thus why, in a particular sense of 'why', the members of the tribe were dancing.

The distinction between nomological (i.e. routine) and rationalizing (i.e. sense-making) explanations is often overlooked or misunderstood. Rationalizing explanations are (erroneously) presented as camouflaged nomological explanations in which the explanans are antecedent conditions of an internal kind (mental states, such as beliefs and desires) rather than external events, such as the dropping of the temperature and the presence of water in a bucket left outside. Given this (mistaken) assumption, the objection to the idea that rationalizations are a distinctive kind of explanation runs as follows. Consider Collingwood's example of the ancient tribe who takes the long and perilous route around a mountain chain rather than crossing it to reach its destination (Collingwood 1946: 317). What the tribe does is explained, so the argument goes, by invoking certain antecedent conditions, the mental states of the agents (their believing that the mountains are inhabited by ill-intentioned devils, and their desiring to reach their destination safely) together with the general psychological law that everyone who desires to reach safely their destination will avoid situations which they regard as dangerous. The explanation, so the argument goes (Hempel 1942), is nomological and has the same logical structure as the explanation of why water freezes when the temperature drops, even if the kind of laws it invokes are of a different (psychological) nature.

This reasoning, which is often invoked to reduce sense-making explanations to routine/nomological ones, rests on a mistake. In the context of rationalizing explanations beliefs and desires are not antecedent conditions of an inner/psychological nature: rather, they play the role of premises in a practical argument that justifies (in an admittedly weak sense of justify) the action. In sense-making explanations beliefs and desires are a different kind of 'cause' altogether. The behaviour of the ancient tribe who take the tortuous and treacherous path rather than cross the mountain chain in order to reach their destination is not explained (in a humanistic context of explanation) by invoking antecedent conditions of an internal/psychological nature (the mental states of *believing* and *desiring*), together with a psychological generalization (whoever is in the mental states of believing x and desiring y will do z). It is explained instead by showing that it is rationally entailed by the propositional content of the epistemic and volitional premises, through the reconstruction of a practical syllogism in which the action is understood as the rational thing to do in the light of those premises. This kind of explanation invokes the consideration that the presence of devils presented (in the eyes of the tribe) a cause for concern. The conduct of the tribe is explained by invoking what Collingwood calls sense I of causation, the sense in which the term is used in statements such as 'Mr Baldwin's speech caused the adjournment of the house' (Collingwood 1940: 290). In statements such as these, the term 'cause' clearly does not have the same meaning as in 'heavy rain causes River Trent to burst its banks', as in the headline of ITV news of 27/09/2012.

When the tribe's decision is explained by invoking sense I of causation a certain kind of puzzlement (why on earth did they not take the safe and fast route to the destination?) is dispelled, in the way in which the curiosity of someone who wonders why Paul made a trip to town is satisfied when one is told that he had unexpected guests for dinner (and wanted to prepare them fish bought from the fishmonger rather than the local supermarket). This kind of explanation shows what the point of Paul's trip to town is, not what Paul normally does when he has guests for dinner. *What* is explained, for Collingwood (the explanandum), depends on *how* it is explained (the sense of causation invoked in the explanation). Because rationalizing explanations are sense-making explanations that invoke a distinctive concept of cause, they have a unique explanandum: actions. Actions, so understood, differ from events not because they are the things that humans do, but because they are the correlative of a certain kind of (humanistic) explanations. They elude nomological explanations not because they are not-natural or supernatural, but because rationalizing explanation brings reality under a different description, one which captures a different category of things.

The target of Collingwood's criticism, namely the view that humanistic explanations of actions are not different in kind from nomological explanations of events, has a long pedigree. Mill (1843 book VI, chapters III and IV) claimed that it is a mistake to think that action explanations are different in kind from explanations of events. All explanations appeal to laws. The fact that humanistic explanations invoke psychological rather than natural laws does not change their logical status. Mill did concede that there are some differences between humanistic explanations and explanations in physics. The difference lies in the degree of accuracy of their predictions. While the explanations of physics are exact, humanistic explanations are not. But this is purely a distinction in the degree of accuracy of their predictions, not in the logical form of the explanation. The philosophically relevant distinction, Mill claimed, is not between irreducible, sui generis humanistic explanations (of actions) and scientific explanations (of events), but between exact and inexact sciences. Humanistic explanations are inexact explanations, just like those of tidology or meteorology, whose predictions are imprecise because of the complexity of antecedent conditions (the configuration of the bottom of the ocean, for example, in the case of tidology, or the direction of the winds, in the case of meteorology). On Mill's account, therefore, actions are species of events, events which have internal causes (mental states such as beliefs and desires) rather than external ones.

It is precisely this picture of the relation between humanistic and scientific explanations that Collingwood rejects. The explanation of action is not a nomological explanation that invokes a peculiar kind of antecedent condition (internal mental states rather than external events) and a particular kind of law (a psychological law rather than a physical one). It is an explanation of a different kind. It is because humanistic explanations have a distinctive logical form that their subject matter is irreducible to that of the natural sciences. The concept of Actions (understood as the correlative of rationalizing explanations) is not a species of the concept Event (in the way in which, for example, red is a species of the genus colour). It is a sui generis concept that defines the distinctive subject matter of humanistic explanations. The non-reductivism defended within a conception of philosophy as presuppositional analysis rests on the assumption that the distinction between humanistic and scientific understanding is a distinction in kind, not in degree. The relevant distinction for Collingwood is not between sciences such as physics, whose laws are strict, and sciences whose laws are hedged by *ceteris paribus* clauses (chemistry, geology, biology and also psychology), but between different forms of knowledge or forms of inquiry which ask and answer different kinds of questions. Presuppositional analysis defends the view that explanation varies according to context or, as Collingwood puts it, that there are different senses of causation that are mobilized to address different kinds of puzzlement. Such analysis informs an argument for methodological pluralism against the claim for the unity of science. This explanatory pluralism is genuinely *methodologically* non-reductive: it rejects the view that explanations which invoke motives as their explanans are of a piece with explanation which invoke antecedent conditions, be these external ones, such as the dropping of the temperature, or internal ones, such as mental states (or their neural realizers). It also denies that explanations of different kinds are in competition with one another. They do not compete epistemically because they answer different questions. They do not compete ontologically because, given the reciprocal relation between *how* and *what* one explains, there is no explanation that is metaphysically privileged. Collingwood's defence of the autonomy of humanistic explanations does not require us to assume that there are as many layers of causation as there are kinds of explanations. It entails only that humanistic and scientific explanations provide answers to different kinds of questions and that, given the reciprocal relation which holds between method and subject matter in any form of inquiry, it is not possible to answer the questions asked by one form of inquiry by adopting the method of another. Given this conception of the relation between different forms of knowledge, the kind of questions that a non-reductive philosophy of mind should address are not questions about whether the mind has causal powers, or about whether the causal efficacy of the mental can be defended against the backdrop of a naturalistic conception of reality. The task of philosophy is *not* to establish how, if at all, mind can fit into the natural world. The questions a philosophy of mind should address are questions about the nature of humanistic explanations, about how they differ from scientific ones and about what their respective explananda are. They are conceptual questions about what it means to explain a phenomenon from a scientific or humanistic point of view, about the kind of questions that science asks and answers and the kind of questions asked and answered by the humanities. These are the kind of questions that a non-reductive philosophy of mind ought to address. But they are not the kind of questions that tend to be addressed by the philosophy of mind.

Reframing the questions of the philosophy of mind

Much contemporary philosophy of mind has been preoccupied by the problem of causal exclusion. Consider the question 'Why did Paul go to the fishmonger?' and the explanation 'because he has guests for dinner'. Do explanations of this kind conflict with neurophysiological explanations? The problem of causal exclusion arises because it is assumed that explanations at the physical level aspire to be complete, to answer all questions and solve all problems, including that of why Paul went to the fishmonger. Given the aspiration of physics to provide complete explanations of reality, the reply 'because he has guests for dinner' becomes problematic unless it can be accommodated within a naturalistic story. To accommodate the way actions are ordinarily explained (by showing what the point of doing them is) within the neurophysiological story, the ordinary explanation must be rewritten in nomological form. This is done in two steps. First, beliefs and desires must be understood as states of affairs which occur before Paul's bodily movements. Once the beliefs and desires are understood as antecedent states of affairs, the rationalizing sense-making explanation 'because he has guests for dinner' is reduced to a routine explanation by claiming it is nothing but a truncated causal/nomological explanation for what happened, i.e. what Hempel (1942) called an 'explanation sketch'. The causal/nomological explanation goes like this: Paul has certain beliefs (that he can find fish at the fishmonger, that his guests are coming for dinner, etc.) and certain desires (to cook fish for his guests). There is a general psychological law according to which whenever someone has certain beliefs and certain desires, they engage in a certain type of behaviour. Ergo, Paul goes to the fishmonger. Second, once the ordinary explanation is shown to be a covert causal/nomological explanation, it is possible to accommodate it in a naturalistic picture of reality by finding correlations between the beliefs and desires (understood as antecedent conditions of a psychological nature) and the brain states. By doing this, the problem of causal exclusion is avoided and so is the need to eliminate ordinary explanations to avoid conflict with neurophysiological ones.

Had Collingwood been alive at the end of the twentieth century, he would have regarded one of the fundamental issues that has dominated analytic philosophy of mind, the problem of causal exclusion, to arise as a result of the failure to disambiguate the explananda of humanistic and scientific explanations. He would have regarded the very idea that explanations of actions such as 'Paul went to town to fetch fish for his guests' are in conflict with neurophysiological explanations to be as absurd as the suggestion that the explanation of the causes of death provided by a coroner is in conflict with the explanation of the causes of death provided by a political journalist. Humanistic explanations are not psychological explanations which apply the same notion of nomological causation to a different set of concepts (beliefs and desires rather than brain states); they are different kinds of explanation altogether, which answer different kinds of questions and satisfy a different kind of curiosity. It is not simply that when one explains why Paul made a trip to town to purchase fish, one invokes antecedent conditions of a psychological nature (his *wanting* to serve fish to his guests and his *believing* that the quality of the fish sold at the fishmonger in town is superior to that sold at the supermarket) rather than neural states; this sort of humanistic explanation has a different logical form, one which invokes a different sense of 'cause'. Therefore, while much contemporary philosophy of mind addresses the problem of causal exclusion, Collingwood would have argued that this problem arises because of certain assumptions concerning the nature of explanation and the relation holding between the sciences: it is only if one assumes, to begin with, that there is a homogeneous notion of causation that does not vary according to explanatory context, that the question of the place of mind in nature (how mind fits within the network of causal explanations in the natural sciences) arises and that the problem of causal exclusion can take centre stage. Rather than trying to solve the problem of causal exclusion, Collingwood would have called for a re-examination of the most general question that has occupied most philosophers of mind, namely the question of the place of mind in nature as it features, for example, in C. D. Broad's *The Mind and its Place in Nature* (1925) or Jaegwon Kim's *Mind in a Physical World* (1998).

This chapter aims to identify the fundamental assumptions which give rise to the question that has dominated much contemporary philosophy of mind, the question of the place of mind in nature and to show how radically different the current forms of non-reductivism are from Collingwood's explanatory pluralism. Contemporary forms of non-reductivism operate with a homogeneous notion of causation that fails to acknowledge that the logical form of explanation is not the same across explanatory contexts. As a result, they face the problem of causal exclusion, a problem which they seek to resolve by adopting a layered view of the sciences. Collingwood's explanatory pluralism, by contrast, operates with a heterogeneous notion of causation which rejects the hierarchical conception of the relation between the sciences that most forms of contemporary non-reductivism accept. In order to understand how tame contemporary forms of non-reductivism are in comparison to Collingwood's explanatory pluralism, we need to take a detour and take a look at contemporary philosophy of mind. The details will unavoidably be sketchy given the nature of our project here, which is not to provide a nuanced discussion of how the question of the place of mind in nature has been answered in the philosophy of mind, but rather to explain why Collingwood urges us to rethink the relation between forms of knowledge and the sort of questions a philosophy of mind should be addressing. I would request the reader's patience at this point, but we shall soon return to Collingwood.

The question of the place of mind in nature

The question of the place of mind in nature is not completely new. Descartes ([1641] 2008) had asked how the mind can interact with the body, given that the mind is immaterial and incapable of making physical contact with something material. In contemporary philosophy of mind addressing this question requires explaining how one might avoid an apparent conflict between folk-psychological or everyday explanations of actions and neurophysiological ones. The question to which an answer is sought arises because of an underlying commitment to two assumptions:

1. The view that the notion of causation is uniform across all explanatory contexts
2. The view that the explanations of physics are complete explanations

The first assumption expresses a commitment to methodological monism, namely the view there is a single notion of causation that does not change in accordance with the kind of questions one tries to answer. The sense of causation that is taken to be uniform across explanatory contexts tends to be a nomological sense of causation. On this view, a view which was defended by Hempel (1942), to explain something, indeed to explain anything, requires us to subsume it under a general law. In a nomological explanation, the explanandum is accounted for by invoking certain antecedent conditions and a general empirical law. For example, the freezing of the water in a bucket (the explanandum) is accounted for by invoking the antecedent conditions (the dropping of the temperature below 0°C) and the general law (that water freezes below 0°C). Nomological explanations are assumed to apply to scientific as well as to humanistic contexts. The everyday explanation of Paul's trip to town, which states that Paul went in order to buy fish for his guests, is deemed to be a nomological explanation which invokes certain antecedent conditions (Paul's desire to cook fish for his guests and his belief that the fishmonger in town sells better fish than the local supermarket) and a general law (anybody who desires x and believes y does z). The logical form of this explanation, that is, the sense of causation invoked, it is argued, is the same as that used when explaining why water freezes. In other words, 'because' in 'Paul went to the fishmonger *because* he wanted to cook a delicious dinner for his guests' has the same meaning as 'because' in 'the water froze *because* the temperature dropped below 0°C'. Given this commitment to a homogeneous sense of causation, the way in which Paul's trip to town is explained is no different from that in which any natural phenomenon (the freezing of water, the explosion of a volcano) is explained, i.e. by invoking certain antecedent conditions and general laws. In the philosophy of mind neurophysiological explanations take the place of the sort of explanations that one gives for natural phenomena, such as the freezing of water, volcanic explosions and flooding. The antecedent conditions are the states of Paul's brain *before* his bodily movements. There are therefore two explanations with the same logical form (the psychological and the neurophysiological explanation). The psychological explanation operates with beliefs, desires and psychological laws. The neurophysiological explanation operates with neural states and neurological laws but the two explanations are not different in kind: they both invoke antecedent conditions, beliefs and desires in one case, brain states in the other, and general laws. Assumption 1 (there is a uniform notion of causal explanation that applies to all explanatory contexts) together with assumption 2 (a commitment to the claim that physical explanations are complete and leave nothing unexplained) give rise to the problem of causal exclusion: it cannot be the case that both the neurophysiological and the psychological explanations are true.

Reductive physicalism as defended by Place (1956) J. J. C. Smart (1959) and H. Feigl (1958) solved the problem of causal exclusion by adopting a hierarchical model of the sciences in which the explanations of physics enjoy ontological primacy, that is, by introducing a third assumption:

3. The explanations of physics are ontologically basic, i.e. they alone capture real causal relations

In this layered model of the sciences there are multiple explanations, but causation proper is not an explanatory relation: it is a *real* relation. Further only the explanations of physics capture genuine *causal* relations. Having ordered the sciences hierarchically, reductive physicalists solve the problem of causal exclusion by arguing that beliefs and desires have causal efficacy in virtue of their neural realizers. There is, for the reductive physicalist, a one-to-one correlation between the explanans invoked in folk-psychological explanations, i.e. beliefs and desires, and the brain states invoked in neurophysiological explanations; the former have causal efficacy because they are identifiable in a lawlike way with their neural realizers. In this naturalistic framework it is the physical realizers of beliefs and desires (the neural states) that do the real causal work. There is therefore no causal conflict between psychological and neurophysiological explanations because mental states such as beliefs and desires, the reductivist argues, are causally efficacious, not qua mental, but qua physical. In this way reductivism seeks to do justice both to the claim that the mind is causally efficacious *and* to the claim that the explanations of physics are complete whilst avoiding causal exclusion. Paul's beliefs and desires are causally efficacious in virtue of being reducible (via empirically discoverable lawlike connections) to neural states, which are what truly or really does the causing. The naturalism in these three background assumptions is both methodological and ontological. It is methodological because it assumes that the sense of causation that is used in psychological explanations is the same as that at work in neurological explanations and therefore that humanistic explanations are not different in kind from scientific explanations. It is also ontological because it claims that only explanations in physics capture real causal relations.

Collingwood's metaphysics of absolute presuppositions rejects these background naturalistic assumptions, methodological and ontological alike. Presuppositional analysis rejects methodological naturalism because it denies that the concept of causation (what it means for one thing to be the cause of another) is uniform across explanatory contexts. Humanistic explanations are not nomological explanations which invoke psychological rather than neurological laws; they are species of justification which rationalize the action by presenting it as the conclusion of a practical argument. Secondly, presuppositional analysis rejects the view that there is a sense of causation that is ontologically or metaphysically privileged; it avoids causal exclusion not by ordering forms of knowledge hierarchically, but by arguing that explanations must be fit for purpose. Given the rejection of these naturalistic assumptions the kind of non-reductivism supported by presuppositional analysis is very different from (and much more robust than) contemporary forms of non-reductivism which, by contrast, tend to accept (either all or some of) the naturalistic assumptions that enable reductivism to explain how the mind can have causal powers without facing the problem of causal exclusion. In the following my task will be to highlight just how weak contemporary forms of non-reductivism are when compared to Collingwood's explanatory pluralism, and why they all singularly fail to address the elephant in the room, viz. the consideration that the sense of causation deployed by scientific explanations is unsuited to address the sort of curiosity that one is trying to satisfy when, for example, one inquires after the point of Paul's going to the fishmonger in town.

Non-reductivism and the elephant in the room

While reductivism is still a widely shared position, it may be fair to say that the orthodoxy in the philosophy of mind tends to be non-reductivist. But the forms of non-reductivism currently defended tend to be extremely bland. Most forms of non-reductivism in contemporary philosophy of mind tend to accept the naturalistic assumptions that govern reductivism while rejecting its conclusions. Let us consider, first, non-reductive physicalism. Non-reductive physicalism suggests that there are no type identities between mental and physical states. Contrary to what the reductive physicalist claims, there are no empirical laws connecting the beliefs and desires invoked in psychological explanations to their neural realizers. This might seem good news for those who think that the mental enjoys autonomy. But is not really so. What motivates non-reductive physicalists to deny that there are any bridge laws connecting psychological states such as beliefs and desires with their underlying neural realizers is *not* the consideration that something is amiss with a commitment to methodological reductivism, i.e. with the idea that there is a uniform notion of causation that is applicable in all contexts. Rather, the non-reductivist's worry tends to be that since it is conceivable that a creature with a very different physiology from humans, say a Martian, could still have the same mental states as humans, say, headaches, then headaches might be instantiated in different kinds of physical states. This worry was addressed by what was deemed to be one of the most promising forms of non-reductivism, namely multiple realization functionalism (Putnam 1975). According to this approach the mental state of being in pain can be realized in different physical systems so that, for example, an octopus and a human, who have very different physiologies, can both still be said to be in pain. Multiple realization functionalism denies there are bridge laws or type identities between mental and physical states without questioning reductive physicalism's commitment to methodological unity in the sciences; it accepts that all explanation is nomological explanation, and that explanations which invoke the concept of mind are of a piece with the nomological explanations used to explain anything in nature. The thought that the logical form of explanation suitable to explain the mental may not be nomological is simply *not* part of the motivation for multiple realization functionalism. Thus, whatever the merits of multiple realization functionalism in addressing the concern that creatures with a different physiological make up from that of humans may still have mental states like headaches, it does not answer the worry that humanistic explanations address different kinds of questions, which arise because of different presuppositions, and that answering these questions requires invoking a different sense of causation. Bearing firmly in mind the point we have just made, namely that this sort of non-reductivism does not even begin to address the consideration that 'because' in humanistic explanations may mean something else than 'because' in nomological explanations, let us now consider how non-reductivism addresses the problem of causal exclusion that the reductive physicalist solved by claiming the mental is causally efficacious qua physical.

The options available to the non-reductivist attempting to respond to the problem of causal exclusion against the naturalistic assumptions which give rise to the question of the place of mind in nature are limited. When such non-reductivists seek to defend the autonomy of the mental, they are forced to choose between arguing that mental states are causally efficacious qua mental (rather than in virtue of their physical realizers, as reductivists claim) or endorsing epiphenomenalism. Neither option is unproblematic. Fodor (1989) took the first route, basing his defence of the causal efficacy of psychological explanations on the consideration that psychological explanations, like explanations in physics, invoke causal laws. Causal laws are generalizations which specify nomologically sufficient conditions for the occurrence of an event (Fodor 1989: 64). There is no reason, Fodor argues, for thinking that this model of explanation should not be applicable to the special sciences (chemistry, biology, etc.) simply because such sciences are unable to provide precise predictions. The fact that the special sciences only project what must happen, everything else being equal, implies only that the covering law under which an event is subsumed should be hedged by *ceteris paribus* clauses. The difference between the special sciences (amongst which psychological explanations of everyday actions are included) and physics is not that whereas the former employ mere generalizations, the latter employ genuine causal laws, but that the laws of physics, being strict, deductively entail the *explanandum*, whereas the laws of the special sciences, being non-strict, only probabilistically entail it. If the nomological model of explanation applies to all sciences, including psychology, then there is no reason to doubt that there are intentional causal laws, and thus to doubt the causal efficacy of the mental *qua* mental; if nomological explanations in physics are causally efficacious, so are explanations in chemistry, biology, geology and, crucially, psychology, for these explanations too are nomological. There is no special problem that is posed by the mental as opposed to the chemical, biological and geological level of explanation, or indeed that of any other special science (Fodor 1989: 59). To support this claim, Fodor offers a sort of reductio ad absurdum of the epiphenomenalist claim: if epiphenomenalism entails that beliefs and desires are 'not real' because what does the causal work are not the beliefs and the desires, but the neurophysiological processes in which such beliefs and desires are realized, then it must also be the case that mountains, lakes, etc., are not real because it is not mountains but atoms that figure in the explanation of the basic sciences. The relevant distinction to be made, therefore, is not between physics and psychology, but between sciences such as physics, on the one hand, whose laws are strict, and sciences whose laws are hedged by *ceteris paribus* clauses, sciences such as chemistry, biology, geology and psychology, on the other. Epiphenomenalism concerning special laws, including intentional laws, is unwarranted in spite of multiple realization functionalism's commitment to a form of token physicalism rather than reductive physicalism.

This defence the causal efficacy of the mental, it is important to note, is based on an argument *for* rather than an argument *against* methodological unity in the sciences; it is an argument based on the consideration that the distinction between the physical explanations of events and the psychological explanations of action is a distinction in degree rather than in kind. There is, in Fodor's defence of the causal efficacy of the special sciences, more than an echo of John Stuart Mill's distinction between explanation in the exact and the inexact sciences. For Mill (1843 book VI, chapters III and IV), as indeed for Fodor, the relevant distinction is between exact and inexact sciences, not between forms of knowing which invoke natural laws and forms of knowing which invoke rationalizations. Even if multiple realization functionalism succeeded in defending the causal efficacy of the mental qua mental whilst avoiding the problem of causal exclusion, it still would not address the elephant in the room: the concern that humanistic explanations deploy a different kind of inference, one which invokes a different sense of causation which needs to be carefully disambiguated from that at work in the natural sciences. From the perspective of Collingwood's explanatory pluralism, multiple realization functionalism hardly qualifies as a form of non-reductivism because it does not challenge the commitment to methodological unity in the sciences.

Be this as it may, this attempt to defend the autonomy of the mental is not just vulnerable to this kind of external criticism, according to which it singularly fails to acknowledge the normative character of the mental; it also suffers from its own internal problems. If the explanations of the special sciences (including those of psychology) are genuinely causally efficacious, then the events which they seek to explain are causally overdetermined by psychological as well as physical laws, and the problem of causal exclusion, which reductive physicalism avoided by arguing that mental states are causally efficacious in virtue of their neural realizers, arises once again. This problem can be solved only by paying an ontologically heavy price, viz. by claiming that there are as many levels of reality as there are explanatory layers. As Heil puts it:

> functionalism is also committed to a distinction of ontological levels. It is not merely that talk of minds and their operations is a higher-level way of talking about what is, at bottom, a purely material system. Rather, higher-level mental terms designate properties taken to be distinct from properties designated by lower-level terms deployed by scientists concerned with the material compositions of the world.
>
> (Heil 1999: 93)

Multiple realization functionalism can avoid the problem of causal exclusion only by introducing multiple layers of reality corresponding to multiple layers of explanation. These considerations may explain why some forms of non-reductivism have looked on epiphenomenalism as an appropriate solution to be endorsed to avoid causal exclusion rather than as a problem to be solved. Chalmer's (1996) naturalistic dualism, for example, argues that there are mental properties which are irreducible to physical properties, but since these do no causal work, they do not threaten the completeness of physics. Naturalistic dualism is not a form of non-reductive *physicalism* because it explicitly allows for a dualism of properties, but it still operates within a naturalistic framework. Since it strips the mind of causal powers, it does not challenge the three assumptions that give rise to the question of the place of mind in nature: it accepts (1) that there is a uniform notion of causation captured in nomological explanations; (2) that the explanations of physics are complete and (3) that they are ontologically privileged. Like multiple realization functionalism, naturalistic dualism does not consider the possibility that the notion of causation is not homogeneous but sensitive to the context of inquiry.

In sum, there are two problems with the forms of non-reductivism operating within the naturalistic assumptions which give rise to the question of the place of mind in nature. The first is that when they try to defend the autonomy of the mental within a naturalistic framework, they are confronted with two equally unpalatable options: to avoid causal exclusion they either have to multiply levels of reality or they have to accept epiphenomenalism. Hopefully this brief (and I am very aware, far too sketchy) foray in the philosophy of mind has given some indication of how a metaphilosophical commitment to certain naturalistic assumptions, be they methodological (the claim that there is only one sense of causation) or ontological (the claim that only explanations in physics capture real causal relations), limits the moves available to non-reductivists for solving the problem of causal exclusion within a naturalistic framework. A great deal of contemporary philosophy of mind has been devoted to establishing whether a naturalistic-friendly non-reductivism can avoid the problem of causal exclusion without accepting that the mental is epiphenomenal, thereby renouncing what is often taken to be a key advantage of reductive physicalism, i.e. the ability to explain how mental states are causally efficacious by reducing them, through empirically discoverable laws, to the underlying physical states (which do the causing). The internal tensions from which non-reductive physicalism suffers have been extensively discussed by Crane and Brewer (1995) and Kim (1988; 1989;

1990; 1992 and 1998) amongst others. The second problem, one that is less discussed but is arguably more fundamental, is that since the naturalistic assumptions which inform non-reductivism are not usually subjected to critical scrutiny, most forms of non-reductivism in contemporary philosophy of mind do not even begin to address the worry that humanistic explanations are distinct in kind from scientific ones. I have referred to this second problem as the elephant in the room. Unlike most forms of non-reductivism, Collingwood's conception of philosophy as a form of presuppositional analysis does not address the quasi-Cartesian question of the place of mind in nature against the background of certain naturalistic assumptions. Rather, presuppositional analysis demands a reassessment of the kind of questions a philosophy of mind should be asking. Before returning to Collingwood, however, we need to look at Davidson because he raised an important challenge to Collingwood's defence of humanistic understanding while acknowledging that the concept of mind has a normative dimension that cannot be swept under the carpet as most forms of non-reductivism in philosophy of mind do.

Davidson's challenge

Davidson articulated an important challenge to Collingwood's explanatory pluralism. This challenge needs to be considered because it is often thought to have dealt a fatal blow against the form of non-reductivism Collingwood defends. Davidson agrees with Collingwood's claim that the explanation of action has a different logical form from the explanation of events in that it requires a rationalization. To this extent, Davidson's non-reductivism, Anomalous Monism, is the closest one finds to Collingwood's position in this regard. But he must also be regarded as one of his most insidious enemies. In *Actions Reasons and Causes* (1963) Davidson launched an important challenge to Collingwood's explanatory pluralism. He claimed that genuine action explanations are not mere rationalizations, as Collingwood thought.

An appeal to rationalization alone, he argued, cannot support the distinction between reasons for acting and the 'real' reasons why a person acts. An action can be brought under different descriptions depending on what one takes the goal of the agent in acting to be. Anscombe (1957) illustrated this claim through a now famous example of a man pumping water. The man pumping water might have been replenishing the water supply or poisoning the inhabitants of the house. These are both plausible descriptions of the action which reflect the ascription of different reasons for acting. The method of rationalization alone (so Davidson's argument goes) cannot determine which rationalization captures the man's intention in acting. In order to capture the distinction between possible reasons for acting and the reasons why a person acts or reasons which are genuinely explanatory, one must single out, amongst the possible practical syllogisms that rationalize the actions, the one on which the agent acted. The practical syllogism on which the agent acted is one in which the epistemic and conative premises capture real psychological states (beliefs and desires) which precede the action which the practical syllogism rationalizes. Rationalizations which are genuinely explanatory (which capture the reasons why an agent acts as opposed to reasons on which they might have acted) are such that the beliefs and desires invoked to rationalize the action are not merely premises in a practical syllogism but also antecedent conditions of an inner psychological nature; they are, one might say, an efficient cause. This is not to say that rationalizing explanations are nomological explanations, but that the connection between the explanans and the explanandum is not exclusively one of rational entailment holding between the premises and the conclusion of an argument. Davidson's argument in *Actions Reasons and Causes* was widely regarded as vindicating the claim that genuine explanations of action cannot be mere rationalizations and thus as undermining the view that a defence of the autonomy of humanistic explanations could be articulated within the framework of a 'metaphysics without ontology', a view which takes the task of philosophical analysis to be that of detecting presuppositions and dispenses altogether with the notion of causation as an inquiry-independent relation which holds between events irrespective of the goals of inquiry (D'Oro 2011 and 2012).[1]

Collingwood, who died in 1943, could not have anticipated Davidson's challenge, but he would *not* have been sympathetic to the claim that in genuine action explanations the explanans plays the dual role of (a) volitional/epistemic premises which rationally entail the conclusion of the practical argument through which the action is rationalized and of (b) antecedent conditions which precede the bodily movement in time. To say *this* would be to conflate the notion of before and after with that of logical entailment: in some explanations, such as those which are at work in the practical sciences of nature, the cause is something that precedes in time the effect; but in other explanations, namely the sort of rationalizing explanations that one finds in humanistic clarification, the cause is the logical antecedent of the effect. To say that in genuine explanations of action the explanans plays the dual role of a premise in a practical argument and of a psychological state is to conflate one kind of explanation, where the cause is the logical antecedent of the effect, with another kind of explanation, where the cause is a state of affairs that is temporally prior to the effect. Collingwood would have probably argued that both correct and incorrect explanations in a given domain of inquiry must have the *same* logical form, that whether an explanation in a given form of inquiry is correct or incorrect cannot change the logical form of the explanation for that domain of inquiry without thereby changing the subject matter. Consider the following example. A car stops. Why did it stop? The car may have stopped because (a) it had a flat battery, because (b) it run out of petrol, because (c) it had a loose cable or because (d) the driver decided to pull in and take a snapshot of the sunset. The last explanation, explanation (d), does not have the same logical form as the first three. It does not invoke the handle conception of causation that belongs to the practical sciences of nature. It treats the

---

[1] I have explored the bone of contention between Collingwood and Davidson in more depth in D'Oro 2012, where I argued that Davidson's success is to be explained largely by his denial that the concept of causation captures explanatory connections rather than real/metaphysical relations.

stopping of the car not as an event but as an action which is explained by showing its point, i.e. by invoking sense I rather than sense II of causation. It is not just a different explanation; it is an explanation with a different logical form that brings what happens *not simply* under a different description, but under a different *kind* of description. By the same token, if a certain behaviour is explained by invoking something that preceded it, rather than something which makes sense of it by showing its point, one provides a different *kind* of explanation, one that alters the nature of the explanandum. Collingwood would have probably argued (and I am obviously speculating here) that Davidson's argument in *Actions, Reasons and Causes* conflates two questions. The first is a conceptual question about the nature of action explanation, a question about what it means to explain something as a certain type or kind of thing, i.e. as an action. In answer to this conceptual question, Collingwood would have claimed that to explain something as an action type is to rationalize it. The second is an epistemological question as to whether one has really understood another agent's token action. Here Collingwood would have agreed with Davidson that different rationalizations entail different descriptions or capture different actions (such as 'poisoning' or 'replenishing the water supply' in Anscombe's example), and that choosing between one rationalization and another may not always be a straightforward matter. But he would have denied that the consideration that there are cases where it is difficult to choose between one rationalization and another provides legitimate motivation for claiming that rationalizing explanations which capture an agent's goal in acting have a different logical form from rationalizations which explain why it would make sense to act as the agent did. In other words, rationalizations which are true to the agent's goal in acting cannot have a different logical form from rationalizations which are not true to the agent's goal in acting. The logical form of action explanation must be the same whether or not the rationalization succeeds in capturing the agent's motives in acting. If one denies this, one changes the explanandum, just as one would if one explained why the car stopped by saying the driver wanted to take a photo rather than looking for a mechanical fault.

If these considerations are correct, then Davidson's challenge is wrongly posed because it rests on the false assumption that correct and incorrect explanations within the same domain of inquiry have a different logical form. Davidson's argument, however, was generally deemed to have dealt a serious blow to the view that the primary task of philosophical analysis is to answer certain conceptual questions about the nature of explanation and that these conceptual questions are more fundamental than any epistemological worry concerning which explanation in any given domain of inquiry is the true explanation.

Davidson's challenge was seen as providing indirect support for Davidson's distinctive brand of non-reductivism, Anomalous Monism, which reinstated a distinction between domain-relative explanatory relations (or as Collingwood puts it, different concepts/senses of 'causation') and real causal relations. Something needs to be said about Anomalous Monism (Davidson [1970]/1980) because it is the form of non-reductivism in contemporary philosophy of mind which comes closest to acknowledging Collingwood's concern that humanistic explanations are different in kind from scientific explanations. Anomalous Monism concedes that to explain actions is to rationalize them and that rationalizing explanations have a normative dimension which is missing from nomological explanations. Unlike multiple realization functionalism it is not motivated by the worry that reductive physicalism may be unable to account for how creatures with a different physiology from humans may have the same mental states, but by Kant's antinomy of freedom and determinism. While Anomalous Monism is sometimes read as a variation on non-reductive physicalism, it is argued (with good reason) by some to be an ontologically neutral monism, i.e. a distinctive position with its own answer to the problem of causal exclusion (see Stoutland 2011; Heil 2013). As an ontologically neutral monism Anomalous Monism is not committed to the claim that only explanations at the level of physics capture real causal relations. Davidson argues instead that while both rationalizing and nomological explanations establish domain specific explanatory relations, the causal relation is an extensional relation which holds between events *simpliciter* independently of how they are described within any one form of inquiry (Davidson 1993: 13). This distinction between domain-specific explanatory relations (or different senses of 'cause') and real causal relations is Davidson's distinctive 'extensionalist' reply to the problem of causal exclusion. Anomalous Monism argues that causal relations hold between events independently of how these are described in the sciences (as actions which are explained via rationalizations or as events which are explained through nomological explanations); it seeks to avoid causal exclusion by denying that the explanations of physics are ontologically basic (it is an ontologically neutral monism); it seeks to avoid epiphenomenalism by arguing that the causal relation holds between particulars independently of how they are described and explained in any given domain of inquiry. Anomalous Monism acknowledges the elephant in the room, insofar as it grants that nomological and rationalizing explanations have a different logical form and is arguably the only form of non-reductivism in contemporary philosophy of mind that comes any way near to addressing the concerns which motivate Collingwood's explanatory pluralism, namely the need for a concept of mind that is recognized as a normative or, as he puts it, criteriological concept (Boucher 1997: 317ff). Yet by invoking the idea of real relations, i.e. relations that hold between events irrespectively of how these are described within a form of inquiry, Anomalous Monism reintroduces the idea of pure being that Collingwood's metaphysics of absolute presuppositions sought to leave behind by arguing that there is a reciprocal relation between method and subject matter, between the form of the explanation and what one wants to explain, the *explanandum*. Once the legitimacy of any reference to pure being is reintroduced the question, 'which explanatory relation (rational or nomological) is true of events *simpliciter*?' demands an answer and the problem of causal exclusion rears its head once again. Anomalous Monism may have abandoned the commitment to the layered model of the sciences which characterizes most forms of non-reductivism in contemporary philosophy of mind in favour of a neutral monism, but it has not abandoned the kind of metaphysics within which the problem of causal exclusion thrives. Presuppositional analysis ruled out the idea that pure being could have any substantive role to play in a defence of explanatory pluralism by showing that the question 'which sense of causation is real or true?' is a nonsense question. Presuppositions, Collingwood argues, provide the verification criteria through which we can find true or false answers to our questions. It is only once a particular conception of causation is assumed, such as the handle conception of causation (sense II), that it is possible to gather evidence for and against a particular causal claim, and establish, for example, that a plant died because it was overwatered, not because it was not watered at all. This is a crucial difference between the kind of non-reductivism that Davidson defends and Collingwood's explanatory pluralism. Collingwood's defence of the autonomy of humanistic understanding is premised precisely on the view that it makes no sense to speak of causal explanations independently of any questions one seeks to answer or of some set of explanatory goals. Anomalous Monism acknowledges the elephant in the room by conceding that rationalizing explanations are not camouflaged nomological explanations, but it remains committed to a conception of metaphysics that is very different from that which characterizes presuppositional analysis. In Collingwood's metaphysics of absolute presuppositions causation is an explanatory relation that is sensitive to the context of inquiry; it is a category that is embedded in the judgements we make, judgements which enable us to establish domain-specific explanatory connections. The kind of connections that are established depend on the questions one is seeking to answer. In the context of humanistic explanations the term 'cause' is employed in what Collingwood calls sense I to indicate a motive that makes sense, rationally speaking, of an action (Collingwood 1940: 285). It is this sense that it is implied when we say, for example, that one has 'cause' for concern, or in statements such as 'Mr Balwin's speech caused the adjournment of the house' (Collingwood 1940: 290). In the practical sciences of nature, such as medicine and engineering, which are concerned with the manipulation and control of the environment, the term 'cause' is employed in sense II to indicate an 'event or state of things by producing or preventing which we can produce or prevent that whose cause it is said to be' (Collingwood 1940: 296–7). Finally, in the theoretical sciences of nature, such as physics, which abstract from human interests, the term 'cause' is employed in sense III and 'that which is caused is an event or state of things and its cause is another event or state of things such that (a) if the cause happens or exists, the effect must happen or exist even if no further conditions are fulfilled (b) the effect cannot happen or exist unless the cause happens or exists' (Collingwood 1940: 285–6). There is, Collingwood argues, no such thing as a science which studies the relations holding between particulars independently of how they are described in a given explanatory context. One cannot, therefore, meaningfully distinguish between causal explanations and causal relations in the way that Davidson's extensionalist reply to the problem of causal exclusion seeks to do.[2]

The discussion of the different senses of 'cause' in *An Essay on Metaphysics* makes explicit the metaphilosophical commitments of Collingwood's defence of the autonomy of humanistic explanations. He does not claim that humanistic explanations establish conceptual connections and are therefore *mere* rationalizations, whereas scientific explanations establish connections between spatio-temporally distinct events (such as the dropping of the temperature below 0°C and the freezing of water). He claims rather that scientific and humanistic explanations bring reality under different categorial descriptions by deploying different kinds of inferences, inferences which correlate with different senses of causation. Thus, while he may be legitimately described as being part of the anti-causalist consensus (Melden 1961; von Wright 1971) which was the target of Davidson's 'Actions, Reasons and Causes',[3] his non-reductivism is best understood as claiming that there are different senses of the term 'cause', which establish different

---

[2] For an account of Davidson's extensionalist reply, see Hutto (2013) and his exchange with McLaughlin (2013).
[3] For a recent discussion of this anti-causalist consensus, see Schumann (2019; forthcoming) and D'Oro and Sandis (2013).

kinds of explanatory connections, not as stating that humanistic explanations establish *mere* conceptual connections which lack ontological clout. We will return to this claim briefly in Chapter 8.

History, not psychology, as the study of mind

The distinction that is relevant to a defence of the autonomy of humanistic explanations, for Collingwood, is not a distinction between exact and inexact sciences which invoke one and the same kind of (nomological) explanation, but one between forms of knowledge in the Latin sense of the term *scientia*, which establish domain-specific explanatory connections in answer to their characteristic questions. We saw that humanistic explanations are rationalizing, sense-making explanations which account for what happens in a very different way from that in which a tidologist explains the movements of the tides or a meteorologist predicts the weather conditions. What is understood in this way, namely through a rationalization, is brought under the categorial description of action. The concept of 'events' is connected to nomological explanations: they are the descriptions under which reality is brought when what happens is explained by invoking antecedent conditions and general empirical laws. Nomological explanations account for an event's occurrence by showing that it is what normally or routinely happens given certain antecedent conditions and general laws. It is in this way that one explains 'why' water freezes when the temperature drops below 0°C. Rationalizing and nomological explanations are not in competition because they explain different categories of things: actions and events. They do not causally exclude one another because they invoke different senses of 'causation'. Just as there is no problem of causal exclusion in the case of the explanations of the theoretical physicist and the AA mechanic, there is no competition between rationalizations and nomological explanations because they are answers to different questions. This is why Collingwood's explanatory pluralism differs from contemporary forms of non-reductivism which operate with a homogeneous concept of causation that is not responsive to the nature of the questions asked in different explanatory contexts. Thus Collingwood does not try to solve the problem of causal exclusion: he denies there is one.

It is in history, not in psychology, Collingwood claims, that one tends to find the rationalizing sense-making explanations that address the sort of questions we ask when we are guided by a humanistic concern with what happens. It is history, therefore, not psychology, that brings reality under the categorial description of action. To illustrate how a humanistic concern differs from a scientific one we might consider the following example: suppose that a tourist from a distant galaxy with no knowledge of the Catholic faith arrives on Earth when the cardinals are gathered in Conclave, and hovers over St Peter's square in her spaceship. One day the tourist notices crowds in St Peter's square cheering and wonders why. She consults extensive video footage going back centuries and notices that whenever there are large crowds in St Peter's square and white smoke comes out of a chimney, the crowds cheer. She formulates a general law: 'whenever there are large crowds in St Peter's square and there is white smoke coming out of a chimney, the crowds cheer' or, in short, 'the smoke caused the crowds to cheer'. This general law, we should readily admit, does not explain, in the sense of 'explain' relevant to a historian, why the crowds cheered. For the crowds did not cheer on account of the white smoke. They cheered *because* the cardinals gathered in conclave elected a new leader of the Catholic Church. While the tourist provides a nomological explanation for the crowds' cheering that might enable us to either predict it or retrodict it, this kind of explanation singularly fails to capture the symbolic significance of the white smoke; it does not explain the cheering of the crowds in the way in which the tourist would like to understand it if she were a historian, i.e. by grasping what the point of it was. If the intergalactic tourist were a historian, she would want to know what the point of cheering at the sight of white smoke is, what the symbolic significance of the white smoke is for the people gathered in the square. And *this* question is not answered by explaining what happens nomologically or as a matter of routine. Or consider possible answers to the question 'why was he kneeling?' Then consider two possible explanations given in answer to this question: 'He always does that when he enters that building' or 'He is paying his respects'. It is the latter explanation that addresses the concerns of a historian, not the former. Here is another question: 'Why were the bodies in the priory's cemetery buried with their heads facing down?' And then consider the kind of answer which would satisfy the curiosity of a historian: 'to atone for their sins'. The goal of this explanation is not to provide practical advice on how to bury sinners so that they can atone for their transgressions. The historian is not a practical scientist of nature concerned with discovering which antecedent conditions must hold for a certain effect (atonement) to come about in the way in which, say, a structural engineer needs to know what kind of building material is adequate to support the weight of a roof. The goal, for the historian, is to find out the significance or meaning of that practice for the people concerned. And this goal is not well served by the conception of explanation at work in the practical sciences of nature because the historian's question is not asking which antecedent conditions should be manipulated to bring about a certain effect. To explain what happens by showing its point, as in saying 'because a new pope was elected', or 'because he was paying his respects', or 'in order to atone for their sins', is to bring reality under the categorial description of action.

Rationalizations can predict, but they predict in a different way

Contrary to popular myth, rationalizations deployed in humanistic explanations of actions, we have seen, are not camouflaged nomological explanations. One of the features of nomological explanations is that they have the same logical structure whether they are applied to the future or the past: if they are future-directed they yield predictions; if they are past-directed they yield retrodictions, but whether they predict the future or retrodict the past they do so in the same way, namely by subsuming the event under a general law. It may be tempting to think that rationalizations differ from nomological explanations because insofar as they are used to understand why agents acted as they did in a historical context, they tend to be directed at the past rather than the future. It would be a mistake, however, to interpret the claim that rationalizing/sense-making explanations (of actions) do not share the same logical structure as nomological explanations (of events) to imply that whereas events can be predicted, actions cannot. Rationalizing explanations can be used to predict what people may do in the future, just as they can be used to understand what they did in the past. But (and this is the crucial caveat) even when they are used prospectively to yield predictions, they do not predict in the same way in which nomological explanations do. Nomological explanations predict what will happen by means of inductive inferences, that is, by means of observations and empirical generalization. Future-directed sense-making explanations anticipate what someone might do by rationalizing it. Expectations based on prospective rationalizations are therefore not the same kind of expectations that we form on the basis of inductive generalizations based on past observations. When the traffic lights turn red for the cars and green for the pedestrians, we expect the cars to stop at the zebra crossing. This expectation is based on a prospective rationalization, according to which the driver *should* stop at the red lights. That this expectation is not based on a nomological explanation is shown by the fact that if the cars do not stop, we will not blame ourselves for failing to predict that outcome, but blame the unruly driver for failing to do what they should have done. This is not the case when we form expectations based on nomological explanations: when the sun does not shine, as we were led to believe by the weather forecast, we do not blame the weather, but the weather forecast. The distinction between rationalizing and nomological explanations is therefore not that rationalizing explanations are directed at understanding past actions rather than predicting future ones, whereas nomological explanations can be used to predict the future as well as to explain the past. The difference lies in the fact that in a rationalizing explanation the action is understood by invoking the idea of how agents ought to act rather than how they normally act. But while predictions based on prospective rationalizations are possible, they should not be confused with the predictions one finds in natural science which rely on inductive inferences.

Successful predictions of human behaviour based on nomological explanations, according to Collingwood, take advantage of rationalizations which explain behaviour as action. It is only once behaviour is understood as an action (for example, bending one's knee as a sign of respect) that a historically meaningful pattern of paying one's respects can be identified. But to identify a pattern of behaviour such as bending one's knee as symbolizing a sign of respect requires understanding the significance of kneeling, and this in turn requires understanding the bending of the knee as an action in the first instance, just as understanding the cheering of the crowds in St Peter's square requires grasping the significance of the white smoke for the people gathered in the square. As Collingwood puts it,

> Types of behaviour do, no doubt, recur, so long as minds of the same kind are placed in the same kinds of situations. The behaviour-patterns characteristic of a feudal baron were no doubt fairly constant so long as there were feudal barons living in a feudal society, but they will be sought in vain (except by an enquirer content with the loosest and most fanciful analogies) in a world whose social structure is of another kind ... a positive science of mind will, no doubt, be able to establish uniformities and recurrences, but it can have no guarantee that the laws it establishes will hold good beyond the historical period from which its facts are drawn.
>
> (Collingwood 1946: 223–4)

Invoking the norms that guide the conduct of past agents enables historians to form expectations about how they tend to act insofar as they acknowledge those norms, just as, if we understand the traffic regulations, we will be able to predict fairly effectively that drivers will stop at red traffic lights. Predictions based on norms which are sensitive to the social context to which they belong will be more precise than those that can be achieved by a positive science of the mind because, as Collingwood points out, the behaviour patterns characteristic of feudal barons 'will be sought in vain ... in a world whose social structure is of another kind'. What Collingwood says here implies not only the claim that rationalizations have a different logical structure from nomological explanations, but also that they are *not* epistemically inferior explanations with a lower predictive power than that of nomological explanations. The best way to predict what someone will do or to retrodict how they did act is to think like they do; and to think like they do requires us to make the same logical connections that they make, and to recognize as binding the same norms as they do. Of course, agents may act erratically rather than rationally and they may transgress norms even when they acknowledge their validity or at least acknowledge their existence, so predictions based on rationalizations may fail. But they are much more likely to hit the mark than predictions based on empirical generalizations which attempt to explain the actions of historical agents in the same way in which natural scientists explain the movement of the planets or the ebb and flow of the tides. Contrary to a popular philosophical prejudice, according to which humanistic explanations lack the accuracy and predictive power of scientific explanations, they are in fact the most straightforward and effective way of establishing why we do what we do in the future as well as in the past. By Occam's razor, everyday explanations of actions which invoke rationalizations are the simplest, most elegant explanations of actions.

The curse of King Midas

Had Collingwood been living at the end of the twentieth century he would have disagreed in many respects with the way in which twentieth-century philosophy of mind is conducted. He would have thought that much contemporary philosophy of mind lacks a proper grasp of the concept of mind. This failure to understand the concept of mind is reflected by the tendency to focus on psychology rather than history as the home of humanistic explanations of actions. He would have disagreed at a very fundamental level, directing his criticisms not at the solutions that various forms of non-reductivism have advanced, but at the naturalistic assumptions which have given rise to the questions they have sought to address and which have created the problems they have set out to solve. The fundamental question that a philosophy of mind should be addressing, for Collingwood, is not that of the place of mind in nature; it is a question about the chains of questions and answers which are characteristic of humanistic and scientific understanding. Once the explanatory frameworks which govern different forms of knowledge are made explicit by means of presuppositional analysis, it becomes clear that there is no conflict between humanistic and scientific explanations because they do not provide competing answers to the *same* questions but answers to *different* kinds of questions.

Humanistic explanations will not wither away with the progress of natural science because they are not low-grade scientific explanations with a poor predictive power. They are explanations of a different kind, which answer different questions, and are in fact better suited at relieving the specific kind of puzzlement they address than scientific explanations. Even if neurophysiologists will one day be in a position to tell us everything that there is to know about the brain, they will still not have answered the question of why Paul went to the fishmonger, if with this question one wants to know what the point of Paul's action is. The question as to why Paul paid a visit to the fishmonger is fully answered by the rationalization that he needed good-quality fish for his dinner party that night; it is not undermined by the consideration that there are still many things that we do not know about how the brain works and that if we had this full knowledge that question would be answered more satisfactorily by invoking a general psychological law and internal mental states which are reducible via bridge laws to brain states. Given the reciprocal relation which holds between method and subject matter in any form of inquiry, it is not possible to answer the questions asked by one form of inquiry by adopting the methods of another. The very attempt to do so simply leads to a change in subject matter. Since actions are the correlative of rationalizing explanation and events are the correlative of nomological explanation, the ambition of natural science to provide answers to questions other than scientific ones will not deliver the complete explanation of reality that it hopes for. On the contrary it will summon the curse of King Midas (D'Oro 2018a): the universal application of its method will ensure that nothing will ever be encountered as an action since everything that is explained by the method of science is an event. To lift the curse of King Midas science will have to renounce the ambition to answer all questions and thus allow some things to be known in a different way, that is, to be encountered as actions.

4

The 'limits' of science

There is nothing spooky about 'actions'

The idea that science cannot explain everything is often received with suspicion, and those who claim that there are things which are beyond the ken of science are usually taken to be committed to the existence of something spooky, such as transcendent or super-sensible entities which essentially lie beyond the reach of empirical investigation. Collingwood argues that actions cannot be explained through the methods of science because to explain something as an action means we must invoke a certain kind of explanation, one that deploys a different sense of causation. The very attempt to explain actions through the method of science transforms the action into something else, just as the touch of King Midas transforms food into non-edible gold. Should we be suspicious of this claim? Are actions really spooky entities which one should try to eliminate from a respectable naturalist metaphysics? This chapter has two goals. The first is to show that a commitment to the claim that science cannot explain everything is not the same as a commitment to the existence of transcendent or super-sensible metaphysical entities. There is nothing intrinsically spooky about actions. It is perfectly legitimate to say that scientific explanations miss the point of Paul's trip to the fishmonger without committing ourselves to the view that there is something ghost-like, not-natural or supernatural about Paul's action. To explain actions requires answering different kinds of questions from those that science addresses, questions that rest on different presuppositions. To say *this* is not the same as saying that actions are beyond the reach of science because they are transcendent metaphysical entities. Nor is it to point to a failure of science per se. Just as nobody, in their right mind, would expect a detective to be able to solve the mysteries of nature, and think any less of them for being unable to do so, likewise it would be equally unreasonable to expect physicists to solve murder mysteries and to think any less of them for being unable to solve them. The fact that the method of physics is suited to answer a certain kind of question, but not others, is not a limitation on the part of physics but a feature of that form of inquiry. Further, the view that physics should answer all questions and that the inability to do so would be a fault or failure is not itself a scientific claim; it is rather the result of a particular metaphilosophical conception of the relation between the sciences, one which, as we have seen, Collingwood is keen to undermine. The second goal of this chapter is to contrast Collingwood's handling of the question of the 'limits' (we place this within brackets precisely because the inability of science to answer non-scientific questions is not strictly speaking a limitation) of science with the way in which the question tends to be approached in contemporary philosophy of mind. Here it is often argued that the fact of consciousness constitutes the greatest obstacle in the way of science's ability to provide complete explanations of reality. The fact of consciousness seems incomprehensible from a scientific perspective because conscious states are accessed in a unique way, namely by introspection, or from the first-person perspective, and are inaccessible from the observational or third-person perspective of science. This view of consciousness as the most intractable obstacle in the way of science's ability to provide complete explanations of reality presupposes that the philosophical distinction between the mind and the body is primarily an epistemological distinction between the inner and the outer, between the first and the third person. The reason why the mind/body problem persists in spite of the progress of natural science, it is therefore argued, is precisely because of this duality of epistemic access to mental states, the supposed duality of access from the inside and the outside. Collingwood eschews this epistemological approach to the mind-body problem and argues instead that the so-called explanatory gap is semantic rather than epistemological (D'Oro 2007). There is an explanatory gap between the mind and the body, but this is not a gap between mental states which are inner and are accessed through introspection, and external bodily movements which are outer and accessed through empirical observations. The distinction between mind and body is a distinction between explanations with a different logical form: the term 'because', as we have seen, has a different meaning in nomological explanations of events than it has in rationalizing explanations of actions.

Soluble and insoluble mysteries

The idea that what cannot be explained by the methods of natural science is mysterious, in a sense of 'mysterious' that is intrinsically objectionable, is largely the legacy of logical positivism. Although few philosophers today would confess to being unqualified defenders of this school of thought, the idea that what science cannot explain is intrinsically spooky can be traced back to the kind of verificationism that A. J. Ayer (1936) espoused, the very views which Collingwood contested in *An Essay on Metaphysics*. Ayer argued that in order to be meaningful a proposition must be empirically verifiable, unless it is a tautology. Ayer's verificationism was a direct attack on metaphysical propositions concerning transcendent entities, since these are neither empirically verifiable, nor are they mere analytic statements which are true in virtue of their meaning or, as Hume would have said, in virtue of the relations holding between ideas. The proposition 'God exists' as it features in the ontological argument for the existence of God is a case in point. The proposition is neither a contingent empirical proposition which is empirically verifiable through the experimental method, nor is it a necessary proposition that simply unpacks the concept of God since it actually makes an existential claim. Since it is neither of these things, the proposition 'God exists' is meaningless and God is precisely the kind of spooky metaphysical entity which should be eliminated from our ontology. By the same token one would have to conclude that 'actions', understood as the distinctive subject matter of a humanistic concern, just like the concept of God in traditional metaphysics, are spooky transcendent entities which, as Hume said of metaphysical treatises, should be committed to the flames.

Ayer's goal was to show that metaphysical disputes are irresolvable pseudo-disputes. They cannot be resolved, not because the problems which they tackle are intrinsically difficult, but rather because there simply are no criteria that we could appeal to which could help settle such disputes. One example of a metaphysical pseudo-dispute, for Ayer, is the debate between idealists and realists (Ayer 1934). There is no empirical evidence that could be invoked to settle a dispute between idealists who claim that the rain is ideal (a collection of ideas in the mind) and realists who claim that the rain is real (that it exists in a mind-independent way) since the rain looks exactly the same whether one is a realist or an idealist metaphysician. The metaphysical dispute between idealists and realists, for Ayer, is therefore very different from a genuine dispute such as that between two art critics who disagree about the authenticity of a painting attributed to Goya. The dispute between the two art critics may be difficult to settle, but it is one that can in principle be settled. There are clear criteria that could be invoked to settle it: the canvass could be dated by using scientific techniques to ascertain whether it was painted in the times of Goya; the nature of the strokes on the canvass could be compared to those of other certified paintings by Goya; historical records that refer to Goya being commissioned to paint such a picture could be consulted; and so on. Unlike the dispute between the two art critics, metaphysical disputes, Ayer argues, are not genuine disputes because there are no criteria by which they could be settled. It is not so much that they are difficult to settle in practice, but rather that they cannot be settled in principle. This is why there is ultimately no progress in philosophy: metaphysical disputes, unlike those which go on in science, cannot be settled one way or the other, not because they are difficult to settle, but because there are no empirical criteria by which they could be settled.

Collingwood would have agreed with Ayer that knowledge requires a criterion of verification; that there must be some criterion, through appeal to which, one can, at least in principle, settle disagreements between knowledge claims. He disagreed, however, with the assumption that the principle of (empirical) verification is *the* criterion to be used to distinguish between genuine disputes, disputes which can be solved and pseudo-disputes which are in principle insoluble. Any claim to knowledge must be justified by invoking evidence in its support, but the standards of evidence, Collingwood argued, are not the same in all explanatory contexts because different forms of knowledge deploy explanations with a different logical form, explanations which answer different kinds of questions and rest on different presuppositions. The criteria for the verification of knowledge claims, in other words, vary in accordance with the kind of questions one is trying to answer: to discard the rationalization that Paul went to the fishmonger because he had guests for dinner one would have to show that the point of his acting as he did was a different one. Perhaps Paul had gone to the fishmonger just before discovering that his *vegan* friends were going to visit him that night so he would not have made a trip to the fishmonger on their account: the point of his trip was not to cook fish for his friends (or to make his dinner guests uncomfortable); it was to sample their produce. But to redescribe what Paul does in this way is not to subsume Paul's behaviour under a different general law, thereby treating it as an event. According to Collingwood criteria of verification are not the same in all contexts, as Ayer implicitly acknowledged by exempting mathematical propositions from the demand that they be *empirically* verifiable. The task of philosophy is to make explicit the presuppositions which govern different forms of knowledge, thereby exposing their domain-specific criteria of verification. As we have seen, he regarded philosophical disputes which arise when different standards of evidence/verification come into contact and seem to conflict to be a result of a failure to disambiguate the explanandum of different forms of knowledge. He would agree that the dispute (if it were to arise) between the AA mechanic claiming that the car stopped because it had a flat battery and the theoretical physicist claiming that the car stopped because the centre of the earth is further removed from the top than the bottom of the hill is a pseudo-problem. But he would not have regarded the question addressed by the AA mechanic, namely whether the car stopped because it had run out of petrol or whether it stopped because it had a flat battery, as an insoluble metaphysical pseudo-mystery simply because this question cannot be answered by the physicist. Nor would he have regarded the question as to who killed John Doe (Collingwood 1946: 266) as an insoluble metaphysical pseudo-mystery because it cannot be answered by either the practical or theoretical sciences of nature. While not many philosophers today would confess to be endorsing the kind of verificationism advocated by logical positivism, it is a commitment of this kind that underpins the widespread view that what science cannot explain is necessarily mysterious in an objectionable way.

If one accepts that criteria of verification vary in accordance with context, and that one cannot expect the same standards of evidence in all forms of inquiry, then humanistic explanations of actions are identified by discarding rationalizations which fail to show what the point of an action is, just as scientific theories are discarded when they fail to explain the phenomena under investigation. A. J. Ayer's verificationism presupposed that there is only one standard of evidence and one criterion of meaning. In so doing, this approach overlooked the fact that its central proposition, namely that 'claims which are not empirically verifiable are meaningless', is in fact a presupposition of a certain kind of (scientific) inquiry. Collingwood's view is rather that the principle of verification, as understood by logical positivism, is an unacknowledged presupposition of a certain kind of (empirical) inquiry. His claim that the presuppositions which govern forms of inquiry lie beyond empirical verification is therefore not a nod to the principle of verification, as understood by logical positivism, as it is sometimes maintained (Beaney 2005). There is a key difference between Ayer's verificationism, according to which propositions which are not in principle (empirically) verifiable are meaningless unless they are tautologies, and Collingwood's claim that the notion of truth and falsity does not apply to the presuppositions which govern forms of inquiry. Such presuppositions are neither true nor false, not because they are unverifiable in principle rather than in practice, as the logical positivists claimed propositions about transcendent entities to be, but because since they are constitutive of the form of knowledge they make possible it makes no sense to verify them. The attempt to verify them generates the kind of paradox discussed in Lewis Carroll's (1895) 'What the Tortoise said to Achilles' where Carroll exposes the absurdity involved in seeking to justify deductively the principle which governs deductive inferences (D'Oro 2014).[1]

Is consciousness the last stop?

There are two assumptions that tend to dominate the question of the limits of science in contemporary philosophy of mind. The first is that what science cannot explain is, by the very fact that it is beyond the reach of science, problematically mysterious. This, as we have seen, is the legacy of logical positivism. The second is that consciousness is the most mysterious of all things, that it is the thing which is most problematic from a scientific perspective. Consciousness is 'the hard nut of the mind-body problem' (McGinn 1989: 349; Chalmers 1995). How can something like a brain process, it is often asked, give rise to qualitative feels such as the taste of mango? The two things are radically different. In Huxley's words, 'how is it that anything so remarkable as a state of consciousness comes about as a result of initiating nerve tissue, is just as unaccountable as the appearance of the Djin, where Aladdin rubbed his lamp in the story' (quoted in McGinn 1989).

---

[1] I have argued along these lines in 'The Logocentric Predicament and the Logic of Question and Answer' (D'Oro) 2014. Martin (1989 and 1998: xxii ff.) also defends the constitutivist view that absolute presuppositions are *basic conceptions* that come with the territory of doing any science. This view is questioned by Beaney (2005). Beaney disputes the view that absolute presuppositions are constitutive of forms of knowledge or inquiry and sees Collingwood's refusal to attribute truth values to absolute presuppositions as betraying a covert commitment to logical positivism.

The reason why consciousness is often regarded as the most mysterious of all things is that conscious states have a qualitative feel which can be accessed only from the first-person perspective and which lies beyond the third-person perspective of science. Any attempt to explain conscious experiences by reference to physical laws encounters an obstacle that is not present when trying to explain natural phenomena. Take a phenomenon such as lightning, for example. Science has shown that lightning is an electromagnetic discharge in the atmosphere by establishing a correlation between the observable occurrence of a bright flash in the sky and high voltage. But unlike lightning, conscious states are accessible only from the first-person perspective and cannot be observed in the way in which lightening can. Establishing correlations between conscious states and brain states is therefore a much trickier business than establishing correlations between the publicly observable phenomenon of lightning and electromagnetic discharge. The existence of conscious experiences, it is often argued, presents science with a mystery. But this mystery is not a soluble one: lightening was once a mysterious phenomenon, but it is no longer so. For we now know that lightning is electromagnetic discharge. Consciousness, by contrast, presents us with an *insoluble* mystery, one which the progress of natural science cannot solve because the way in which conscious states are accessed, from the inside, locates them *in principle* beyond the reach of scientific explanation. First personal access to conscious states therefore presents science with an insurmountable barrier to explaining consciousness scientifically, a barrier which scientific progress cannot remove. Unlike the phenomenon of lightning (which is publicly observable), the fact of consciousness presents science with an insoluble mystery (one that scientific progress cannot remove) rather than a soluble one (a mystery which can in principle be solved by the progress of science). It is the last stop on the scientific journey towards the complete naturalization of reality.

There have been different reactions to Huxley's challenge. Some have argued that physicalism cannot meet this challenge (Jackson 1986; Kripke 1980; Chalmers 1996). Since physicalism aims to provide complete explanations of reality, but actually fails to explain the phenomenon of consciousness, it must be false. Frank Jackson's (1986) 'knowledge argument' makes use of a thought experiment featuring a colour scientist, Mary, who knows everything neurophysiological that there is to know about colour. However, having been confined from birth to a black and white environment, she has never had a colour experience and does not know what, for example, it is like to have an experience of redness. The thought experiment is devised to show that there is a kind of knowledge, knowledge of *qualia*, that Mary cannot have even though she knows everything that there is to know about colour from a physical point of view. Knowledge of how a sunset looks, or roses smell, and so on, is beyond the reach of physicalism. Since science is supposed, at least in principle, to be able to provide complete explanations of reality, and since the knowledge argument shows there is a kind of knowledge that is in principle, rather than simply in practice, beyond the reach of scientific explanation, physicalism stands refuted.

Another argument aimed at showing that physicalism cannot provide complete explanations of reality was formulated by Saul Kripke (1980) who exploits an asymmetry between scientific identities such as 'heat is the motion of molecules', 'water is H_2O', and mind-body identities such as 'pain is the firing of C-fibres', to undermine the identity thesis. Kripke's argument is that both in the case of scientific and psychophysical identities there is a feeling of contingency about them. There is a feeling of contingency because it seems plausible that we could conceive a world in which water is not H_2O, heat is not molecular motion and pains are not the firing of C-fibres. Yet there is a difference because whilst the feeling of contingency about scientific identities can be explained away, the felt contingency in the case of psychophysical identities cannot. In the case of scientific identities when we believe ourselves to be conceiving of a world in which water is not H_2O or heat is not molecular motion what we are in fact doing is conceiving of undergoing an experience which is qualitatively similar to that of heat but is not caused by molecular motion. The air of contingency in the case of scientific identities is merely apparent. This, however, is not so in the case of psychophysical identities since in the case of pain, pain *just is* the sensation of pain. We can thus conceive of a world in which there is pain but no C-fibres. Since such a world is conceivable, psychophysical identity statements are false.

Panpsychists such as Galen Strawson (2006) or Philip Goff (2017) have more recently intervened in this discussion by arguing that the reason why the existence of conscious states seems so intractable has to do with certain ontological assumptions concerning the ultimate constituents of reality. If the ultimate constituents are thought to be material, then the existence of consciousness looks inexplicable. The proposed solution is to adopt a different ontology to suggest that reality is always already imbued with consciousness at a very fundamental level. Panpsychists do not claim that the ultimate constituents of reality are conscious in the way in which, for example, humans and other mammals are conscious, but that if the ultimate constituents share very rudimentary levels of consciousness, then the question as to how sophisticated forms of consciousness could arise from dead matter no longer looks intractable, as it now becomes a question of degree rather than kind. Some panpsychists claim that this solution is not in conflict with physics: panpsychism does not question the fundamental laws of physics; what it claims, rather, is that the ontological constitution of the particles whose behaviour physics describes in its laws is not what the materialists think it to be. Panpsychism alters the ontology of the fundamental constituents of reality whilst remaining committed to the view that the laws of physics can provide exhaustive explanations that can answer all relevant questions. If one removes the assumption that reality is material, and postulates instead that the ultimate constituents of reality are imbued with mind, consciousness no longer appears mysterious.

Others have denied that the apparent inability of physicalism to account for the phenomenon of consciousness entails it must be false. Explanatory gap theorists agree that the progress of science will not dissipate the mystery surrounding the fact of conscious experiences but also deny that the inability to bridge the gap between first personal access to conscious experiences and the third-person perspective of science poses a threat to physicalism. Thomas Nagel, for instance, claims not that physicalism is false, but that 'we do not have the beginnings of a conception of how it might be true' (Nagel 1979: 177). Similarly, for James Levine (1983), it is the ability of physicalism to explain the phenomenal character of experience that is at stake, not its truth. These views are echoed by Colin McGinn (1989), who argues that our inability to comprehend how 'the aggregation of individually insentient neurons (could) generate subjective awareness' is not itself an argument against reduction. It is rather an indication of a limit on the part of our cognitive faculties, a kind of cognitive blindspot that prevents us from grasping the psychophysical nexus and which 'makes us prone to an illusion of mystery'. According to explanatory gap theory physicalism is true, but just leaves certain aspects of our experience unexplained. The mind-body problem arises

> because we are cut off by our very cognitive constitution from achieving a conception of that natural property of the brain (or of consciousness) that accounts for the psycho-physical link. This is a kind of causal nexus that we are precluded from ever understanding, given the way we have to form our concepts and develop our theories. No wonder we find the problem so difficult!
>
> (McGinn 1989: 529)

In sum, while many philosophers disagree about whether the fact of conscious experiences poses a threat to physicalism, they tend to agree that the reason why there is a *philosophical* mind-body problem, as opposed to a *scientific* problem (as in the case of lightning and electrical discharge), lies in the fact of consciousness and of a distinctive mode of access to conscious states. There is an epistemological gap between the way in which mental states are accessed, viz., from the third-person perspective, which tells us about what goes on in the brain on the one hand, and what is accessed from the first-person perspective (colours, tastes, etc.) on the other. Collingwood rejects the assumption that governs this entire debate, namely that the reason why there is something philosophically interesting to discuss when it comes to handling the relation between the mind and the body is that this relation is one that should be characterized as one between the inner and the outer. The mind/body distinction is not an epistemological distinction between modes of access, but a semantic distinction between concepts, those of actions and events, which bring reality under different categorial descriptions. The reason why there is something philosophically interesting to discuss about the mind/body distinction is that rationalizing and nomological explanations have distinctive explananda (actions and events) and that the questions which these explanations seek to answer presuppose different conceptions of causation.

The gap is semantic, not epistemological

To understand the nature of the action/event distinction, and Collingwood's take on the mind/body problem, we need to take a step back and revisit his account of the nature of philosophical distinctions as presented in *An Essay on Philosophical Method* (1933). Philosophical distinctions, Collingwood argues, are not empirical classifications. When Aristotle distinguished between generosity and courage as types of virtues, he was not sorting actions into empirical classes in the way in which one sorts Lego blocks into blue and red ones. Aristotle was not suggesting that all instances of generosity involve parting with one's cash and that one could sort out generous from non-generous actions by observing people handing over money to others. Similarly, when Kant distinguished between the principle of duty and that of utility, he was not sorting actions into empirical classes: those which are expedient and those which are dutiful. As the well-known example of the shopkeeper who gives the correct change to a customer because he realizes honesty is a good for business is meant to illustrate (Kant [1785] 1964, book I, 4:397), one and the same deed could exemplify either the principle of duty or that of utility. To distinguish between generous and ungenerous actions for Aristotle or between dutiful and prudential actions for Kant is not the same as sorting T-shirts and jeans to place into different drawers. The distinction between actions and events, for Collingwood, is just like the distinction between different kinds of virtues (for Aristotle) or between the principle of duty and that of utility (for Kant): the action/event distinction is an intensional or purely semantic distinction to which there correspond no determinate empirical classes. The distinction between humanistic and scientific explanations and their respective domains of inquiry (actions and events) is a distinction between concepts which bring reality under different descriptions and which could potentially overlap in all of their instances. The task of philosophy precisely is to distinguish between concepts which coincide in their instances.

Since philosophical distinctions do not sort things into classes, they defy the rules which apply to the relation between genera and species in the traditional theory of classification (Collingwood 1933: 31). In the traditional theory of classification, the adjacent species of a genus tend to be mutually exclusive. Natural history, for example, classifies organisms into animals and vegetables, animals into vertebrates and invertebrates, vertebrates into mammals, birds, reptiles and so on. These adjacent species tend to capture mutually exclusive classes (the class of vertebrates is different from the class of invertebrates; the class of animals is different from the class of vegetables). While there may be some overlap between adjacent species in this type of classification (the platypus is an animal that suckles its young like a mammal and lays eggs like a bird), these cases are 'exceptional and limited' (Collingwood 1933: 30). Overlap of classes, on the other hand, is a 'regular' feature of philosophical distinctions (Collingwood 1933: 36). The task of philosophy is to distinguish between concepts which coincide in their instances. It is the task of the philosopher to distinguish, for example, between the principle of duty and that of utility, even in a hypothetically wonderful scenario in which virtue is always rewarded and all actions performed for the sake of duty also turn out to benefit the doer. Similarly, in the case of the distinction between the mind and the body, it is the task of philosophy to distinguish between these concepts, even if they are jointly instantiated and there is no separate class of things which has a mind whilst lacking a body.

Philosophical distinctions (such as the distinction between dutiful actions and expedient ones) relate to the things which they describe in a very different way from that in which empirical classifications (such as the description of an animal as either oviparous or a mammal) do. When the adjacent species of an empirical concept (such as mammal and oviparous) coincide in their instances (as is the case with the platypus, an animal that suckles its young like a mammal and lays eggs like a bird) the resulting phenomenon is that of a hybrid. By contrast, when two philosophical descriptions or concepts coincide in their instances, the result is not a hybrid, but rather the same thing known in different ways. As Collingwood puts it:

> man's body and man's mind are not two different things, but the same thing ... as known in two different ways. Not a part of man, but the whole of man is body in so far as he approaches the problem of self-knowledge by the methods of natural science. Not a part of man, but the whole of man is mind, in so far as he approaches the problem of self-knowledge by expanding and clarifying the data of reflection.
>
> (Collingwood 1942: 11)

To say that what human beings do can be described in two different ways, as actions or as events, is not the same as saying that human beings are partly body and partly mind, in the way in which a centaur is partly horse and partly human and the platypus is partly mammal and partly oviparous. To say that the concept of action and that of event can coincide in their instances (or overlap in their classes) is to say rather that human behaviour may be described either as action (if rationalized) or as event (if subsumed under general laws) just as the way in which the action of the shopkeeper who gives the correct change to his customer could be described as exemplifying either the principle of duty (do the right thing) or that of utility (honesty is good for business). Just as the action of the shopkeeper is not partly dutiful and partly expedient but rather expedient when considered from the point of view of its consequences and right when considered from the point of view of one's duty to others, so what one does can be brought under different descriptions: as action when one tries to discern its point, or as event, when one describes it as happening as a matter of routine. The distinction between mind and body, between actions and events, for Collingwood, is neither an empirical classification nor is it an epistemological distinction between the inner and the outer, but a semantic distinction analogous to that between the concept of duty and that of utility. Actions remain beyond the reach of scientific explanations *not* because the mind's conscious experiences can only be accessed from the first-person perspective, but because when something is explained as an action it is brought under a different categorial description. And this is why actions will remain forever beyond the ken of science: not because science can only explain part of what humans do (the part of the body in the centaur which is horsey rather than that which is human) but because they home in on a completely different explanandum. The action/event distinction does not cut nature at its joints. Just as in Anscombe's (1957) example there is only one man responding to the descriptions 'replenishing the water supply' and 'poisoning the inhabitants of the house', so the distinction between actions and events, between mind and body, does not divide into separate parts the entity that it describes in these two different ways.

Murder mysteries and scientific mysteries

Collingwood handles the question of the limits of science in a very different way from that in which it is approached by most contemporary philosophers of mind. As we have seen, much contemporary philosophy of mind tends to make two assumptions: first that the definition of what it means for something to be mysterious is for it to lie beyond the power of science to explain; and, second, that consciousness is the most mysterious of all things because it requires first personal access. This dual access entails that consciousness presents us with a distinctive kind of mystery, one that, unlike past scientific mysteries, cannot be solved by the progress of natural science. Collingwood rejects both assumptions. The sheer inability of science to explain something does not make it mysterious. A theoretical physicist cannot answer the question as to why Alexander Litvinenko was poisoned, or at least it cannot satisfactorily answer it in the way in which the investigative journalist would like to have it answered in order to declare the mystery solved. But the fact that physics cannot discover the motives behind Litvinenko's poisoning (thereby solving the murder mystery) does not mean that there is something intrinsically mysterious about Litvinenko's death. It just means that it is not possible to resolve the mystery of his death in the same way in which physics dispels the mysteries of nature.

There are different kinds of mysteries; murder mysteries, just to use one example, are not like the mysteries of nature. If you want to find out who murdered Litvinenko you should hire a detective, not a quantum physicist. The sheer fact that science does not answer all possible questions we may ask does not entail that the questions which cannot be answered scientifically are pseudo-mysteries. Collingwood would therefore have rejected Ayer's view that if a dispute cannot be settled by the methods of science, it is likely to be a metaphysical pseudo-dispute. There is a legitimate question about who was responsible for Litvinenko's death; the fact that a theoretical physicist cannot answer it with the resources of theoretical physics does not mean that searching for a humanistic explanation betrays a pre-scientific belief in spooky entities. Nor does the fact that science cannot answer all our questions point to a failure of science per se. It is the *philosophical* expectation that science should be able to answer all possible questions that is at fault here. Collingwood addresses the question of the limits of science by invoking the kind of contextualism made possible through his commitment to metaphysics as the study of absolute presuppositions. Just as for Aristotle's doctrine of the mean the appropriate food portion for an Olympic athlete should not be the same as that for a sedentary armchair philosopher, so according to metaphysics as the study of absolute presuppositions, one should not expect the method of the physicist to be fit to answer the questions of the detective. Collingwood also rejects the second assumption that governs most approaches to the mind-body problem in contemporary philosophy of mind, namely that the mind/body distinction is an epistemological distinction between different ways of accessing mental states, from within and from without respectively, a distinction that is invoked by some explanatory gap theorists to account for why the mind-body problem endures in spite of the progress of science. Collingwood would have agreed there is an explanatory gap between the concept of mind and body that cannot be closed by the progress of natural science, but he would have disagreed about the nature of this gap. The mind/body distinction is a semantic distinction between concepts which bring reality under different descriptions rather than sort things into the empirical classes of human actions and natural events; it is a distinction between the explananda of the sciences of nature and of the mind, not an epistemological distinction between two different modes of access, the inner and the outer. The explanatory gap, for Collingwood, is semantic, not epistemological: the 'because' in action explanations such as 'the crowd in St Peter's square cheered *because* a new pope was elected by the cardinals gathered in conclave' does not have the same meaning as the 'because' in 'the crowds cheered *because* the smoke coming out of chimney was white'. The latter has the same logical structure as 'the ice melted *because* the temperature rose above 0°C'; it simply states what normally happens when certain antecedent conditions hold. These considerations concerning the nature of the philosophical distinction between the mind and body, as Collingwood construed it, will have to be borne firmly in mind in the next chapter, where we will explore Collingwood's claim that action, as the expression of thought or mind, is the subject matter of historical inquiry.

5

History as the study of mind

The past is an ambiguous term

It is history, for Collingwood, that is the true science (in the Latin sense of the term *scientia*, i.e. a body of knowledge) of the mind because it is history that studies actions qua expression of thought, and studies them in a radically different way from that in which events are known and explained through the scientific method. Since history is normally taken to be the study of the past, not the study of mind, and the philosophy of history is consequently often understood as a discipline that addresses the methods by which 'the past', not 'the mind' per se, is known, we need to provide an explanation for why history, at least as Collingwood understands it, is a humanistic discipline which is concerned with understanding agents and their actions, qua expression of thought or mind. For, even if one were fully on board with the claim that the distinction between actions and events is the correlative of the methodological distinction between nomological and rationalizing explanations respectively, one may still find the claim that history is the study of actions, qua expression of thought or mind, somewhat puzzling. So why does Collingwood claim that history is the study of mind, that all history is the history of thought or that actions are the subject matter of history – all claims that make one and the same point in different ways and are largely interchangeable. 'The past', Collingwood argues, is an ambiguous expression: what happened in the past can be investigated in radically different ways. Just as present reality can be brought either under the categorial description of action or that of event, so a concern with the past may be guided by either a humanistic concern with actions or a naturalistic concern with events. For example, the past is studied not only by historians of the First World War or of the Elizabethan period, but also by evolutionary biologists and big bang physicists. There are such things as the histories of human evolution and of the origins of the universe. The history of the evolution of the human species from the Neanderthals to Homo Sapiens, and the history of the origins of the universe are all histories, in some sense of the term 'history', the sense in which anything that is concerned with the past is a form of history but, Collingwood would argue, they are not histories, namely in the same sense in which the histories of the ancient Egyptian or Roman civilizations are histories. The Egyptologist and the evolutionary biologist do not share the same method and they home in on very different explananda respectively. The past as studied by the palaeontologist who traces the evolution of an animal species through the study of their fossilized remains, and the past as studied by a historian of ancient civilizations are as different as a bean burger is from a hamburger. Both the hamburger and the bean burger are burgers in the sense that they are kinds of patties or fritters; similarly, both evolutionary history and the history of ancient civilizations are histories in the sense that they are both concerned with the past. But just as the hamburger is not a bean burger so the evolutionary past is not the same as the past studied by the Egyptologist. The natural past (the explanandum of natural science) and the historical past (the explanandum of history as a humanistic discipline) are as different as the bean burger, is from the hamburger. One should not be misled by the fact that both the evolutionary biologist and the Egyptologist are concerned with the past, and thus imagine that they are investigating the same sort of thing, any more than one should not be misled by the fact that both the hamburger and the bean burger are kinds of patties or fritters into thinking that they are prepared using the same ingredients. When it is claimed that 'Pompei came to a sudden end as a result of a sudden volcanic eruption', one is making a rather different kind of judgement than when one says that 'the Egyptians mummified their dead to ensure they could have a safe passage to the afterlife'. The latter judgement is a rationalization that belongs to a humanistic history which is concerned with the past qua action; the former belongs to a natural history that is concerned with the past under the description of events (in spite of the fact it makes a claim about an ancient Roman city and its inhabitants). The fact that both these judgements are about the past does not mean that they involve the same kind of inference, and are concerned with one and the same concept of 'past'. Just as the term 'cause' is not the homogeneous term that it is often supposed be, so the term 'past' has different meanings in different explanatory contexts. In distinguishing between the historical and the natural past, Collingwood's goal was not to bring about a linguistic reform aimed at banning a concern with the *natural* past, with, say, the evolution of the human species, or with the origins of the universe, from being called 'history'. His goal was not to ban the term 'history' from being used in the generic way in which the term 'burger' is used (as a general term for fritters or patties which includes both bean burgers and hamburgers), but to acknowledge the distinction between the *historical* and the *natural* past as the explananda of different kinds of knowledge or forms of inquiry. Nor was Collingwood proscribing practising historians who work in the faculty of humanities from saying anything about the natural past. Practising historians often shift from one kind of inference, or one sense of causation, to the other, as required by the relevant context. For example, they explain the destruction of Pompei as a result of the eruption of Vesuvius, in basically the same way as a natural scientist would. It would be preposterous for a historian of Rome to explain the destruction of Pompei in the way in which they would explain why the crowds in St Peter's square cheer at the sight of white smoke, since Vesuvius had no 'cause', i.e. no reason, to erupt, at least not in the sense in which the crowds in St Peter's square had good 'cause' (in what Collingwood calls sense I of the term 'cause') to rejoice. History, as Collingwood understood it, is not to be identified with the academic discipline one finds in university departments. It is rather a form of knowledge, a way of coming to know reality by making use of certain kinds of judgements or inferences that are distinct in kind from those typically found in the natural sciences. Collingwood's point is that the past can be brought under different descriptions, that there is a distinctive kind of past, namely the historical past, which is the domain of inquiry of a humanistically oriented history; this kind of past is the correlative of *history* understood as the study of thought, mind or action. It is the past as it is pre-eminently studied by the Egyptologist or the historian of Ancient Rome and is the subject matter of a certain kind of history whose methods of investigation differ from the sort of history which is concerned with the natural past. These different histories have different presuppositions, presuppositions which shape the methods used to explore the past. The scientific investigation of the past abstracts from the understanding and self-understanding of past agents. When forensic archaeologists, for example, examine human remains, they are not concerned with the burial practices of the agents whose tombs they excavate and whose bones they carbon-date; historians (humanistically oriented historians), by contrast, investigate past reality as it was understood by the agents whose bones the forensic archaeologist carbon-dates (just as a palaeontologist does with the fossilized remains of dinosaurs); historians are concerned with human remains in the context of burial rituals and the symbolic significance of the objects found in burial sites. A humanistically oriented history seeks to understand the past through the lens of the historical agents who inhabited it; in so doing, history approaches the past as another country, so to speak, with different cultures and mores.

The past as another country

Collingwood never used the expression 'the past is another country' but it is well suited to capture his approach to the nature of historical understanding and thus his claim that scientific and historical approaches to the past rest on different presuppositions. Scientific inquiry rests on the presupposition of the uniformity of nature. Natural scientists assume that water freezes at 0°C and ice melts above 0°C.

They can rely on this regularity to make inferences about the natural past, to claim, for example, that since the polar caps were larger in pre-industrial times, the average temperature in the north pole must have been lower than it currently is. Historians (humanistically oriented historians) cannot rely on this principle to form expectations about the behaviour of past agents. They cannot, for example, assume that in 1950s America a black person had the same rights to take an empty seat on a bus as a white person did:

> It is the task of the historian to discover what principles guided the persons whose actions he is studying, and not to assume that these have always been the same. To forget this is to fall into the error of naturalistic or materialistic history: a history which replaces principles by causal laws, and assumes that these laws, like the laws of nature, are constant.
>
> (Collingwood 1946: 475)

Understanding what Rosa Parks did, what her refusal to give up her seat to a white person meant, requires understanding what the established practices and rules of engagement on public transport were at that time in that place, and how they differ from what they are now. The historian, in other words, cannot presuppose that the norms or practices to which past agents are held accountable or expected to conform are the same as those that apply in the present. Collingwood thought that this presupposition, namely that norms of engagement lack uniformity across time as well as space, governs the understanding of all agents; it is a condition of the possibility for understanding agency, whether past or present. He would not have denied that understanding the past poses additional epistemic obstacles: past agents cannot be engaged in a conversation and the records available may be poor. There are past agents whose actions will remain unfathomable to us. But when we do understand past agents, we understand them very much as we understand contemporary agents who do not share our same norms. Collingwood's answer to the question 'how do we understand the *historical* past?' is that we understand it through the eyes of past agents, and that we understand past agents in the same way as we understand our contemporaries, i.e. by locating their actions in their *own* context of thought. Understanding the past historically requires suspending our own conception of reality in the way in which the audience of a period play suspends disbelief in order to enter the world (the thought context) of the characters. Just as it would not be possible to understand the actions of Nora in Ibsen's *The Doll's House* without bearing in mind the role of and expectations on women in society at that time, so for Collingwood, it would not be possible to understand the actions of historical agents without any familiarity with the relevant context of thought. Turning one's gaze to past agents makes one more acutely aware of the presupposition that governs the understanding of other agents in general whether past or present; it helps to grasp that to understand others one must interpret their actions in the context of the norms and rules of engagement to which they take themselves to be accountable, not those of the interpreter or historian.

It is because the actions of past agents, unlike the events of the past per se, have to be understood in the context of thought, that actions have what Collingwood refers to as an 'inside' that events lack (Collingwood 1946: 213). This claim is often interpreted literally as stating that actions are bodily movements which are accompanied by internal psychological processes which cannot be accessed from the third-person perspective. As a result, Collingwood is understood to be saying that the historian is tasked with recovering these inner processes which, unlike visible bodily movements, are not available for observation. This rather unguarded use of the inside/outside metaphor has given rise to a string of quasi-Cartesian readings of Collingwood's concept of mind which see Collingwood as the rightful target of Ryle's criticism of the doctrine of the 'ghost in the machine' (Ryle 1949). But one only needs to scratch beneath the surface of his metaphorical use of language to see that he did not share the early modern conception of the mind as a kind of 'inner theatre'. What fixes the meaning or significance of Caesar's crossing of the Rubicon, qua action, is not a psychological process or a train of thought that Caesar was reciting to himself whilst wading across the Rubicon on his horse. The historian understands what Caesar was doing in the way in which someone chairing a paper at an academic conference understands that a member of the audience intends to ask a question when raising their hand: by knowing the conventions which govern the asking of questions. By the same token a historian understands Caesar's crossing of the Rubicon as signalling a hostile intention against the Republic because they understand the rule by which Roman generals were bound. Caesar's crossing of the Rubicon is understood (historically) as an action because it is understood in the context of Roman law and the rules which banned Roman generals from crossing a border with their army:

> The historian, investigating any event in the past, makes a distinction between what may be called the outside and the inside of an event. By the outside of the event I mean everything belonging to it which can be explained in terms of bodies and their movements: the passage of Caesar, accompanied by certain men, across a river called the Rubicon at one date, or the spilling of his blood on the floor of the senate house at another. By the inside of the event I mean that in it which can only be described in terms of thought: Caesar's defiance of Republican law, or the clash of institutional policy between himself and his assassins. The historian is never concerned with either of these to the exclusion of the other. He is investigating not mere events (where by a mere event I mean one which has only an outside and no inside) but actions, and an action is the unity of the outside and the inside of an event. He is interested in the crossing of the Rubicon only in its relation to Republican law, and in the spilling of Caesar's blood only in its relation to a constitutional conflict.
>
> (Collingwood 1946: 213)

The reason why Caesar's crossing is understood as an action rather than an event is not because the historian has recovered an inner psychological process, a train of thought that Caesar recited to himself, but because the historian interprets it in the context of a legal norm rather than a law of nature. As this example of how to understand Caesar's crossing of the Rubicon in a historical way makes clear, the 'inside' of the event (what a humanistically oriented history aims to explain) is understood in relation to the laws of the Republic, to what it means to abide by them or to challenge them. In order to understand what Caesar did as an action, rather than as a mere bodily movement, one needs knowledge of the rules and regulations that applied to Roman generals under the Republic; the historian needs to know that they were forbidden to cross a border with their army. Understanding Caesar's action historically, in other words, requires 'insider' knowledge of the Roman world. Having this kind of 'insider' knowledge is not the same as being able to peek inside Caesar's mind, to see through Caesar's exterior appearance into what is going on in his head (Ahlskog and D'Oro 2022). As we have seen, just as the chair of a presentation at an academic conference knows that when a member of the audience raises their hand they are signalling that they would like to ask a question, and they know this, not because they have some sort of x-ray vision or powers of telepathic access to the minds of the audience, but because they are familiar with the rules of engagement which govern academic conferences, so the historian knows Caesar's crossing of the Rubicon as an action (as signalling a hostile intention towards the Republic) rather than just as an event (as a group of people on horses crossing a stream) in virtue of knowing that the stream is a border and that crossing it with armed men in that way is a transgression of Roman law. The meaning of Caesar's action is not concealed in or 'inside' his skull; it is not a beetle in a box: to get to the meaning of Caesar's action the historian needs *insider* knowledge of the Roman world, what Collingwood refers to as the context of thought, not access to what goes *inside* Caesar's head, such as a train of thought he might have recited to himself while crossing the Rubicon, such as saying to himself 'there, I am crossing the Rubicon in order to conquer Rome'.[1]

Collingwood's claim that to understand the past historically, qua action, requires understanding the inside or thought side of the

---

[1] The distinction between insider knowledge and knowledge of what goes on inside people's head is explored in Ahlskog and D'Oro (2022).

event has given rise to the suspicion that he believed actions to be events with a ghostly inside and that it is this ghostly inside that the historian tries to get at by re-enacting the thoughts of historical agents (Gardiner 1952a and 1952b). But, as Collingwood's example of what it means to understand Caesar's action in the passage quoted above makes clear, to say that the historian is concerned with the inside of an event is just a metaphorical way of stating that to explain the action historically is to understand it against the background of norms, in this case the laws of the Republic. Understood *historically* the action of Caesar (the crossing of the Rubicon) challenged a legal norm, but it did not falsify a natural law. Norms are not empirical generalizations; they are not undermined by acts of defiance in the way in which natural laws are falsified by counter-instances. Counter-instances to empirical laws require that the law is discarded: the discovery of a black swan, for example, falsified the empirical generalization 'all swans are white'. The infringement of a norm, by contrast, does not count as a refutation of the norm: the fact that people steal does not undermine the rule that one ought not to steal in the way in which the discovery of a black swan falsifies the generalization that all swans are white. When astronomers explain the motions of the planets they invoke laws, not norms. When historians explain the behaviour of past agents, they invoke norms, not laws. Sometime the expression 'norms of nature' is used. But when it is so used, the term 'norm' is either deployed loosely or one is overlooking the distinction between obeying or challenging (a norm) on the one hand and confirming or falsifying (a law) on the other. To understand Caesar's action historically is to understand how it stands in relation to a norm. When the historian does this, Collingwood claims, he gets to the 'inside' of the event and, in so doing, explains what Caesar did as an action.

Collingwood's distinction between the inside and the outside of an event is therefore merely a metaphorical way of capturing (or recapturing) the distinction between different kinds of explanations and their respective explananda. It takes what Bernard Williams calls a 'clinically literal minded' reader (Williams 2006a: 183) to assume that by the 'inside' of an event Collingwood meant some secret thought process hidden behind the bodily carapace of the agent. Collingwood's account of re-enactment has suffered from this unfortunate reading. As a result of this myopic interpretation, the 'inside' of an event has been identified with an internal psychological process inaccessible from a third-person perspective, and the claim that actions (which unlike events have an inside as well as an outside) are the subject matter of history has been construed as claiming that the task of the historian is to retrieve these inner psychological processes by re-enacting them. Collingwood's claim, by contrast, was to undermine the view that we can understand others, be they our contemporaries or past agents, by ignoring the context of thought. He was spelling out the conditions of the possibility for a humanistic understanding of the past which brings reality under the description of action and arguing that if we wish to understand something as an action (be this past or present) one cannot ignore the intensional context of explanation. When reading Collingwood's philosophy of history, one therefore needs to bear firmly in mind what we pointed out in the previous chapter, namely that the action/event distinction is not an epistemological distinction between internal mental states which are normally accessed from the first-person perspective and external bodily movements which are accessed via the third-person perspective of science: it is a semantic distinction between the explananda of the sciences of nature and mind.

Re-enactment and the problem of other minds

To understand the actions of historical agents, we have seen, is just a special case of understanding others in general. Collingwood's account of historical understanding, or as he calls it, re-enactment, may therefore be regarded as his contribution to the problem of how to understand the minds of others and therefore as contributing to the discussion of what often goes under the name of 'the problem of other minds'.[2] As it might be expected from what we have argued so far, Collingwood's answer to the question of how it is possible to understand others is very different from the standard approach to the problem of how other minds are known or understood. In contemporary philosophy of mind the problem of how to understand other minds is often construed as the problem of how one can know what goes on inside the minds of others, given that each one of us only has first personal access to our own mental states. One frequently suggested solution to this difficulty is that we know in our own case that a particular environmental input, say, being stepped on the foot by someone wearing a football boot, gives rise to a certain kind of behaviour, i.e. screaming, grimacing, etc. In our own case we also know that there is an intermediate stage in this process, namely the feeling of pain. We can then infer, by analogy with one's own case, that there is an intermediate stage between environmental inputs or stimuli and behavioural outputs in the case of others too. Given the same kind of environmental inputs, and the same kind of behavioural outputs, we can, by an analogy with our own case, also infer that the other is undergoing a qualitatively similar experience. The standard objection to this standard solution to the problem of how we understand the minds of others is that it is based on a very weak inductive inference. To be powerful or convincing, an inductive argument must be supported by a wide observational sample: the wider the sample, the stronger an argument's inductive power, so the objection goes. From Collingwood's perspective the standard solution to the problem of other minds is inadequate not because it lacks sufficient inductive support, as the standard objection to the standard solution states, but because by construing the mental as a hidden efficient cause of an outward bodily movement it misses

---

[2] Collingwood does not address the question of whether there are other minds: 'Could it be the case, for example, that what we are surrounded by sophisticated automata that simply behave as if they had minds?' His account of re-enactment is aimed at explaining not whether there are minds but how they may be understood.

the point of the concept of action, and, as a result, fails to capture what it means to understand others as 'acting'. The standard solution presupposes that to ascribe to someone a particular mental state (a non-observable inside) is to say that they have engaged in a type of behaviour that characteristically occurs when the agent is stimulated in a certain way by analogy with one's own case. Collingwood's challenge to this proposed solution for understanding the minds of others is not that the analogy on which it is based is inductively weak, but that this causal model of the mind does not capture the concept of action. He agreed that actions, unlike events, are the expression of thought or mind but, as we have seen, argued that the meaning of action is retrieved not by establishing certain empirical/observable patterns between environmental inputs and behavioural outputs, but by interpreting the action in the light of norms: it is by being familiar with Roman law that historians understand that Caesar's crossing of the Rubicon signalled a hostile intention towards the Republic, just as it is by knowing the conventions that govern academic conferences that the chair of a paper at an academic conference understands that when a member of the audience raises their hand they are signalling their intention to ask a question.

In claiming that to understand past agents requires locating what they do in the context of thought Collingwood was making an important conceptual point about what it means to understand what others do under the categorial description of 'action'. He was not addressing the epistemological question as to whether a token action has been correctly interpreted, for example, as an attempt to let air in rather than an attempt to let a fly out. Only once the *conceptual* question concerning the appropriate form of explanation for actions as a type or category of thing is settled, can one turn to address the *epistemological* question of whether a token action has been correctly interpreted. Identifying the logical form of explanation appropriate for actions *as a category of things* is not the same as knowing whether explanations of token actions are successful. Perhaps some of the crowd's members in St Peter's square were not cheering because a new pope had been elected, but because they were watching the football on their mobile phones and their team scored a goal shortly after the white smoked appeared. Perhaps Caesar's crossing of the Rubicon did not signal an intent to march onto Rome, but something else. There is of course always room for historical/humanistic explanations of token actions to get it wrong. Collingwood's point is not that re-enactment is an infallible method, but rather that something does not even count as an explanation of an action (let alone a *correct* explanation of action) unless it invokes the context of thought. To even ask whether one might have historically misunderstood the actions of past agents (was Caesar perhaps just going for a midnight stroll and had simply forgotten to dismiss his army?) one must have a grasp of what it means to understand them as actions in the first instance. Collingwood's account of re-enactment, his answer to the question 'how do we understand the actions of others?', is meant to ward off not possible misunderstandings of token actions, but rather what we would call the mother of all misunderstandings, i.e. the categorial misunderstanding of actions as a species of event that can be explained by observing certain empirical patterns between environmental inputs and behavioural outputs, rather than by familiarizing oneself with the thought context of the agents. It is only in the context of thought that a case of kneeling, for example, can be understood as a genuflection, that the crowds cheering in St Peter's square can be understood as welcoming a new pope and that Caesar can be understood as marching onto Rome rather than going across the river for a stroll. To begin with the epistemological/sceptical question – (how do I know that the historian has understood an agent from the past?), before settling the conceptual question 'what does it take to understand others?' – is to put the (epistemological) cart before the (conceptual) horse. For one cannot even begin *historically* to misunderstand an action unless one has a firm grasp of what it takes *historically* to understand it in the first instance. It is this higher-level (categorial) failure to grasp what it means to understand the past historically, i.e. as action, or from a humanistic point of view, that Collingwood exposes in *The Idea of History* by denying that actions are species or kinds of events.

Scissors-and-paste history

The past, as we have seen, can be known under different presuppositions. The presupposition that is key to the scientific investigation of the past, i.e. to the study of the *natural* past, is the principle of the uniformity of nature. The scientific investigation of the (natural) past presupposes that the laws of nature are uniform, that they apply to all times and places, future, present and past. When a cosmologist investigates the big bang, or when a palaeontologist carbon-dates certain fossilized remains to establish their age, they begin from the latest scientific knowledge and apply it to the past, on the assumption that their theories can explain the events of the past just as well as they can explain those of the present. In approaching the past from the perspective of the latest and most advanced scientific knowledge they may correct misunderstandings about the origins of the universe or about the presumed age of a fossil reached on the basis of earlier scientific theories, theories which were subsequently discarded as a result of the progress of science. Science progresses by falsifying previous scientific theories and replacing them with others that have greater explanatory power. More accurate knowledge of the *natural* past is reached through scientific advances that falsify earlier scientific findings. When investigating the past, a scientist is not concerned with how past agents' conceptions of reality informed their explanation of natural phenomena. Twenty-first-century volcanologists revisiting the causes of the eruption of Vesuvius which led to the disappearance of Pompei and Herculaneum, for example, would disregard contemporary explanations of this natural phenomenon, be they of a religious nature or based on outdated science. The explanations of the eruption of Vesuvius given in 79 AD are irrelevant to the present-day scientific investigations of its causes. Volcanologists revisiting the cause of Vesuvius' eruption are justified in ignoring explanations of Vesuvius' eruption given at the time or in discarding them as false hypotheses based on obsolete science if they diverge from conclusions they have reached. A humanistically oriented historian, by contrast, cannot approach the past in this way. An

Egyptologist cannot reject the ancient Egyptians belief in the afterlife in the way in which Copernicus rejected the Ptolemaic conception of the universe. The goal of a humanistically oriented historian (simply a historian from now on) is not to establish whether the beliefs of the Ancient Egyptians are true, whether there is an afterlife and whether embalming the dead will guarantee them a safe passage to it. It is rather to understand how these beliefs shaped the lives of the ancient Egyptians and motivated them to build such elaborate burial sites. Thus whilst volcanologists investigating the causes of past eruptions, such as Vesuvius', explain what happened in terms of the best science available to them, rather than in the light of the scientific knowledge available at the time of the events' occurrence, the belief system of past agents is indeed key to understanding the past historically. When historians forget this fundamental difference between the presuppositions of science and those of history, and seek to explain past occurrences in the way in which a scientist investigates the events of the past, they end up writing what Collingwood calls scissors-and-paste histories, histories which include in their narratives only what is deemed to be possible in the eyes of the historian. Thus, for example, if the historian does not believe in the possibility of miracles, they will treat witness statements about the occurrence of miracles as false observational statements and simply discard them as untrue or unreliable rather than attempt to understand their significance for the agents. On this approach a historical testimony that is deemed false in light of the historian's own belief should be excised or disregarded; only what makes sense in light of the historian's own thought should be pasted in – hence the name scissors-and-paste history.

Scissors-and-paste histories are presentist histories, histories written from the perspective of the historian, rather than the perspective of the agents; the scissors-and-paste historian's attitude towards the past is like that of a natural scientist who examines past phenomena by his or her own scientific standards and discards the explanations that past agents gave for them as false if they conflict with the conclusions reached by applying their own standards of evidence. The primary task of a humanistically oriented history, Collingwood claims, is not to judge whether the testimony of past witnesses is true or false, whether or not there is an afterlife, for example, but to understand the significance that mummification had for the ancient Egyptians. If one imports the presuppositions of scientific investigation to the study of the historical past, one engages into a kind of pseudo-historical investigation of the past which makes a certain kind of humanistic understanding of past agents impossible in principle. We will return to Collingwood's critique of presentism in the next chapter. For the moment, however, it is important to note that the point that Collingwood establishes is that scissors-and-paste histories misunderstand historical agents on a grand scale: they do not merely misconstrue *this* or *that* action; their error is a categorial one: they seek to explain actions as if they were events to be understood under the presupposition of the uniformity of nature, rather than explain them in relation to norms, be they epistemic, moral or otherwise, which vary from time to time. Collingwood's task in *The Idea of History* is to correct this fundamental conceptual obstacle in the way of understanding the past historically. His argument for the autonomy of history takes the form of a reductio: if you want to explain why the ancient Egyptians mummified their dead and built pyramids, you cannot do so in the same way in which a natural scientist explains the occurrence of solar eclipse or the eruption of a volcano: you cannot abstract from the understanding and self-understanding of historical agents.

Collingwood's concern with the past is neither metaphysical nor epistemological but conceptual. He is not concerned with the ontological status of time (whether, for example, it is a growing block or whether time is more comparable to space and the passage of time is just an illusion). Nor is his primary concern of a sceptical/epistemological nature, addressing the question: how can the past be known given that it is not present? Epistemological themes are clearly present in his work but the overriding concern of his philosophy of history is a conceptual one: what is the nature of historical understanding? What does it mean to understand the past historically?[3] How does a humanistic concern with the past differ from a scientific concern with the past? His claim is that understanding the past historically is a special case of understanding the minds of others, and that philosophers have misunderstood what it means to understand the past historically because they have modelled the sciences of mind on an analogy with the sciences of nature (Collingwood 1946: 206 ff.). In so doing, they have overlooked the distinction between the natural and the historical past and investigated the actions of past agents as if they were events which could be explained by observing correlations between environmental inputs and behavioural outputs.

How to misunderstand others. Historically

Collingwood's proposal for a science of historical understanding is to lay out the criteria for a humanistic as opposed to a scientific investigation of the past. A humanistic approach to the past is concerned with actions; it explains what happened in the past in terms of the significance an occurrence had for the agents concerned. The crossing of the Rubicon, we have seen, is understood in relation to a legal norm, not in relation to a natural law and its significance as an action is lost to the method of observation and inductive generalization. Just as the significance of the white smoke for the crowds gathered in St Peter's square eludes the inductive scientist who establishes behavioural patterns through repeated observation (whenever white smokes emanates the crowds cheer), so the significance of Caesar's crossing the Rubicon is lost if the river is not understood in relation to Roman law, namely as marking a border. Caesar's crossing of the Rubicon gives the senators *cause for concern*, just as the white smoke gives the crowds in St Peter's square *cause for rejoicing*. The relevant sense of causation is sense I: the

---

[3] For a contemporary defence of this conceptual angle, see Ahlskog (2021).

cause rationalizes the phenomenon it explains; it is not an antecedent condition in either sense II or III.

Understanding Caesar's crossing as an action requires familiarity with Roman law, just as understanding why the crowds in St Peter's square cheer at the sight of white smoke requires familiarity with the catholic faith, with the conventions which govern the election of the Pope and how this is communicated to religious believers. Had Collingwood been alive in the latter part of the twentieth century he would have regarded Quine's suggestion that understanding others requires engaging in a form of interpretation which bypasses the thought context of the agents (radical translation) as a recipe for misunderstanding others, historically. Quine ([1960]/2001) sought to defend the idea of a form of translation that is radical in the sense that it completely bypasses the thought context of the historical agents by focusing on the case of an alien culture, a culture so remote that the only explanatory tools available to a field linguist seeking to put together a translation manual would be those of empirical observation. When trying to translate a word whose meaning is unknown, the field linguist would record the observable empirical circumstances in which a word is uttered. For example, the linguist observes a member of that culture utter the word 'gavagai' in the presence of a rabbit and writes down 'rabbit' in his translation manual. He codifies linguistic behaviour in the manner in which a botanist catalogues plants and a zoologist classifies animals. Much as the anthropologist from Mars observing earthlings cheering at the sight of white smoke emanating from a chimney in Rome records that crowds cheer when white smoke appears, so the field linguist can only appeal to behavioural data: native of that culture utters 'gavagai' in the presence of a rabbit. Quine's account of radical translation is not limited to the case of an alien culture; it is in this way, according to Quine, that we do not simply understand agents from alien cultures, but indeed all agents, including our contemporaries. Thus, though the idea of radical translation is illustrated through the scenario of a field linguist confronted with a completely alien culture, radical translation is not something that one has to use only as a last resort. The scenario of the field linguist illustrates the conditions under which all translation operates. The general point behind Quine's idea of radical translation, as Hilton puts it, 'is to give an approach to language which is evidently empirical, to see how much can be made of the idea of meaning' (Hylton 2007: 199). Collingwood is adamant that one cannot understand the significance of an item of behaviour, be this linguistic or otherwise, as an action by adopting this stimulus/response model of explanation. To understand a case of kneeling as a genuflection requires much more than observing that people routinely kneel when they enter a building; to understand the facial expressions of the crowds in St Peter's square as jubilation at the election of a new Pope one needs to know more than that a particular environmental input (white smoke coming out of chimney) is typically followed by a certain behavioural response (cheering). Collingwood did not claim that humanistic understanding of the past qua action (genuflecting rather than bending one's knees) can always be achieved. He explicitly conceded that some periods of history are hard to fathom:

> Certain historians, sometimes whole generations of historians, find in certain periods of history nothing intelligible, and call them 'dark ages'; but such phrases tell us nothing about those ages themselves; though they tell us a great deal about the persons who use them, namely that they are unable to re-think the thoughts which were fundamental to their life.
>
> (Collingwood 1946: 218–9)

But while Collingwood conceded that humanistic understanding of the past (qua action) is not *always* possible, he saw no reason to infer from this consideration that the past can *never* be so understood that the stimulus response model of explanation is appropriate in all cases and that the only way to understand our contemporaries as well as past agents involves an exercise in radical translation. For Collingwood, the inability to understand the past historically *in some cases*, say, those of cultures which are completely alien (which he clearly concedes) does not entail that the past cannot be understood historically *in all cases* (as Quine wants to claim). The impenetrability of certain periods of history to the humanistically oriented historian, for Collingwood, does not provide sufficient grounds for the wholesale rejection of humanistic understanding that Quine seeks to justify through the example of the field linguist trying to fathom a completely alien culture. One cannot enjoin a wholesale rejection of humanistic understanding simply by pointing out that in some cases, say those of completely alien cultures, or periods of history for which there are no written records, it is not possible to acquire or develop such an understanding. What should be recognized as responsible for the failure to do so, in such cases, is not the suitability of the method but the lack of relevant evidence.

Quine's account of radical translation is often seen as providing indirect support for his attack on the notion of meanings as suspicious ontological entities which lie hidden in the minds of historical agents: if all that a field linguist needs to translate the word 'gavagai' is access to the environmental inputs (the presence of a rabbit) and the behavioural response (the uttering of a word), there is no need to endorse the early modern myth of the mind as an inner theatre and to assume the existence of entities inaccessible to the experimental method. But such an argument for the elimination of meanings relies on conflating the claim that understanding other agents historically requires *insider* knowledge (knowledge of the thought context) with the claim that understanding the minds of others requires accessing ontological entities hidden *inside* the heads of historical agents. Humanistic understanding of the kind that Collingwood advocates relies on *insider* knowledge of the rules, regulations and practices which governed the lives of historical agents, not knowledge of what goes *inside* the head of agents; it assumes neither the existence of suspicious ontological entities nor does it require a special intuitive/empathetic method to gain access to these hidden psychological processes.[4] Historians understand

---

[4] For a recent argument against the reading of re-enactment as empathy, see Retz (2017).

why (in a specific sense of 'why') the crowds were cheering when white smoke appeared from a chimney because they have an understanding of the catholic faith; they understand why (in a specific sense of 'why') Caesar crossed the Rubicon because they have an understanding of Roman law, and what it means to abide by it or to disobey it. Insider knowledge of the Catholic faith and of Roman law does not require privileged access to the minds of others of the kind that can be enjoyed only by introspection, or from the inside, as opposed to knowledge that can be gained through empirical observation, or from the outside.

Quine's argument for radical translation arguably rests on a conflation or confusion of these two different meanings of 'inside' (Ahlskog and D'Oro 2022). He denies the radical translator (whose task is to render a word into the home language without any prior knowledge of the target language) '*insider* knowledge' in the sense of prior familiarity with the norms (linguistic or otherwise) that govern the agent's behaviour on the grounds that presupposing familiarity with the cultural context of the native speaker would be tantamount to being able to peek *inside* the minds of historical agents. But this, as we have seen, is a mistake. For Collingwood the significance of an action is understood in the cultural context of the agent, just as the meaning of raising one's hand at an academic conference is understood in relation to the practice governing question and answer sessions. The meaning of an action is identified or determined in this way, not by gaining access to hidden psychological processes. This places Collingwood and Quine on two divergent paths. Since, Quine argues, the only evidence for imputing meanings to others is based on observations of their behaviour, and behavioural evidence cannot legitimate the ascription of a particular set of intensions over another, translation is necessarily indeterminate. The behavioural evidence available to the field linguist attempting to translate the word 'gavagai', for example, is insufficient to determine whether, when uttering the word 'gavagai', the native means a whole rabbit or undetached rabbit parts. For Quine there is no fact of the matter about translation because since empirical evidence systematically underdetermines translation, and since there is no other criterion applicable for understanding others, there is no such thing as the correct translation. For Collingwood, Caesar's action has a meaning that is determined in relation to Roman law. Of course, historians could misunderstand the actions of past agents at times, but it is at least in principle possible to determine those meanings, and to do so without assuming some privileged access to Caesar's mind or the existence of dubious ontological entities inside his head. Collingwood was remarkably unsceptical about the possibility of knowing the historical past. Historical knowledge, in his view, was knowledge of the past qua action: to understand the past historically is not a task that is substantially different from that of understanding our contemporaries: to do so we must recognize or appreciate their worldview, the norms they took themselves to be accountable to, and suspend disbelief in the way that we do when watching a period drama. In claiming that historical knowledge of the past is in principle possible because the significance of past actions can be determined by reference to the context of thought which belonged to them, Collingwood's account of historical understanding puts itself on a collision course with much that has happened in philosophy of history in the second half of the twentieth century where the sceptical view that the meaning of the past is not fixed or determinate, that there is not one past, but many, has tended to echo Quine's thesis of the indeterminacy of translation. In the next chapter we turn to consider how philosophy of history changed after Collingwood death, why certain sceptical assumptions concerning the possibility of knowing the past have prevailed and why Collingwood would have been very critical of the relativistic outlook that has dominated reflections on the possibility of historical knowledge.

6

The past as it always was

The 'different kinds of past' claim *versus* the 'many pasts' claim

A key feature of Collingwood's explanatory pluralism is the rejection of the claim that the fundamental presuppositions governing forms of inquiry lay claim to truth values. As we saw in Chapter 2, the question one should ask is not 'which concept of causation/form of explanation is real or true of an inquiry-independent reality?', but rather 'which sense of causation is fit for purpose?' At a time when the notion of truth has encountered radical criticism both in the philosophical and the political arena, Collingwood's denial that absolute presuppositions are truth apt may be easily misread as an attempt to undermine the idea that there are *scientific* truths or *historical* truths which can be objectively known. This chapter undertakes to show that Collingwood's claim that absolute presuppositions lack truth values should not be confused with the sceptical and relativist views which are challenged by Ophelia Benson and Jeremy Stangroom in *Why Truth Matters* (2006). His commitment to the possibility of *historical* truths is evident in his philosophy of history where, against the sceptical/relativist trend that has strongly marked the debate in the latter half of the twentieth century, he defends the view that the historical past is, at least in principle knowable, *as it was*. Collingwood argued that there are different kinds of past, namely the historical and the natural past, each being the correlative of different kinds of explanations. His defence of the view that the historical past is distinct from the natural past should *not*, however, be conflated with the revisionist claim that there is not one past but many, as many pasts as are retrospectively constructed by each generation of historians writing from different standpoints in time and with different concerns in mind. The revisionist view argues that the past is not a given but essentially and inevitably a construction. Since it is a construction, it is constantly reconstructed from different presents, as the arrow of time moves on. Historical revisionism is largely the result of a commitment to a form of presentism, according to which the starting point for all knowledge of the past is the standpoint of the historian's own present. Collingwood was not a revisionist about our knowledge of the past; he believed that the context that is relevant to understanding the past historically is that of the historical agents, not that of the historian or interpreter, and when considered from the perspective of the historical agents, the past does not change from a later perspective in time.

This chapter isolates three assumptions that inform the revisionist conception of the historical past that proved to be so influential in the philosophy of history after Collingwood's death and shows that Collingwood does not share any of them. The first is that the categorial framework of the historian is like a skin that cannot possibly be shed or even temporarily suspended in order to see things from the perspective of the historical agents themselves. Collingwood, as we shall see, rejects this view. He argues that what is known, the content of knowledge, can be separated from the context of its discovery and that it is therefore possible to understand the world from the agents' point of view even if one cannot re-live their experiences.

The second assumption that governs much contemporary revisionism is that there is an asymmetry between historical and scientific knowledge: whereas scientific theories are verifiable, historical narratives are not. This asymmetry between scientific theories and historical narratives is motivated by the consideration that narratives construct the past by weaving together events and that, whereas the events (the building blocks out of which the narratives are constructed) can be verified, the narratives themselves cannot be, because they are not building blocks, so to speak, but the cement which the bricklayer brings to the building site. Collingwood rejects the view that history is epistemically disadvantaged vis-à-vis science, that whereas scientific theories are in principle verifiable, historical theses, being narrative constructions, are not. As we have seen in Chapter 2, he does claim that the notion of verifiability does not apply to the presuppositions which govern forms of inquiry. The presuppositions which govern the historical method, just like those which govern scientific method, are neither true nor false. But to say *this* is not to say that there are no verifiably true claims either within science or within history. Explanations, we have seen, are 'because' answers to 'why' questions, questions which arise because certain presuppositions about what it means to establish explanatory connections are made. Explanations in history can be verified by the application of the historical method, just as explanations in science can be verified by the application of the scientific method. There is therefore no asymmetry between scientific and historical knowledge; it is just that the criteria for the verification of historical claims are not the same as the criteria for the verification of scientific claims.

A third assumption that governs the revisionist conception of the historical past is that rejecting an empiricist conception of history (according to which the significance of past events can be read off the facts without any need for narration) entails accepting that the categorial framework needed to gain historical knowledge must be that of the historian in the present. For example, the categories required to turn a fact such as the assassination of Archduke Ferdinand into a historical knowledge claim proper, say, the claim that it marked the beginning of the First World War, requires seeing things from the perspective of a later historian. Collingwood also rejects this assumption. Like narrativists he rejects the empiricist conception of history as mere chronicle and agrees that knowledge requires an explanation and interpretation of the facts. But he denies that the categories that are relevant to the historical understanding of the past are those of the present.

Having identified three common assumptions which govern the commitment to historical revisionism, the chapter contrasts the revisionist view that there are many pasts with Collingwood's claim that there are different *kinds* of past, the *natural* and the *historical* past, which are known through the explanatory tools of science and the humanities respectively. Collingwood's distinction between *kinds* of past, the historical and the natural past, does not entail the revisionist claim that there are many pasts: to know the past historically is to know it from the perspective of past agents and their categories, a perspective from which the past remains *as it was*. In showing that Collingwood was not a sceptic concerning the possibility of acquiring objective knowledge of the past *as it was* this chapter indirectly aims to dispel the suspicion that a commitment to the view that absolute presuppositions are not truth apt entails giving up on the idea of verifiability altogether.

The decline of speculative philosophy of history and the epistemic priority of the present

Revisionism is largely the result of a commitment to 'presentism'. In order to understand why Collingwood would have rejected the revisionist conception of history that has largely prevailed in the philosophy of history after his death, we need to understand first what presentism is and how it took hold. Presentism, in this context, is not a view in the metaphysics of time, according to which only the present exists; it is rather the epistemological view that past events are and should be interpreted from the standpoint of the present. So understood presentism was arguably the result of the decline of 'speculative' philosophy of history. Speculative philosophy of history typically regarded historical events as progressing towards some kind of goal (such as the realization of freedom) and took the task of a philosophy of history to be that of describing a process of development unfolding along a specifically identifiable or even predetermined path. On this view (admittedly a rather simplistic view of speculative philosophy of history that I am simply reproducing here) the end goal of the historical process is already implicit in its beginning, just as the development of an oak is implicitly contained in the acorn. On this conception of the historical process, the standpoint in time from which the development of history is captured in historical writing does not alter the historical process. A historian writing once the historical process has come to fruition, at the end of history, so to speak, will be in a better position to grasp the nature of historical development, but while the historian who stands at the end of history is in a better position to grasp the nature of the historical process, the historian's standpoint in time does not affect how the events unfold: they were always going to unfold that way, just as an acorn, other things being equal, was always going to develop into an oak. As narrativists like to put it, speculative philosophies of histories viewed the course of history as the text of a play waiting to be performed (Mink 1987: 193–4; Roth 2020: 15). With the decline of speculative philosophy of history, the perspective of the present became more prominent: since there is no set itinerary for historical events to follow, and no final destination, every historian stands at the end of history and locates or relocates the past in a narrative she writes from her standpoint in time. The historian's standpoint changes as the arrow of time moves on and each historian narrates the past in a different way.

While presentism has taken slightly different forms, it tends to be a pervasive assumption today. A key moment in the emergence of presentism came with Danto's introduction of the concept of narrative sentences. These are statements such as 'The Thirty Years War began in 1618' (Danto 1965) which can only be known to be true retrospectively and could not possibly be known to be the case by a person living in 1618. Narrative sentences bring earlier events, such as the assassination of Archduke Ferdinand of Sarajevo, under new descriptions such as 'the event which triggered the Great War', descriptions which were in principle unavailable to a contemporary chronicler unaware of the later ramifications of an event. The time lag between the event's occurrence and the writing of history becomes therefore a condition of the possibility for bringing the bare empirical fact (the assassination of Archduke Ferdinand) under a thicker historical description such as 'the event which triggered the Great War', something which could be known only after the war had started, or the 'First World War' which could be known as such only after a second world-wide conflict had taken place. Danto's claim that the past is brought under different descriptions from a future perspective has been recently mobilized by Paul Roth, who deploys it to support the revisionist conclusion that there are multiple versions of the past, as many versions as the different descriptions under which it can be brought from different standpoints in time (cf. Roth 2020, chapters 1 and 2). In the philosophical hermeneutics of Hans Georg Gadamer (1960/2013) presentism takes a slightly different form. Here the encounter with the past resembles the encounter with a text from a past tradition, one which was conceived within a different horizon of meaning. The task of the interpreter is to understand the past by approaching it from their own horizon of meaning. Rather than bracketing their cultural horizon the interpreter should bring it to the hermeneutic table. The text, for Gadamer, is productively or meaningfully understood once a fusion of horizons is accomplished. The 'prejudices' in the sense of the for-conceptions of the interpreter are enabling conditions of interpretative understanding, not hindrances to it and 'a text is understood only when it is understood in a different way' (Gadamer 1960/2013: 320) by each generation of interpreters. For Danto the time elapsing between the event's occurrence and that of a later historian gives the latter a vantage point which was unavailable to contemporary observers; for Gadamer the horizon of the interpreter is an enabling condition of interpretation. A different variation of presentism is to be found in Hayden White who was critical of what he derogatively dismissed as an 'antiquarian' interest in the past and claimed that the past should be appropriated for practical purposes. The focus on a distinctively historical past, a past that should be understood in its own terms, according to White, places history into a 'quarantine as a guide to present activity and future aspiration' (White 1973: 415). Whether motivated by epistemic concerns concerning the knowability of a reality that is no longer available for observation, or by a political concern with reviving historical studies by putting the past at the service of contemporary political goals, the present has enjoyed a privileged epistemic position in the philosophy of history.

The epistemic priority that the standpoint of the present has enjoyed has spearheaded a principled revisionism according to which the past must be understood in a different way by each generation of historians if it is to be understood at all.

Revisionism, so understood, is not evidence-driven. It is a dogmatic, aprioristic commitment to the necessity of reinterpreting the past from the perspective of the present, as we shall see shortly.

An aprioristic revisionism and evidence-based revisions

It is important to distinguish between the principled aprioristic historical revisionism spearheaded by a commitment to presentism that took hold with the decline of speculative philosophy of history and the rise of narrativism, and evidence-driven historical revisions. Evidence-driven revisions are an acknowledgement of the fact that historical knowing, like any other form of knowing, is not infallible that historians may make mistakes, which can be rectified by re-examining the available evidence, or that our conception of the past may change as a result of new previously unavailable evidence coming to light. Collingwood was not hostile to evidence-based revisions to our conceptions of the historical past. He was, however, opposed to the kind of aprioristic revisionism that is underpinned by a commitment to the epistemic priority of the present. The context that is relevant to understanding the past historically, according to Collingwood, is the context of the historical agents, not that of the interpreters. This context does not retrospectively change. The significance of Caesar's crossing of the Rubicon, for example, is determined by Roman law; it does not change as the arrow of time moves on and the laws of the land subsequently change. It is the idea that the meaning of Caesar's crossing of the Rubicon is defined once and for all in this way, by reference to the context of Caesar and his contemporaries, which is threatened by the kind of principled revisionism based on a commitment to presentism.

This principled revisionism makes knowledge of the past as it was (for the ancient Greeks, Romans, etc.) impossible in principle. Principled revisionism does not claim that knowledge of the past as it was cannot always be achieved in practice; it rules this kind of knowledge out a priori by denying that access to the past from the perspective of historical agents is possible in principle because the past must necessarily be narrated from the perspective of the present. Collingwood clearly accepted that knowledge of the past is not always possible in practice:

> Every period of which we have competent knowledge (and by competent knowledge I mean insight into its thought, not mere acquaintance with its remains) appears in the perspective of time as an age of brilliance; the brilliance being the light of our own historical insight. The intervening periods are seen by contrast as, relatively speaking and in different degrees, 'dark ages': ages which we know have existed because there is a gap of time for them in our chronology, and we have possibly numerous relics of their work and thought, but in which we can find no real life because we cannot re-enact that thought in our own minds.
>
> (Collingwood 1946: 328)

What he objected to was the view that knowledge of the past *as it was* is impossible in principle. As we saw in Chapter 5, the task of understanding past agents, for Collingwood, is not different in kind from that of understanding contemporary agents: 'Historical knowledge is not concerned only with a remote past. It is by historical thinking that we re-think and so rediscover the thought of Hammurabi or Solon, it is in the same way that we discover the thought of a friend who writes us a letter, or a stranger who crosses the street' (Collingwood 1946: 219). Contemporary agents, just like past ones, need to be understood from their own point of view. Unless one is willing to commit to the claim that it is impossible to understand contemporary agents who do not share the same culture as the historian in their own terms, there is no reason to hold, as Gadamer did, for example, that each generation of historians necessarily must understand the past in a different way in order to understand it at all or, as Quine (1960, chapter 2; 1990, part III) claimed that translation from past cultures must remain necessarily indeterminate.

What is at stake between the kind of principled revisionism spearheaded by a commitment to presentism and Collingwood's claim that the categorial framework of the historian is the wrong lens through which to approach the historical past, is whether or not it is possible for the historian sufficiently to distance herself from her own perspective to interpret past agents from their own categorial framework. Collingwood was persuaded this was a possibility and his account of the identity of thought can be read as an attempt to show *how* this is possible by undermining the view that the propositional content of thought is inextricably tied to the spatio-temporal position of the thinker. It is to this claim that we shall now turn.

Re-enactment and the content of thought

Collingwood firmly believed that it is possible for the historian to bracket her own point of view and to 'see' the world from the perspective of the historical agents, just like audiences at a theatrical performance of a period play are able to suspend disbelief. The assumptions which underpin this commitment must now be made explicit. For the historian to be able to rethink reality from the perspective of historical agents, to know it as they did, there cannot be too rigid a connection between the knower, the historical agent and *what* they know. The content of thought must be separable from the spatio-temporal context of the knower. This is precisely what Collingwood argues when he claims that the propositional content of thought, unlike 'feelings' or 'sensations', which do have a definite spatio-temporal location, is re-enactable.

In *The Idea of History* Collingwood distinguishes between what he calls (and these are terms of art) 'thought in its immediacy' (sensations and feelings) and 'thought in its mediation' (henceforth: thought). It is thought, not feelings or sensations, which, he claims, is the proper object of historical understanding. He identifies two important differences between sensations/feelings and thought. Sensations and feelings have a definite location in space and time: 'What we feel is always something existing here and now, and limited in its existence to the place and time at which it is felt' (Collingwood 1938: 158–9). Because feelings/sensations have a definite location in space and time, they cannot be re-experienced in the way in which thought can be re-thought: 'You cannot remember the terrible thirst you once endured; but you can remember that you were terribly thirsty' (Collingwood 1942: 34). Second, feelings are private while thought is not:

> The cold that one hundred people feel ... is simply a feeling in them, or rather, a hundred different feelings, each private to the person who feels it, but each, in certain ways, like the rest. But the 'fact' or 'proposition' or 'thought' that there are ten degrees of frost is not a hundred different 'facts' or 'propositions' or 'thoughts'; it is one 'fact' or 'proposition' or 'thought' which a hundred different people 'apprehend' or 'assent to' or 'think'.
>
> (Collingwood 1938: 158)

It is thought, not sensations or feelings, which is the object of historical understanding. One cannot, for example, re-enact Archimedes' excitement upon first coming across the idea of specific gravity. But while Archimedes' experience cannot be repeated, one can rethink/ re-enact Archimedes' thought of specific gravity, an insight that he had whilst taking a bath, and understand it, even if one is not taking a bath or experiencing Archimedes' elation:

> The first discovery of a truth, for example, differs from any subsequent contemplation of it, not in that the truth contemplated is a different truth, nor in that the act of contemplating it is a different act, but in that the immediacy of the first occasion can never again be experienced: the shock of its novelty, the liberation from perplexing problems, the triumph of achieving a desired result, perhaps the sense of having vanquished opponents and achieved fame, and so forth.
>
> (Collingwood 1946: 297–8)

Unlike feelings and sensations thought is not tied to the context of discovery:

> The immediacy of thought consists not only in its context of emotions (together, of course, with sensations, like the buoyancy of Archimedes' body in the bath) but in its context of other thoughts. The self-identity of the act of thinking that these two angles are equal is not only independent of such matters as that a person performing it is hungry and cold, and feels his chair hard beneath him, and is bored with his lesson: it is also independent of further thoughts, such as the book says they are equal, or that the master believes them to be equal; or even thoughts more closely relevant to the subject in hand, as that their sum, plus the angle at the vertex, is 180 degrees.
>
> (Collingwood 1946: 298)

As this passage makes clear, Collingwood refuses to tie the propositional content of thought too closely with the experiential circumstances of the knower. While he could not have been aware of later developments in epistemology, claims such as this one run counter to the commitments of 'standpoint epistemology' according to which the content of knowledge, what one knows, is inextricable from the social standpoint of the knower (Harding 1991). Had he been living in the 1990s Collingwood would most likely have been very critical of the idea that a male historian could not understand the suffragettes' fight for the political emancipation of women. He considers the objection that the propositional content of knowledge cannot be extricated from the spatio-temporal standpoint of the thinker, namely the argument that abstraction necessarily leads to falsification and pre-empts it by claiming that if this were the case, then it would never be possible to rethink the thoughts of past agents because to rethink the same thoughts would require replicating the precise spatio-temporal context in which those thoughts were formulated:

> It has been said that anything torn from its context is thereby mutilated and falsified; and that in consequence, to know any one thing, we must know its context, which implies knowing the whole universe. I

do not propose to discuss this doctrine in its whole bearing, but only to remind the reader of its connexion with the view that reality is immediate experience, and its corollary that thought, which inevitably tears things out of their context, can never be true. On such a doctrine Euclid's act of thinking on a given occasion that these angles are equal would be what it was only in relation to the total context of his then experience, including such things as his being in a good temper and having a slave standing behind his right shoulder: without knowing all these we cannot know what he meant ... Very likely he never thought of his fifth theorem without some such context; but to say that because the theorem, as an act of thought, exists only in its context we cannot know it except in the context in which he actually thought it, is to restrict the being of thought to its own immediacy, to reduce it to a case of merely immediate experience.

(Collingwood 1946: 298–9)

The doctrine that the propositional content of knowledge is inextricable from the context of discovery, Collingwood claims, cannot be maintained consistently: the proponent of this doctrine, for example, cannot defend it against an opponent or criticize the alternative viewpoint of his opponent for any doctrine 'is what it is only in a total context that cannot be repeated and cannot be known ... if an act of thought is what it is only in relation to its context, the doctrine he criticises can never be the doctrine taught by his opponent' (Collingwood 1946: 299). The term 'context' is potentially misleading. On the one hand Collingwood is clearly committed to the view that context is important. If we are to understand historically the significance of Caesar's crossing of the Rubicon, or the reasons why the crowds in St Peter's square cheered at the sight of white smoke, we need to understand, in the first case, that the Rubicon marked a border and that Roman law proscribed generals from crossing it with their army and, in the second, that the appearance of white smoke signifies the election of a new leader of the Catholic Church. This context, the context of thought, is clearly relevant and necessary to understanding the past historically. On the other hand, one need not be a centurion in Caesar's army, or a believer standing in St Peter's square, to understand what Caesar was engaged in doing or what the white smoke symbolizes.[1] The context of feelings and sensations, unlike that of thought, is not re-enactable, nor is that necessary for historical understanding. Principled/aprioristic revisionism betrays a commitment to a form of standpoint epistemology, according to which the content of knowledge – what is known – cannot be shared between differently situated agents because they do not share the context of feelings and sensations, i.e. because they are differently situated. This is a view that Collingwood rejects; for he believes rather that thought, unlike feelings and sensations, is re-enactable and can be shared across differently situated knowers. One need not be an ancient Egyptian or an ancient Greek in order to think like the ancient Egyptians or the ancient Greeks: we can bracket our own ways of thinking and adopt those of historical agents, just as we suspend disbelief when watching a period play. Collingwood's account of re-enactment rejects what we have identified as one of the key assumptions which dominated the philosophy of history after his death, namely that it is not possible to shed our conceptual skin and understand things from the perspective of the historical agents themselves. The kind of context that is required to understand others, Collingwood argues, is the context of thought, not of feelings and sensations; there is no principled epistemological barrier to re-enacting the thoughts of past agents, just as there is no principled epistemological barrier to re-enacting the thoughts of our contemporaries.

On the alleged asymmetry between scientific and historical knowledge

Another assumption which informs the revisionist conception of historical writing that had has been so influential since Collingwood's death is the view that the unavailability of the past for present observation is more problematic for the possibility of historical knowledge than it

---

[1] For a discussion of Collingwood's account of re-enactment, see van der Dussen (1995), Skagestad (1975 and 2020 chapter 4), Saari (1989) and Dray (1995).

is for that of scientific knowledge. Natural scientists do not observe the disappearance of the dinosaurs any more than historians observe the assassination of Archduke Ferdinand. But past natural events can be retrodicted by applying the same laws used to predict the future, whereas the historical past cannot be retrodicted in that way: one cannot retrodict that a revolution had to happen in the way in which one can retrodict that the earth's temperature must have been lower if the size of the polar caps was larger at a certain moment in time. Given that the historical past is unavailable for observation, and also that it cannot be reproduced under experimental conditions, historical claims unlike their scientific counterparts, cannot be verified. This assumption is encapsulated by Hayden White who claims:

> I do not see how the truth of our knowledge of the past or more specifically the historical past – not to mention their meaning – could be assessed other than relatively to the cultural presuppositions of those who made them and in the light of the presuppositions of those who wish to assess them. This is not an argument for universal relativism, since I am perfectly willing to accept the criteria of both correspondence and coherence as ways of assessing the truth of knowledge about entities still open to ostensive indication and direct perception and those which are in principle 'reproducible' under laboratory experimental conditions.
>
> (2014: xi)

The assumption at work here is that historical knowledge is problematic in a way in which scientific knowledge is not. Historical claims are not just harder to verify than scientific claims; rather, they are in principle unverifiable because the past which the historian narrates can neither be observed, nor can it be reproduced experimentally. For example, whereas scientific claims such as 'the dinosaurs became extinct because the average temperature of the Earth dropped below the comfort levels of coldblooded creatures' can be found to be true or false, historical claims such as 'Archduke Ferdinand was assassinated because he was believed to pose a threat to the devolution of powers' or 'The ancient Egyptians mummified their dead to ensure a safe passage to the afterlife', cannot.

Collingwood rejects this asymmetry between historical and scientific knowledge and holds instead that criteria of verification vary in accordance with forms of inquiry. History, understood as a form of inquiry with its own set of presuppositions, is not in an epistemically disadvantaged position in comparison to science. A historian can confidently determine that it is true that the crowds in St Peter's square cheered because a new Pope was elected, and that it is false that the pyramids were huge banquet halls. It is just that the way in which these claims are verified and falsified is very different from that in which a natural scientist rules out, as false, the claim that the size of the polar caps was smaller in 1566 when the average temperature of the earth was lower. To explain why the pyramids were not huge banquet halls Egyptologist will invoke the differences between the function of a tomb and that of a palace, where banquets were indeed held. An environmental scientist, by contrast, will explain that the ice caps shrank with global warming because ice melts as temperatures rise. Therefore it must have been true that the size of the polar caps was larger. There are, for Collingwood, verifiably true and false claims in history, just as there are in science; both are forms of knowledge governed by their own distinctive criteria about what it means to explain and to determine whether an explanation should be accepted or rejected. Both science and history rest on presuppositions about what it means to forge explanatory connections and reach conclusions on the basis of them. Historical knowledge differs from scientific knowledge not because the historical past is constructed, rather than discovered, but because the presuppositions on which scientific knowledge of the past rests differ from those on which historical knowledge of the past is based. The presuppositions which govern the scientific investigation into the (natural) past imply that the laws by which a phenomenon is explained do not change. The presuppositions which govern the investigation of the (historical) past imply that past agents are responsive to norms, which may well change over time. These presuppositions lay out the criteria by reference to which historical explanations can be verified. Collingwood, we have seen, would have agreed with A. J. Ayer that knowledge requires criteria of verification; but he would have disagreed with the claim that there is only *one* criterion of verification.

The view that there is an asymmetry between scientific and historical knowledge, that science and history do not have the same epistemic standing as forms of knowledge, is premised upon a localized form of anti-representationalism, one which applies to history only, because the historical past is neither available for observation nor can it be reproduced under laboratory conditions. Collingwood's rejection of realism with respect to historical knowledge is not based on the consideration that claims about the historical past are unverifiable because the historical past, unlike the natural past, is neither available for observation nor reproducible under experimental conditions. His metaphysics of absolute presuppositions is committed to a global form of anti-representationalism based on the view that there is no such thing as knowledge of pure being, no knowledge claims that can be established non-inferentially, or independently of the explanatory framework of a form of inquiry. Just as the natural past is the *explanandum* of science, so the historical past is the *explanandum* of history. History, understood as a form of inquiry with its own set of presuppositions, is therefore not in the peculiar and unfortunate position of having to struggle to establish objective claims in the absence of criteria for the verification of historical theses. There is no asymmetry between historical and scientific knowledge of the past. The fact that history and science stand on the same epistemic footing becomes clear if one reads Collingwood's philosophy of history against the background of his commitment to explanatory pluralism and takes the task of a philosophy of history to be that of spelling out the presuppositions on which a certain kind of humanistic understanding of the past rests and how these presuppositions differ from those of natural science.

Narrative construction and the empiricist myth of the given

Another factor which contributed to the popularity of the revisionist conception of history is the assumption that revisionism is the unavoidable corollary of the rejection of a conception of history as a value free empirical inquiry. This assumption, I argue, rests on a non-sequitur. There is no need to commit to the view that the past must be written and re-written from the perspective of the present in order to reject an empiricist conception of history writing. Collingwood clearly shows that to know the past as it was for the historical agents is not the same as knowing it independently of all conceptual mediation. It is rather to know it through the categories of the historical agents, instead of those of the historian.

The narrativist conception of historical writing which prevailed in the latter half of the twentieth century attacked the empiricist conception of history as a value-free data-gathering activity. To be clear, narrativism does not deny that gathering the facts is an important aspect of the historian's task. What it questions is the meta-level view that the significance of historical events can be simply read off the facts and argues instead that the meaning of historical events is constructed through the act of historical narration. For narrativism the idea that there is one past only, which can be unproblematically read off the facts, goes hand in hand with what Sellars (1956) called the empiricist 'myth of the given' (according to which the building blocks of knowledge are grasped by the mind raw, without any conceptual mediation). If one rejects the empiricist myth of the given and accepts that all knowledge is conceptually mediated, so the argument goes, one must also accept that there is not one past, but many pasts, as many as are retrospectively re-constructed through the concepts and values that historians bring to the examination of the data.

Narrativism reasonably argues that to have historical knowledge is not just a question of knowing certain facts; knowing a fact *historically* requires placing it into a pattern or context that makes sense of it. This is the role of narratives which are said to synthesize the manifold of empirical data in the way in which, for Kant, the categories of the understanding bring together the manifold of intuitions received via the senses. Just as for Kant (though this is arguably a tendentious reading of Kant on which I shall not comment), the unity of the experiential object is brought about through the synthetic activity of the mind, the significance or meaning of the facts emerges through the act of narration. To reject the view that the historical past comes into being through the narrative, it is claimed, would be tantamount to subscribing to a crude form of empiricism according to which the mind has no role in the production of knowledge and the task of the historian is simply to describe the facts as they are. The empiricist conception of history, in other words, is committed to a mythical conception of the past as it is in itself. While radical forms of narrativism see the construction as something that floats free above the facts, moderate forms claim that there are constraints on how the past can be narrated. Neither of these positions denies that there are data, the building blocks out of which historical narratives are constructed, but they differ in the way in which they present the activity of the bricklayer, so to speak, and how free she is in positioning the bricks out of which the narrative structure is built. Narrativists tend to agree that there is a distinction between data gathering and data arrangement just as there is between picking flowers and creating a bouquet. But just as the flowers can be arranged in different ways in order to create different kinds of bouquets, so too can the data out of which narratives are produced.

Accepting that there is only one way to narrate the story of what happened would be tantamount to endorsing the empiricist myth of the given according to which the facts simply speak for themselves. But, so the narrativist argues, there is no such thing as an uninterpreted/unnarrated historical past. Just as if you undo the bouquet you are left with individual flowers, so if you take away the historian's narrative you are left not with a history but with a mere chronicle of events. As we shall see in the next section, Collingwood too rejects a meta-level conception of history as mere fact-gathering. But he does not draw the same revisionist conclusions as narrativism, namely that the past must necessarily be re-written from the perspective of the present.

The past *as it was* and the past as it is *in itself*

Knowing *what* happened historically, for Collingwood, is not simply a matter of knowing *that* something happened; it requires explaining why it happened. Just as, for example, knowing that the water in a bucket froze does not amount to having *scientific* knowledge of that fact (to have scientific knowledge of that fact is to know that the water froze because the temperature dropped below 0°C), likewise to know the fact that Archduke Ferdinand was assassinated on 28 June 1914 is not to have *historical* knowledge of that fact. To know that fact *historically* requires providing an explanation of why the Archduke was assassinated, to argue, for example, this was done to free Bosnia and Herzegovina from Austro-Hungarian rule. Collingwood agrees that historical knowledge proper is not knowledge of mere facts. He notoriously claimed that when the historian knows what happened, 'he already knows why it happened' (Collingwood 1946: 214). But the facts of the past, according to Collingwood, are understood historically when they are understood through the categories of the historical agents, their worldview, not those of the historian. One cannot, for example, understand why the assassination of Archduke Ferdinand triggered the Great War without understanding the system of alliances in place at the time, just as one cannot understand why Caesar's crossing of the Rubicon posed a challenge to the Republic without any familiarity with Roman law at the time. To have historical knowledge of Caesar's crossing of the Rubicon is not simply to know the fact that a roman general on a horse crossed a stream which was later glorified with the name of a river. To understand that fact historically is to bring it under a thicker description (it was an act of aggression against the Republic). But to bring it under a thicker historical description (it was such an act of aggression) requires knowing that the Rubicon marked a border, that Roman generals were banned from crossing it with their army. Similarly, to retrospectively understand why the assassination of Archduke Ferdinand triggered a world conflict one needs to understand the various treatises in place at the time of his rule. Now, to endorse Collingwood's claim that the historian's own categories are the wrong filters through which to understand the past is not to deny that retrospectivity has a role in historical writing, that a historian, writing at a distance from the events, enjoys a certain kind of vantage point. Retrospectivity clearly has a role in historical inquiry. Danto is correct in claiming that one could not have known on 28 June 1914 that the assassination of Archduke Franz Ferdinand would have triggered the Great War. It is conceivable that the assassination of the Archduke may not have triggered a world war if the repercussions of the system of alliances in place at the time had been clearly anticipated and careful negotiation had been undertaken to pre-empt a large-scale conflict. But it would not be possible retrospectively to identify that event as a trigger without locating in the political context of the time. This is the context in which the facts have to be located in order for the past to be understood historically. It would be a mistake, therefore, to read Collingwood's claim that when a historian knows what happened he already knows why it happened as endorsing the claim that the significance of the past is grasped from the standpoint of the historian's present: the framework which enables the understanding of the past historically is the framework of the agents. While Collingwood rejects the empiricist view that history is a mere chronicle, he denies that the glue which holds the facts together essentially derives from the historian's conceptual toolkit. Collingwood's account of historical understanding rejects the form/content distinction that narrativism inherits from Kant (or at least from a certain reading of Kant's claim concerning the transcendental unity of apperception). The assassination of Archduke Ferdinand could not have the historical significance it has (the trigger for the Great War) were it not for the political context (the system of treatises and alliances) of its time, just as Caesar's crossing of the Rubicon has the significance it has in the context of Roman law. To understand Caesar's crossing of the Rubicon historically is to understand it in the way in which a Roman familiar with Republican law would have understood it. Similarly, to understand the significance of the archduke's assassination is to understand it in relation to its contemporary repercussions. The conceptual mediation that enables the facts (the crossing of the Rubicon; the assassination of the archduke) to be understood historically is that relating to the perspective of the Romans living at the time of the Republic, not that of the historian. The categories through which the past is understood are baked into the facts, just as the eggs, sugar and flower are baked into the cake, not poured over them like a glaze. But to claim that the past can be known as it was, from the perspective of the agents, is not the same as saying that the past can be known in itself, independently of any conceptual mediation; it does not require us to endorse the empiricist myth of the given. It is one thing to reject a conception of history as mere chronicle; it is another to assert that we cannot understand the world as it was understood by the Greeks, Romans and so on. The latter claim is not entailed by the former. If what underlies narrativism's commitment to revisionism is the assumption that rejecting the empiricist myth of the given requires endorsing the view that there are multiple pasts, this assumption is based on a non-sequitur. One can accept that historical knowledge requires conceptual mediation, that the past cannot be known in itself, whilst rejecting the claim that what the crossing of the Rubicon signified to a Roman of the time changes as the arrow of time moves on, changing in accordance with the perspective of a historian writing in the Middle Ages, in modernity and so on.

In this chapter we have identified some key assumptions that govern the form of revisionism which has dominated philosophy of history after Collingwood's death. The first concerns the epistemic priority of the present and the view that the historian cannot extricate herself from the conceptual framework of the present to see things from the perspective of historical agents. The standpoint of the historian in the present, for

Collingwood, is the wrong filter through which to view the past; the categorial mediation that is relevant to the understanding of past agents is that of the agents' themselves, not that of the historian. The past is at least in principle knowable from the perspective of past agents by bracketing the historian's own system of beliefs and imaginatively immersing oneself in the framework of thought within which the historical agents moved. The assumption that it is not possible to understand past agents from their own point of view reflects the idea that understanding another person requires undergoing the same experiences as the person in question, something that Collingwood explicitly denies. The second assumption is that there is an asymmetry between historical and scientific knowledge of the past because unlike scientific theories, the narratives retrospectively constructed by historians are in principle unverifiable. Collingwood rejects the asymmetry between history and science that governs much contemporary revisionism. Presuppositional analysis shows that there is no need to liken history to a form of narrative and to deny that it is a genuine form of knowledge which advances verifiable claims, just like science does, in order to defend the autonomy of historical understanding. As a result, his defence of the autonomy of history does not lead to scepticism concerning the possibility of acquiring objective knowledge of the past, but rather to an acknowledgement that verification criteria vary in accordance with explanatory contexts and goals of inquiry. History is a form of knowledge with its own criteria of verification. It is the presuppositions of historical inquiry which are not verifiable. But the same applies to the presuppositions of scientific inquiry.

The third assumption is that to reject an empiricist conception of history as mere fact-gathering requires accepting that there are many pasts, rather than one, which are retrospectively re-constructed from the standpoint of the present. Collingwood denies that rejecting the empiricist myth of the given entails ipso facto accepting that there are many pasts, rather than one. Just as suspending disbelief when reading a work of fiction or attending the performance of a period play requires seeing things from the perspective of the characters or actors, rather than adopting a view from nowhere, suspending one's prejudgments is not tantamount to accepting some mythical notion of the past as it is in itself.

The past, for Collingwood, is an ambiguous term. There are different *kinds* of past, the *natural* and the *historical* past, which are the correlative of different forms of explanations, explanations which rest on different presuppositions, presuppositions which provide criteria appeal to which enables one to establish true and false claims in their respective domain of inquiry. The claim that the historical past as the correlative of a humanistic explanation is distinct from the natural past as the correlative of scientific explanations should not be confused with the revisionist's view that there are many pasts, as many as are retrospectively constructed by narratives written from the perspective of the present. In contrast to the constructivism that has prevailed in the philosophy of history after his death Collingwood was committed to the claim that the past can, at least in principle, be known as it was. Endorsing the kind of explanatory pluralism which is made possible by his conception of metaphysics as the study of presuppositions does not, therefore, lead to scepticism. Such scepticism seems rather to be generated by the rejection of the view that there are domain-specific criteria by reference to which explanatory hypotheses, whether scientific or historical, can be assessed for their truth or falsity. The importance of the distinction between the natural and the historical past will be explored in Chapter 8 and defended against a form of nouveau naturalism which denounces the distinction as based on unacceptable anthropocentric assumptions. But before concluding let us just recall the broader point that this chapter seeks to establish over and beyond the philosophy of history.

We began by saying that one of the goals of this chapter is to allay fears that Collingwood's rejection of the applicability of the notion of truth to absolute presuppositions may make him into an enemy of the idea that there are verifiable knowledge claims, in any domain of inquiry, which can be found to be true or false through the methodological means that the experts in those forms of inquiry avail themselves of. Nowhere is Collingwood's commitment to the objectivity of knowledge clearer than in his philosophy of history where he upholds the view that there is one past that can be known as it was for the historical agents. Collingwood's distinction between the natural and the historical past is very different from the constructivist claim that there are many pasts. The claim that there are many pasts rests on a commitment to a form of standpoint epistemology according to which one can only know reality from the temporally situated standpoint of the present. Collingwood's claim that there are different kinds of past, the historical and the natural past, on the other hand, rests on the reciprocity thesis (as described in Chapter 2), namely the claim that there is a reciprocal relation between method and subject matter, that it is not possible to know the significance of Caesar's crossing of the Rubicon by adopting the methods of physics any more than it is possible to explain the death of a star by deploying a certain kind of humanistic understanding. The reciprocity thesis entails that different forms of knowing have different explananda: events are the correlative of scientific method and actions are the correlative of a humanistic-oriented historiography. The claim is that if one changes one's methodological assumptions or the presuppositions which govern a form of inquiry, one ipso facto changes the explanandum, not that there are as many 'truths' about the past as there presents from which the past is retrospectively known. Collingwood's claim for the autonomy of historical knowing is, as we shall see in the next chapter, part and parcel of an argument against scientism, not of an argument for historical relativism.

7

Beyond scientism and historicism

What it really takes to overcome scientism

Scientism is normally described as a belief in the epistemic superiority of scientific knowledge and its right to impose its methods onto the territory of the humanities. It is not a scientific claim but a philosophical claim concerning the relation between science and other forms of knowledge. Let us describe this approach, defined as a philosophical belief concerning the epistemic standing of the natural sciences and their right to trespass onto the territory of the humanities, as scientism in the narrow sense. Collingwood is well known for articulating a defence of the autonomy of history against the claim for methodological unity in the sciences and thus for advancing an argument against scientism so understood. Scientism, however, can also be understood more broadly to designate a belief in the epistemic superiority of *any* one form of knowledge and their right to trespass onto the territory of another. In this broader sense historicism, understood as a form of historical fundamentalism according to which everything is ultimately knowable by the method of history, or as the claim that all knowledge is historical knowledge, is a form of scientism in reverse, as it were. Historicism, so understood, is not an argument against scientism; it *is* a form of scientism. Collingwood was opposed to scientism not only in the narrow sense, i.e. as the illegitimate trespassing of scientific explanations onto the subject matter of the humanities, but also to scientism broadly understood, as the trespassing of any form of knowledge onto the territory of another, and thus to historicism understood as form of historical fundamentalism. He was just as opposed to the philosophical view that everything can be known by the method of history as he was opposed to the claim that everything can be known by the method of science. He challenged epistemic fundamentalism in all forms. He rejected the philosophical commitment to a layered/hierarchical view of the sciences which privileges the explanations of physics in favour of the view that the choice between one kind of explanation and another is made by determining which kind of explanation is fit to answer the question that is being asked. His agenda was not to replace one 'ism' as in scientism in the narrow sense, with another 'ism' as in historicism, understood as a malignant form of historical fundamentalism, but rather to defend the benign claim that the actions of past agents have to be understood in the context of their own thought. His goal was not to bring about a sort of epistemological coup aiming at replacing the form of knowledge in charge (scientific knowledge) with another (historical knowledge). The goal was rather to rebalance the epistemic relations of power by showing that there is a time and a place for scientific explanations and a time and a place for humanistic explanations of the kind one often finds in history. His argument for the methodological autonomy of historical knowledge, as we have seen, is based on a commitment to a conception of philosophy as a form of presuppositional analysis aimed at uncovering the assumptions which govern different forms of inquiry and at showing that both history and natural science are sciences in the Latin sense of the term *Scientia*, meaning a body of knowledge with a distinctive method and subject matter. The relation between scientific and humanistic understanding is to be understood against the background of the claim that natural science and history have different presuppositions, which serve different explanatory goals, and which give rise to distinctive questions. This aspect of Collingwood's defence of the methodological autonomy of history is often misunderstood, and he is usually read as advocating a form of historical fundamentalism intent on reversing the epistemic power relations between science and history. This chapter argues that Collingwood articulates a defence of the autonomy of humanistic explanations against scientism in the narrow sense without turning the tables on science, i.e. without endorsing a form of inverted scientism which aims to reduce scientific knowledge to historical knowledge.[1] His aim is to undermine scientism both narrowly conceived, as a form of imperialism of the natural sciences, and broadly conceived, as the belief that any one form of knowledge has the right to extend its methods onto the subject matter of another.

The image of Collingwood's thought that I present is therefore very different from the metaphilosophy with which he is usually associated, according to which all knowledge (including knowledge acquired by the methods of science) is historical knowledge and history simply steps in the shoes of the freshly usurped dictator whilst leaving the epistemic power structures intact. This claim is the natural outcome of what has been argued so far, namely that Collingwood's non-reductivism is a genuine form of explanatory pluralism.

Inverted scientism

Before explaining why Collingwood was not covertly committed to historicism, understood as a form of scientism in reverse, it is important to understand why it is worth defending him against this accusation, one that is often voiced by saying that he was a 'radical historicist'. Radical historicism claims that there is no such thing as transhistorical knowledge, or knowledge that reaches beyond the parochial temporal standpoint in which it emerged. This commitment to the claim that all knowledge is historically relative has certain counterintuitive implications. We often want to make claims from our peculiar standpoint in time and yet extend these claims beyond our own standpoint. A scientist, for example, may want to claim that the Earth revolves around the Sun, that the system in which the Earth finds its place is heliocentric, rather than geocentric in character, as it was believed to be in pre-Copernican times. However, radical historicism

---

[1] This theme is explored in D'Oro G. and Connelly J. (forthcoming).

(as a form of relativism) precludes one from correcting the beliefs of others, thereby making it impossible to claim, for example, that pre-Copernicans believed the Sun revolves around the Earth, but they were mistaken about this since their theories have since been refuted. Claims such as this one are not possible if one endorses a form of historical fundamentalism according to which all knowledge, including scientific knowledge, is relative to a certain standpoint in time. Some philosophers have endorsed historicism, understood as a form of historical relativism reaching 'all the way down' to scientific beliefs and embraced some of its most counterintuitive implications. Bruno Latour (2000), for example, rejected the claim that pharaoh Rameses II died of tuberculosis, on the grounds that the tubercle bacillus was not discovered until 1882 and hence bacilli are not the sort of things that can be invoked to explain the pharaoh's death or indeed any deaths prior to the arrival of microbiology.

This kind of historical relativism seems to be motivated by the assumption that one cannot make assertions such as 'Rameses II died of tuberculosis, although the Ancient Egyptians simply did not know about this particular disease' without committing oneself to the view that nature can be known in itself, that scientific knowledge (unlike humanistic knowledge) delivers conceptually unmediated knowledge of reality as it is 'in itself', rather than conceptually mediated knowledge of reality as it is 'for us' in different moments in time. Those who embrace the counterintuitive implication that people only died from tuberculosis after 1882[2] tend to do so on the assumption that a consistent commitment to the claim that all knowledge is conceptually mediated, that there is no such thing as unmediated/unconceptualized knowledge of reality, requires us to commit to a form of historical relativism or radical historicism. As we shall see, the assumption that in order to correct past scientific beliefs one must be committed to the view that scientific knowledge delivers knowledge of pure being is a

---

[2] For a discussion of the counter-intuitive implications of dissolving science into the history of the philosophy of science, see Tosh (2007).

non sequitur: there is no need to appeal to pure being in order to be able to claim that the planetary system is heliocentric in spite of what pre-Copernicans believed, or that Rameses II died of tuberculosis notwithstanding the fact this is not what the ancient Egyptians believed. Collingwood's conception of philosophy as presuppositional analysis shows exactly how it is possible to make such critical claims without assuming knowledge of pure being or being in itself to be possible.

Avoiding historical fundamentalism without reintroducing the spectre of pure being

Collingwood's conception of philosophy as presuppositional analysis informs a form of explanatory pluralism. This explanatory pluralism does not entail that Koch's bacilli cannot be invoked to explain why Rameses II died before the discovery of the tubercle bacillus in 1882, but only that, when Rameses' death is so explained, it is *not* explained historically because historical explanations must invoke categories that would have been available to the agents at the time. The historian who explains the death of Rameses II by referring to bacilli that had not been discovered at the time of the ancient Egyptians has changed her explanatory hat and is no longer viewing reality qua historian, i.e. from the perspective of the agents, but this is not to say that Rameses' death cannot be explained in this way from a different explanatory standpoint. The explanation that pharaoh Rameses II died of tuberculosis is illegitimately anachronistic from a historical perspective because it is not one that an ancient Egyptian could possibly have given, but it is a legitimate *scientific* explanation for his death. It is an explanation that answers different kinds of questions from those asked by history as a form of inquiry, questions which arise because a different set of presuppositions are made. What one presupposes, when one says that the Koch bacillus was the cause of Rameses' death, is that nature is uniform, that the laws of nature apply in the times of the Ancient Egyptians as well as those in which the Koch bacillus was discovered.

The historical past and the natural past, as we have seen in the previous chapter, are known in different ways. When investigating the historical past the humanistic historian views reality through the lens of the historical agents, their belief systems and the social norms to which they were held accountable. When investigating the natural past the natural scientist abstracts from the thought context of the agents and views reality as subject to immutable laws of nature. To understand the past historically, by contrast, is to understand it in its own thought context: to import concepts which are alien to that thought context, for example by interpreting the action of agents in the light of scientific knowledge they did not possess, involves an anachronism and is poor historical practice. But there is no such thing as anachronism in science where outdated scientific theories are not past practices one must familiarize oneself with for the sake of understanding how they motivated the actions of past agents, but poor explanatory hypotheses that have to be discarded as false or significantly revised. Bringing the presuppositions of historical understanding to bear upon the practice of science is as damaging as applying the presuppositions of science to the study of the historical past. As we saw in chapter five, when historians adopt the presupposition of the uniformity of nature to investigate the historical past, they end up writing what Collingwood calls scissors-and-paste histories, histories which fail to understand historical documents in the context of the agents. Conversely, when the presuppositions of history are brought to bear upon the study of the natural past, one loses sight of the idea that nature is uniform, that the laws of nature, unlike norms of conduct, do not change, and thus that the causes of diseases, such as tuberculosis, do not vary from one period of history to another. Philosophy takes note of the presuppositions which govern different forms of inquiry and in so doing it shows not only that history cannot be reduced to science but also that scientific inquiry cannot be reduced to a form of historical knowing. A historicism which denies science its autonomous domain of inquiry just is an inverted scientism. Unfortunately, it is precisely this kind of historicism that Collingwood has been traditionally associated with.

Understanding why he avoided the error of replacing the 'ism' in scientism with the 'ism' in historicism without reintroducing the notion of pure being requires us to be clear about the status of the presupposition 'nature does not change' or 'nature is uniform across time and space'. The claim that 'nature does not change', for Collingwood, is a presupposition which governs explanation in the natural sciences, and should not be confused with a commitment to reference invariance of the kind found in the causal theory of meaning as articulated in the works of Kripke (1980) and Putnam (1975). Reference invariance, as defended by these writers, has been invoked to counter the view that since the meaning of scientific terms changes across paradigms, it is not possible to compare scientific theories which belong to different historical contexts.[3] Natural science, for Collingwood, must presuppose that nature does not change; it must presuppose that nature is uniform and thus that all scientific theories describe (in different ways) the same invariant object. But the commitment to the principle of the uniformity of nature is a presupposition of scientific inquiry; it is a claim *not* about the nature or essence of objects per se, but about how they must be conceived and thematized within scientific inquiry. It is a claim that belongs to 'metaphysics' as a science of presuppositions.

Collingwood's metaphysics of absolute presuppositions preserves the distinction between the method and subject matter of science and the method and subject matter of history, without locating science and history on the opposite sides of the fact/value distinction, i.e. without claiming that whereas historical inquiry delivers conceptually mediated knowledge of reality, scientific investigation reveals the nature of pure being. The scientific investigation of nature abstracts from the way in which nature was construed by past historical agents because it is a presupposition of scientific inquiry that nature is uniform, that natural laws, unlike norms of conduct, apply at all times and places. To say *this*

---

[3] On this, see Kuukkanen, J.-M., 'Meaning Change in the Context of Thomas S. Kuhn's Philosophy', (PhD Dissertation. University of Edinburgh, 2006).

is not to claim that scientific knowledge is value neutral knowledge of pure being or being in itself; it is rather to say that it is a mode of inquiry which furnishes knowledge under a different set of presuppositions from those of history. While science has a conception of reality that is distinct from that of history (nature or its laws are immutable for the natural scientist; norms of behaviour are not so for the historian), the distinction between scientific and historical knowledge is not based on a crude separation of fact and value, reality as it is in itself and as it is for us.

All knowledge, including scientific knowledge, has presuppositions: there is no such thing as presuppositionless knowledge of reality or of being qua being. Being is known under the presuppositions of history and science. But to say *this* is not the same as saying that all knowledge is relative to a place and a time. The relativity, insofar as it makes sense to speak of relativity, is to the goals of inquiry and the presuppositions operative in different explanatory contexts, not to place or time. While historians would fail to do their job properly if they assumed that the belief system of feudal barons was the same as that of twentieth-century New Yorkers, natural scientists must presuppose the very opposite, namely that the reality they investigate is unchanging. Neither of these claims, namely (a) that reality as viewed by historical agents changes and (b) that reality is unchanging and independent of how it is viewed by historical agents, is an ontological claim concerning the nature of reality; both claims capture presuppositions which govern forms of inquiry. As such they belong to metaphysics understood as a study of presuppositions rather than as the study of pure being. Collingwood's conception of philosophy as a form of presuppositional analysis supports the claim that there is a division of labour between the scientist and the historian of science. While it is the remit of the natural scientist to assess past scientific claims for their truth or falsity, and to critique them, it is not the task of history to do so. Qua scientists we can claim that pre-Copernicans were mistaken in believing the solar system to be geocentric but qua historians of science the focus is not on whether that belief was right or wrong, but in how those assumptions shaped the scientific practices of the historical agents because the job of the historian of science, qua historian, is to understand. There is consequently no reason to believe that a defence of humanistic understanding must be committed to a form of epistemic relativism according to which the scientific practices of past agents are beyond criticism.

No asymmetry between the epistemic and the moral case

Some philosophers have argued that there is a truth in value/moral relativism, that while it is possible to criticize past scientific beliefs, it is neither possible nor meaningful to judge past agents for their ways of life.[4] There is no indication that Collingwood regarded the moral case to be any different from the epistemic one. Just as he was not advocating a form of epistemic relativism, he was not defending a form of moral or ethical relativism either. The claim that past agents have to be understood in the context of thought does not imply that their beliefs (moral or epistemic) cannot be criticized (as a relativist would claim), but only that the primary task of history as a form of inquiry (which is not to be confused with history as the academic discipline taught in university departments) is to understand the role that such beliefs played as sources of agential motivation, not to critique them. Perhaps what underlies the suspicion that a commitment to contextualism, understood as the view that past agents have to be understood in their own thought context, leads to a form of radical historicism in the ethical domain, is the view that understanding necessarily leads to forgiveness, that 'to understand all is to forgive all'. The view that *tout comprendre c'est tous pardoner* is certainly implicit in the sort of theodicy that Leibniz ([1686]/1991) developed, where

---

[4] This view is sometimes attributed to Williams ([1985] 2006b). For a discussion, see D'Oro and Connelly (forthcoming).

knowledge (if one could acquire it) of God's reasons for choosing to actualize this world rather than another provides a justification for things being as they indeed are. But the idea that to understand is ipso facto to forgive is not one that informs Collingwood's account of what it means to understand past agents by rationalizing their actions. Historical understanding does not justify the actions of past agents in this existential/ontological sense. The goal of rationalization in historical inquiry is to explain why it made sense to act in a certain way in the light of certain epistemic and motivational premises, not to endorse those premises. Just as a historian need not believe the premise 'the mountain chain is populated by evil spirits' to be true, in order to understand how it deterred past agents from crossing it, so a historian need not endorse any of the moral principles which informed the conduct of past agent in order to understand how they informed their actions. Collingwood's defence of the methodological autonomy of history advocates a division of labour between history (including the history of science) and science, not a form of historical relativism either about epistemic beliefs or moral values. The fact that it is the task of history to understand, rather than to critique the moral beliefs of past agents, does not entail that the moral values of past agents are ipso facto beyond criticism. There is no asymmetry between the epistemic and the moral case. Just as in the epistemic case there is a division of labour between the scientist and the historian of science, so in the moral case there is a division of labour between the task of the historian and that of the cultural critic. Contextualism (understood as the claim that past agents are understood historically when they are understood in relation to their own thought context) does not entail relativism. There is therefore no need to approach the past anachronistically from the perspective and categories of the present, as it is sometimes claimed (Rée 1991), in order to allow for the possibility of a critical engagement with the past. What is required is rather an acknowledgement of the fact that all well-directed criticism presupposes adequate (historical) understanding of its target.

There is no epistemological coup

When understood in the context of metaphysics as the study of presuppositions Collingwood's argument for the methodological autonomy of history with respect to natural science does not entail a topsy-turvy dissolution of science into history and the subsequent replacement of one *ism* (as in radical histori*cism*) with another (scient*ism*). *From a historical point of view* nature is like a cultural artefact that must be understood in the context of thought. The *history of the philosophy of science* is a historical inquiry concerned with *the idea of nature*, how nature was conceptualized in different times and places; the historian of science (just like historians in general) works under the presupposition that the context of thought changes, that the conception of nature of the ancient Greeks is different from the conception of nature we now have. For the practising scientist, on the other hand, nature is an invariant object and different scientific paradigms reflect not the historically changing idea of nature but progressively more sophisticated descriptions of an invariant reality investigated under the presupposition of the uniformity of nature. Once the switch in presuppositions is properly recognized, there is no conflict between the history of science (from the perspective of which the conception of nature changes over time) and science itself (from the perspective of which nature is uniform), just as there is no conflict between scientific and humanistic knowledge more generally.[5]

Collingwood's defence of the autonomy of historical explanations is often erroneously presented as an attempt to bring about a kind of epistemological coup that reverses the power relations between science and history by handing over to history the position of epistemic

---

[5] For the view that history and science rest on incompatible ontologies, see Kuukkanen, J.-M., 'Historicism and the Failure of HPS' in *Studies in History and Philosophy of Science* XXX (2015), 1-9.

privilege once occupied by science. As a result he is often understood as advocating a form of historical fundamentalism according to which all knowledge (including scientific knowledge) is ultimately historical knowledge. This reading misunderstands Collingwood's argument at its core: Collingwood's conception of metaphysics as presuppositional analysis does not advocate a reversed scientism in which history moves from the position of the oppressed to that of the oppressor. Just as the subject matter of history (actions) is the distinctive explanandum of humanistic understanding, so the subject matter of science (events) is the distinctive explanandum of scientific knowledge. Neither is reducible to the other.

Presuppositional analysis undermines the *philosophical* belief that scientific knowledge is epistemically superior and that science can answer all questions; it does not degrade scientific knowledge by arguing that it is a covert form of historical knowledge. In rejecting the view that scientific knowledge is a covert form of historical/humanistic knowledge, this chapter substantiates one of the central claims of this book, namely that Collingwood matters because he articulates an argument against scientific imperialism without committing the opposite error of reducing scientific knowledge to historical knowledge. The need to switch between the presuppositions which govern the scientific and the humanistic approach to the past, in accordance with our explanatory goals, is crucial to Collingwood's defence of the nature/culture distinction, as discussed in the next chapter.

8

The historical past and the nature/culture distinction at the time of the Anthropocene

Old and new challenges to explanatory pluralism

It has recently been argued that the distinction between the historical and the natural past, a distinction that is crucial to Collingwood's defence of humanistic understanding, rests on unacceptable anthropocentric and 'speciesist' assumptions. I shall refer to this recent criticism of the idea of a distinctive historical past as 'the new challenge', in order to distinguish it from the older criticism of the autonomy of historical explanations that was articulated by Hempel in the 1940s and 1950s, a criticism which I shall refer to as 'the old challenge'. Proponents of the new challenge (Chakrabarty 2009; Bonneuil and Fressoz 2016; Latour 2017) argue that the advent of the Anthropocene, a geological period in which humankind has become a significant force that is capable of initiating fundamental environmental changes in the entire terrestrial context, forces us to rethink how history should be conceived and how it should be written. Narratives of historical development should go well beyond the relatively recent *human* past (with which history has been traditionally concerned) and view human history in the context of a deeper, longer-term geological time. Advocates of the new challenge argue that the distinction between the historical and the natural past relies on questionable anthropocentric assumptions that treat human beings as if they were not basically or essentially *natural* beings. They condemn the distinction between the historical and the natural past as an unacceptable dichotomy committed to a form of human exceptionalism which pits the human being against the rest of nature. After briefly revisiting the older criticism of the argument for the methodological autonomy of history vis-à-vis natural science, this chapter turns to consider this new challenge, one which seeks to undermine the distinction between the historical and the natural past by arguing that it is based on an unacceptable anthropocentrism. I argue that this new challenge, like the old one, fails to understand the nature of Collingwood's defence of the autonomy of humanistic understanding. While Hempel's challenge to the methodological autonomy of history failed to see that historical explanations (of actions) are explanations of a different kind, not covert nomological explanations or 'explanation sketches', the new challenge to the autonomy of historical understanding conflates the idea of the historical past with that of the human past and the concept of a *humanistic* historiography with that of *human* history. Correcting the misunderstanding of Collingwood's argument for the autonomy of historical understanding and defending his actual position against this latter-day charge of anthropocentrism and speciesism is not just a pedantic scholarly exercise. Only if there is a distinction between the historical and the natural past, can there also be a distinction between the historical and the natural future. If there were no distinction between the historical and the natural past, no disciplinary boundaries between history and science, and no distinction between historical and other kinds of agents, then the anticipation of the future would become a mere spectator sport analogous to the activity of predicting the weather. Disambiguating the historical and the natural past is therefore not a mere exercise in achieving conceptual clarity: it is an exercise in conceptual clarity with real-life consequences precisely because theory does have implications for praxis.

The old challenge and the nature of Collingwood's explanatory pluralism

Just a year before Collingwood's death Hempel (1942) published a very influential article which rejuvenated Mill's argument for methodological unity in the sciences. Hempel claimed that there is one model of explanation, the nomological model of explanation, which can be applied across the board, in science as well as in history. As we saw in Chapter 2, according to the nomological model, to explain something causally is to subsume the explanandum under a general law. This model is tense-less in the sense that it can be employed either to predict the future or to retrodict the past. The fact that historians are typically concerned with the past rather than the future does not entail that historical explanations are different in kind from the nomological explanations used in science. The historian's focus on the past and the scientist's focus on the future obscure the fact that scientific and historical explanations share the same logical form. Historical explanations, Hempel argued, appear to differ from scientific explanations because historical explanations tend to be 'explanation sketches'. A historian who claims that the dust bowl farmer migrated to a different area because the weather conditions were adverse is giving only a partial or incomplete explanation, i.e. a sketch of an explanation. The complete explanation would state that the dustbowl farmers were faced with certain antecedent conditions (adverse weather) and that populations tend to migrate to areas which are more conducive to the thriving of life (general law). Once the explanation is completed in this way it is seen to be no different in form from nomological explanations of natural phenomena, such as the melting of ice, which are explained by invoking antecedent conditions (in this case, the raising of the temperature) and a general law.[1] Hempel's paper was published just one year before Collingwood's death in 1943, so there was no opportunity for him to offer a relevant reply to Hempel. Collingwood's defence of a humanistically oriented historiography was taken up by W. H. Dray in an influential book (1957) and a series of papers (1958; 1963; 1980) which are now largely forgotten, but which exposed the cracks in the

---

[1] Hempel originally argued that nomological explanations are deductive explanations in which the explanandum is strictly entailed by a universal law and the antecedent conditions. He later conceded that covering laws in history are at best probabilistic laws and that in historical explanations the explanandum is only probabilistically entailed by the general laws and the antecedent conditions from which it is deduced, thereby allowing for a distinction in degree (but still not in kind) between the human and the natural sciences.

argument for methodological unity in the sciences. As W. H. Dray pointed out in the decades after Collingwood's death, Hempel's argument for methodological unity in the sciences singularly failed to understand the nature of Collingwood's defence of the autonomy of historical understanding. Collingwood conceded that the mark of a historical explanation is not that it is concerned with the past rather than the future. The past, Collingwood was the first one to point out, is studied by natural science as well as history. But Collingwood denied that the past as understood, for example, by a cultural anthropologist or medieval historian, is the same past as that which is investigated by physicists concerned with 'the big bang': historians do not retrodict Caesar's crossing of the Rubicon in the way in which astronomers retrodict the explosion of a star that occurred millions of years ago. For the sake of predicting the future and retrodicting the past physicists assume that nature is uniform, that the laws of nature are the same in the Victorian and Edwardian period and that water will freeze at 0°C under the reign of King Edward VII as well as that of Queen Victoria. For the sake of understanding historical agents, by contrast, historians assume that agents are responsive to norms and that the norms by which historical agents lead their lives may well differ significantly from their own. From the point of view of the physicist 'nature has no history' (Collingwood 1946: 476). This is not because natural beings are unaffected by the passage of time (fruits first ripen and then rot) nor because nature never changes (the Earth was a very different place millions of years ago than it is now), but because the scientific investigation of nature operates under the assumption of the uniformity of its underlying laws. By contrast, the historical investigation of the past operates on the assumption that agents are interpreting and self-interpreting beings who are responsive to norms, and that these norms are not historically invariant. Collingwood's defence of the autonomy of historical understanding is premised upon the assumption that the explanation of action differs from scientific explanation of events, not because explanations of actions are incomplete (nomological) explanations, but because they are explanations of an altogether different kind, i.e. they are rationalizing, sense-making explanations. A distinctive feature of this explanatory pluralism is that it does *not* claim that whereas nomological explanations are causal explanations which establish empirical connections between distinct events (say the drop in temperature and the freezing of the water), explanations of actions are *mere* rationalizations that bring the explanans under a different description (as in the case of Anscombe's example of the man whose action may be described either as 'replenishing the water supply' or 'poisoning the inhabitants of the house'). Collingwood's explanatory pluralism claims rather that nomological and rationalizing explanations bring reality under different categorial descriptions, as we do, for example, when we redescribe what was thought to be a case of accidental killing as a case of murder. The redescriptions 'replenishing the water supply' and 'murdering the inhabitants of the house' describe, or redescribe, the same category of thing: actions. They are *different descriptions of the same kind*. Accidental killing and murder are not just *different descriptions*, but *descriptions of different kinds*. The redescription of an accidental killing as a murder requires invoking a different sense of 'cause', one which brings reality under an altogether different *kind* of description by explaining it in a different way, i.e., as an action rather than as an event. It is because the description of accidental killing and murder bring reality under different categorial descriptions that it makes no sense to say 'he murdered her accidentally', whereas it does make sense to say 'he murdered her by administering poison'. Whereas one can murder the inhabitants of a house by replenishing their water supply with a poisoned concoction, one cannot murder someone by accidentally killing them. These constraints on what it is and is not possible to say meaningfully reflect certain articulations in the way reality is conceptually mapped. It is precisely because Collingwood's explanatory pluralism identifies this kind of conceptual articulation in the way in which we describe reality that it differs from most forms of non-reductivism in contemporary philosophy of mind. As we saw in Chapter 3, contemporary forms of non-reductivism tend to assume that all sciences, from physics to psychology, explain by invoking the same sense of causation and that the task of a philosophy of mind is to explain how the causal laws formulated in the vocabulary of the special sciences (chemistry biology *and* psychology) can be reconciled with those of physics. Rather than seeking to address the problem of causal exclusion against the background of certain naturalistic assumptions concerning the nature of explanation and the relation between forms of knowledge, Collingwood argues that humanistic explanations (of actions) do not compete with scientific explanations (of events) because they address different kinds of questions, which are answered by using explanations with distinctive logical forms, and which rest on different presuppositions. Much of Chapter 3 sought to make explicit the connection between Collingwood's defence of the autonomy of historical understanding and his distinctive metaphysics, a connection that arguably has not been fully appreciated to this day.

The Anthropocene challenge to the nature/culture distinction

The idea of a distinctive historical past which informed the defence of a humanistically oriented historiography against the old challenge has more recently come under attack on the basis of reflections about what it means to live in the Anthropocene, a new geological epoch characterised by cataclysmic human-induced climate changes which could potentially lead to the extinction of human life on Earth. Definitive stratigraphic proof for the end of the Holocene and the beginning of the Anthropocene has yet to be produced, and there is no consensus amongst geologists as to the identifiable beginning of this new epoch, some dating its onset to the time of the first nuclear explosion in 1945 (Zalasiewciz et al. 2015), some to the year 1784, the date of the invention of the steam engine as a symbol of the beginning of the industrial revolution (Crutzen 2002: 23), and others dating its onset further back to 1610, when a drastic fall in the indigenous population following Columbus' 'discovery' of America led to a decline in atmospheric CO_2 and the cooling of the climate known as the 'little ice age' (Lewis and Maslin 2015). While there is no clear consensus as to whether the Anthropocene has succeeded the Holocene and if so, what its precise starting date is, the Anthropocene has increasingly been described as that slice of geological time in which humans have become causal forces so powerful as to be able not only to selectively intervene in nature, but also to radically alter its course. Whether or not the Anthropocene will be given scientific recognition as a distinctive geological era is ultimately a matter for geologists to determine. What we are concerned here is not the scientific claim that the Anthropocene is a new slice of geological time, in which the effects of human activities are fundamentally affecting the very nature and character of the Earth, but rather the philosophical claim that the realization that human beings are themselves forces of nature capable of altering the Earth's climate implies that we should cast aside the distinction between the historical and the natural past either as philosophically dubious or as an obsolete categorial distinction that no longer serves our present needs.

There is a soft and a hard version of the new challenge. The soft version claims that traditional histories, the history of the Egyptian and the Roman civilizations, for example, and long-term geological or environmental histories, should be regarded as inextricably entwined. For if these two histories are kept in complete isolation from one another, then it is very difficult to expose human activity as a crucial factor in climate change. It is only when these different histories are seen to be entangled that it is possible to see, for example, that 'James Watt's design of the steam engine in 1784' coincides with the 'beginning of growing global concentrations of carbon dioxide and methane' in the air trapped in polar ice (Crutzen 2002: 23), or that the cooling of the climate known as 'the little ice age' followed the drastic fall in the indigenous population after Columbus' 'discovery' of America (Lewis and Maslin 2015: 175–6). This kind of interrelation is not new. But whereas traditional histories tended to mention the way in which nature impinges upon civilization (and discussed, for example, the ways in which draughts impacted upon Pharos' abilities to rule effectively in ancient Egypt), Anthropocene narratives change the direction of this relationship: they expose the influence that civilization exerts on nature rather than that of nature on civilization. The soft version of the new challenge does not deny that longer term, 'deep' geological histories and the history of civilizations are different kinds of histories, with different methods, suited to answer different kinds of questions: an argument against the compartmentalization of knowledge is not the same as an argument against disciplinary boundaries. The hard version, however, is a different prospect and considerably more radical than its soft counterpart. It argues not merely against the compartmentalization of knowledge which prevents the historian of ancient civilization from knowing anything about the findings of geologists, but against the very idea of disciplinary boundaries which was specifically invoked to defend the possibility of a humanistically oriented historiography against the old Hempelian challenge. While the old challenge sought to reduce historical explanations to scientific ones, the new challenge, in its most radical form, aims to undermine the disciplinary boundaries between science and history by doing away with the distinction between kinds of explanations which demarcate the domain of history (traditionally understood) from that of science.[2] In an attempt to eschew (what it erroneously regards as a form of) supernaturalism, the new challenge undermines the very possibility of historical agency by replacing the sui generis category of 'historical agent' with an undifferentiated concept that includes microbes, characters in novels and military commanders alike.

Since we stand on the threshold of an environmental catastrophe, so the argument goes, humans should see themselves in the context

---

[2] I take Dipesh Chakrabarty, Christophe Bonneuil and Jean-Baptiste Fressoz to be articulating, *for the most part*, a soft version of the challenge, calling for entanglement of nature and history, and Bruno Latour as articulating the more radical version, calling for the abolition of any distinction between them. The dividing line between these two versions of the challenge, however, is not always clear cut, and the distinction between the two is more like one that ought, in principle, to be made than one that is actually drawn in practice. For a more recent contribution to this debate, see Tamm and Simon (2020).

of a longer term, geological history of planet Earth, one in which the history of kings and queens unfolds within what is merely the batting of a geological eyelid. During what, from a geological perspective, is an infinitesimally short period of time, human beings engaged in revolutions, waged wars, and plotted against each other. During this period of time those same human beings enslaved members of their own species with a different skin colour, developed class systems which exploited large sections of humanity for the benefit of a select few and created myths to provide ideological support for racial segregation and class exploitation. This is the focus of traditional histories: the domain of human affairs or the time of the human species on Earth and their internal quarrels and conflicts. Historical narratives at this momentous time, where humanity is on the cusp of self-destruction, should focus on a different kind of time, a time long before any of the written records of the kind that professional historians study, in order to uncover the 'deep history' of humankind (Chakrabarty 2009: 212). Anthropocene-inspired criticisms of the idea of a distinctively historical past therefore tend to highlight the brevity and comparative insignificance of human time – a time during which humans became the predominant species, a species whose skills in mastering the natural environment eventually led them to imagine themselves as being somehow other-than-nature.

As well as urging historians to shift their attention away from historical to geological time, proponents of the new challenge seek to undermine what they see as the unacceptable dichotomy between the subjects of traditional history (human agents) and the object in question (nature), a dichotomy that they see as integral to the distinction between the natural and the historical past. The realization that human activity is responsible for global warming and the ensuing 'natural' catastrophes undermines the distinction between the traditional agents of history (humans) and the immutable backdrop against which their deeds take place (nature). As Chakrabarty puts it, climate scientists, in positing 'that the human being has become something much larger than the simple biological agent than he or she has always been …', are 'unwittingly destroying the artificial but time-honoured distinction between natural and human history'

(Chakrabarty 2009: 206). In traditional histories nature is generally portrayed as an unchanging 'silent and passive backdrop' (Chakrabarty 2009: 203) against which human history unfolds; it only makes sporadic appearances in historical narratives when it either facilitates or somehow hinders human endeavours. The weather, for example, is mentioned in histories of the Second World War because on 7 December 1941 the clear skies made the Japanese attack on the American base in Pearl Harbour easier or, in histories of the Great War, because persistent rain weakened the structural integrity of the trenches on the western front. But in traditional histories nature is generally portrayed as a constant backdrop against which human affairs unfold. It is seen as the 'other' of history: whereas civilizations change, the seasons alternate in an eternal recurrence of the same natural cycle, indifferent to human turmoil and unaffected by it. This view of nature as the other of history, an external and static backdrop indifferent and impermeable to human action, is shattered by the discovery that human activity itself is the catalyst for global warming, that deforestation and the industrialization of farming play a role in the process of climate change that is not different in kind from the one that, for example, microbes play in the development of diseases. The science of climate change shows that just as the balance of nature would remain inexplicable without taking into account the 'actions' of living organisms, so the disruptions to the natural cycles that have for so long been taken for granted could not be explained without the agency of humans. The Anthropocene facilitates the realization that human agency is the catalyst of climate change, that humans are geological forces of nature (Latour 2017: 92 ff.), just as Pasteur demonstrated that sugar could not be transformed into alcohol without the presence of yeast. The dividing line between a dead or deanimated nature that can be explained by appealing to physics and chemistry alone and history, as something that by contrast is to be understood teleologically, as the achievement of the goals of human agents, is shattered by the twin realization that just as the balance of nature could not be accounted for without taking into consideration the actions of living organisms, so the disruption to this balance cannot be accounted for without taking into account the activities of humans. The onset of the Anthropocene therefore challenges not only the distinction between human agents as the subject of history and a dead/deanimated nature that is supposed to be understood mechanistically rather than teleologically; it also challenges the distinction between the agents that feature in traditional histories and other kinds of agents: microbes, yeast and so on.

As the distinction between history and nature, between historical and other kind of agents, comes under attack, so does the view that there are different modes of understanding that correspond to the (allegedly) distinctive explananda of the *Naturwissenschaften* and the *Geisteswissenschaften*.

Bruno Latour claims that the way one understands the working of General Kutuzof's mind in Tolstoy's *War and Peace* is not significantly different from the way one understands how the Corticotropin releasing factor works. The reason why one might find it easier to grasp the psychology of the general in Tolstoy's novel than a scientific text describing the function of the factor releasing Corticotropin is simply due to lack of familiarity with the scientific context (Latour 2017: 49 ff.).[3]

The distinction between nature and culture has also become the target of gentle mockery once the question 'don't the historical beings who feature as main characters in traditional histories have a natural environment as well as a culture?' is teasingly posed. Sloterdijk, for example, asks whether Dasein does not have a habitat as well as a 'world' in the Heideggerian sense (a language, a culture a history). 'When you say that the Dasein is thrown into the world, into what it is actually thrown? What is the composition of the air it breathes there? How is the temperature controlled?'[4] The nature/culture distinction presupposed by the notion of a distinctively historical past leads not only to an unacceptable dichotomy between humans and

---

[3] Of course, a humanistically oriented historiographer would retort that since what is needed in the context of humanistic explanations is familiarity with the space of reasons, lack of familiarity with the scientific context is irrelevant to the task at hand: what is at stake precisely is what kind of context one should invoke when explaining General Kutuzof and the Corticotropin releasing factor.

[4] Sloterdijk, quoted in Latour (2017: 123).

the rest of nature; but also treats historical agents as if they were ethereal creatures who do not need to eat, breathe and perform any physiological functions, or so the argument claims. These objections are closely interlinked: if there are no distinctive *historical* agents, then there is no significant difference between culture and habitats and no distinctive methods for studying them are required as a result.

The new challenge questions the methodological distinction between different modes of understanding as based on an unacceptable ontological distinction between humans and the rest of nature. Once the ontological distinction between subject and object in its various manifestations (historical time vs geological time, historical subjects vs the external object (nature); historical agents vs other non-historical agents, humans vs other lesser beings) is rejected, so too are the methodological distinctions that underpin the disciplines which study nature and culture, the *Naturwissenschaften* and the *Geisteswissenschaften*. From the perspective of the new challenge, the nature/culture distinction which was expressly formulated as such at the end of the nineteenth and the beginning of the twentieth century and which was invoked to defend the idea of a distinctively *historical* past is at best humanity's ultimate delusion of grandeur and at worst a self-destructive ideology invoked by the human species to justify the exploitation of nature, just as the idea of the free market functioned as the ideology through which the emerging bourgeoise sanctioned the exploitation of the working classes. Bonneuil and Fressoz, for example, advocate going 'beyond the great separation' of nature and culture, of 'the natural sciences with their non-human objects' and the 'a-natural' humanities and social sciences, the former postulating 'physical continuity between human and other entities', the latter 'defined by a metaphysical discontinuity between humans and everything else' (Bonneuil and Fressoz 2016: 32). The Anthropocene, they argue, once it is recognized 'as the reunion of human (historical) time and Earth (geological) time, between human agency and non-human agency, gives the lie to this – temporal, ontological, epistemological and institutional – great divide between nature and society' (Bonneuil and Fressoz 2016: 32). The *temporal* divide between human and geological time, the *ontological* divide between humans and the rest of nature, the epistemological/*methodological* divide between the humanities and science all stand or fall together, the result of the same unacceptable dualist metaphilosophical standpoint.[5]

The same boring old conceptual distinctions?

Does the nature/culture distinction that is presupposed by the defence of a humanistically oriented historiography and a distinctive historical past either rest on or entail an ontological distinction between humans and the rest of nature? To see why the considerations raised by the new challenge fundamentally misconstrue the assumptions on which the idea of a distinctive historical past rests one needs to understand what kind of distinction the nature/culture distinction is. Nature and culture, for Collingwood, are the explicanda of two different modes of inquiry with distinctive methods and investigative goals.[6] The nature/culture distinction captures an articulation in the way reality is conceptualized in different forms of inquiry; it does not 'cut reality at the joints'. It is not a Cartesian[7] (real or metaphysical) distinction entailing that historical subjects/agents could exist without a physical body, that there could be culture without nature, a 'World' (in the Heideggerian sense)[8] without a habitat, in the way in which Descartes argued that the concept of mind, being really distinct from that of the body, could be conceived as existing apart from the body. Defending

---

[5] This objection, as we shall see below, rests on a hypostatization of the methodological differences between explanatory practices that are not needed to defend the claim that the *Geisteswissenschaften* and the *Naturwissenschaften* have distinctive and irreducible explicanda.
[6] I have explored the reciprocal relation holding between method and subject matter in idealist philosophy of histories in D'Oro (2015b). For an account of this in Oakeshott ([1962]/1991; 1975; [1982]/1999), see Kaldis (2012).
[7] Descartes ([1641] 2008), Meditation 6. On the real distinction, see Murdoch (2009).
[8] For Heidegger's discussion of the world, see Heidegger ([1927] 1962, §43).

the nature/culture distinction does not, for example, entail denying that the Egyptians and the Mesopotamians ate and breathed, or that their bodies aged and eventually decayed. What it entails, rather, is that it is not with their physiological functions that the Egyptologist (qua humanistically oriented historiographer) is concerned. As Collingwood says:

> a great many things which deeply concern human beings are not, and never have been, traditionally included in the subject-matter of history. People are born, eat and breathe and sleep, and beget children and become ill and recover again, and die; and these things interest them, most of them at any rate, far more than art and science, industry and politics and war. Yet none of these things have been traditionally regarded as possessing historical interest. Most of them have given rise to institutions like dining and marrying and the various rituals that surround birth and death, sickness and recovery; and of these rituals and institutions people write histories; but the history of dining is not the history of eating, and the history of death-rituals is not the history of death.
>
> (Collingwood 1999: 46)

Collingwood's point is not that it is not possible to write natural histories. Nor is he advocating a linguistic reform and arguing that the term 'history' should be reserved to denote histories of a certain kind, those which have been concerned with rituals rather than physiological facts. But while we may continue to speak as we wish, we should be wary of the bewitchment that words can exercise on our intelligence[9] and of assuming that because we use one and the same word, 'history', there is no difference between the subject matter of the Egyptologist, or of the historian of ancient Rome, and that of the palaeontologist. Nor does it follow from the fact that the humanistically oriented historiographer and the natural scientist have different interests that there exist different kinds of beings, material and immaterial beings,

---

[9] 'Philosophy is a battle against the bewitchment of our intelligence by language', Wittgenstein (1963, §109).

res cogitans and *res extensa*, that correspond to their different subject matters. Defending the irreducibility of the *Geisteswissenschaften* to the *Naturwissenschaften* is not tantamount to assuming an ontological separation between humans and the rest of nature; it is rather to make the point that the concept 'historical agent' is sui generis and irreducible to that of 'natural agent' and to advance an argument for the existence of disciplinary boundaries that reflect the different concerns and investigative goals of science and the humanities. Collingwood's argument against methodological unity in the sciences is premised on the metaphilosophical assumption that there is a reciprocal relation between method and subject matter, that nature is the *explanandum* of science, just as culture is the *explanandum* of history; it is *not* premised on the assumption that the methods of the *Geisteswissenschaften* and the *Naturwissenschaften* are different because mind and nature are metaphysical entities which can be known 'as they are' independently of the investigative goals of history and natural science. Defending the nature/culture distinction and the possibility of a humanistically oriented historiography does not mean providing an argument for metaphysical dualism,[10] or being committed to it by default. It is to argue, rather, for what we might call the disunity of science, for the claim that science and history ask different kinds of questions and therefore that, just as the questions asked by scientists are not answered by the methods of history, so the questions asked by historians are not answered by adopting the methods of science.

Yet, quite often, when one mentions the old debate for and against methodological unity in the sciences one is met with an intellectual yawn: *how boring, how old hat, you are stuck in the 1950s! Since then much work has been done to show that there are different models of causal explanation that do not invoke generalizations, such as, for example, counterfactual accounts of causation. Since the argument for the unity*

---

[10] For an account of how to disconnect a methodological claim for the disunity of science from a metaphysical claim for ontological dualism, see D'Oro, G., Giladi, P. and Papazoglou A. (2019).

of science as articulated by Hempel was based on a nomological account of causal explanation, defending the inapplicability of this nomological model to a humanistically oriented historiography is tantamount to fighting a strawman. The nomological model of explanation, so the objection goes, has long been superseded, and the debate between those who defended it and those who attacked it is stale. But whatever one might think about the nomological model of causal explanation (it is not my intention to take sides on whether causation should be understood in terms of regularities or counterfactuals), adopting a counterfactual rather than a nomological account of causation does *not* undermine the distinction between the space of reasons and that of causes, the very distinction which was at stake in the old debate for and against methodological unity in the sciences. Recall the example we gave in Chapter 3 of the intergalactic tourist who hovers in her spaceship over Earth at the time when the cardinals are gathered in Conclave. The tourist notices large crowds cheering and wonders why, since she noticed no such cries of jubilation the previous day. Yet the weather was the same, the air temperature similar and the merchants selling silk scarves were positioned in exactly the same spots. She consults video footage of the previous days and notices one difference: the colour of the smoke. On the day in which the crowds cheered, unlike the previous days, the smoke was white, rather than black. Having spotted this difference the tourist concludes that the crowds cheered *because* the smoke was white and that, had the smoke been black, they would not have cheered. She has provided a counterfactual causal explanation for the cheering of the crowds. Now, even if one were to concede that the intergalactic tourist could isolate the colour of the smoke as the relevant counterfactual (why not the fact that, on the day the crowd cheered, the silk scarves on the merchants' stands were a different colour, or the bored kids screaming their heads off were positioned in a sunny rather than a shady spot of St Peter's square?), this counterfactual still does not explain, in a particular sense of 'explain', why the crowds cheered. For the crowds did not cheer on account of the white smoke. They cheered because the cardinals gathered in conclave elected a new leader of the Catholic Church.¹¹ This kind of counterfactual explanation, just like explanations based on empirical generalizations, still singularly fails to capture the symbolic significance of the white smoke; it does not explain the cheering of the crowds in the way in which the tourist would like it to be explained if she were a historian.¹² If the intergalactic tourist were a historian she would ask what the white smoke meant to the crowd, what its symbolic significance was, just as a historian of Rome is interested not merely in the fact that in 49 BC some men with shields and horses waded across a stream, but in what the crossing of that stream by a provincial governor meant to a Roman senator. The historical context of explanation is an intensional context in which the reaction of the crowds to the white smoke is understood against the background of the Catholic faith, just as Caesar's crossing of the Rubicon is understood in the context of Roman law. A counterfactual explanation that limits itself to an extensional context, to the occurrence of white smoke emanating from a chimney, for example, but ignores the intensional context (the significance of the white smoke for the Catholic faith) would fail to explain it in the way that would satisfy the curiosity of the intergalactic tourist if the tourist were after a certain kind of *historical* explanation. Understanding the past historically, as Winch puts it, is a reflective or conceptual task:

> Historical explanation is not the application of generalizations and theories to particular instances: it is the tracing of internal relations. It is like applying one's knowledge of a language in order to understand a conversation rather than like applying one's knowledge of the laws of mechanics to understand the workings of a watch.
>
> (Winch [1958] (1990): 133)

Collingwood's defence of a humanistically oriented historiography rests on the consideration that in order to understand an event historically

---

[11] For a discussion of the role of the intensional context of explanation in historical narratives, see Ahlskog J. and D'Oro (2021 and 2022).

[12] Quine's account of 'radical translation' (1960, chapter 2) exemplifies this purely extensional model explanation.

one must go beyond a purely extensional context of explanation. This consideration is not rendered obsolete by the claim that since counterfactual causal explanations need not invoke covering laws, the argument against methodological unity articulated by Dray, Winch and others was directed at a strawman. Counterfactual causal explanations, just like nomological ones, miss the significance of the white smoke and of the crossing of the Rubicon if they do not consider how things appear or look like to interpreting and self-interpreting beings, to the sort of being who (as Heidegger put it) has 'an understanding of Being'. A history of how humankind sleepwalked into global warming along the lines of Christopher Clarks's *The Sleepwalkers: How Europe Went to War in 1914* (Clarks 2012), cannot simply be a history of the consequences that deforestation, the industrialization of farming and the burning of fossil fuels have on the Earth's climate precisely because only agents who can rethink who they are and reconceptualize their relationship to their habitat could possibly be awoken from their environmental slumber. The facts of climate science can be understood as a wake-up call to alter the way one lives only if one presupposes precisely what advocates of the new challenge at times appear to be to denying i.e. that there is a distinctive kind of (historical) agent that is the correlative of a distinctive kind of (historical) explanation, one, a being, to say it with Heidegger again, who has an understanding of Being.

The argument for the possibility of a humanistically oriented historiography was not an argument in support of some sort of ontological or metaphysical dualism, but an argument in support of the existence of disciplinary boundaries between science and history, one motivated by the consideration that historians and scientists have different concerns. Since interdisciplinarity is the buzz word of the day, and an argument for the existence of disciplinary boundaries could easily be misconstrued as an attack on the very idea of interdisciplinarity, it is important to take some time to explain that defending the idea of disciplinary boundaries does not mean belittling the importance of cooperation amongst disciplines. Consider, for example, the relationship between crime detection and forensic science. Detectives enlist the help of forensic scientists to establish the location and time of a crime. By learning that the grit under the victim's fingernails originates from a remote area of the country that was inaccessible to the prime suspect at the time of the crime, a detective will then be able to rule out the suspect from their investigation. The detective's goal is not to know the chemical composition of the grit; it is to solve the murder mystery, but she would not be able to infer that the prime suspect could not have been present at the crime scene without the assistance of the forensic scientist. Architects choose cladding materials with fire-retardant properties or glass panels which prevent homes from losing heat. But it is not their job to know what chemical composition the cladding panels must have in order to be fire-retardant, or what scientific properties the glass must have to prevent the heat from escaping. Cooperation of this kind, between say, the detective and the forensic archaeologist (or the architect and the chemist), does not require us to deny that mutually supportive spheres have different goals. When understood in this way, interdisciplinarity requires us to acknowledge the distinctive goals of, say, the detective and the forensic archaeologist, the architect and the chemist; in fact, interdisciplinarity makes no sense except against the background of disciplinary boundaries. The goals of those who argue that, in response to the Anthropocene, we should develop new 'environmental humanities' (Bonneuil and Fressoz 2016: 288) can perfectly well be achieved by putting the knowledge that is generated in biology, chemistry and physics at the service of architects, town planners, garbage disposal firms, just as the police can avail itself of the assistance of forensic science. Chakrabarty is absolutely right in saying that 'the crisis of climate change calls on academics to rise above their disciplinary boundaries because it is a crisis of many dimensions' (Chakrabarty 2009: 215). But rising above disciplinary boundaries is not the same as undoing them. There is no need to dissolve the historical past into the geological past or to undo the nature/culture distinction in order to change human habitats and foster environmentally friendly ways of living. What is required is joining the dots between, for example, chemistry and architecture so that the knowledge gained in one sphere can be mobilized to achieve the goals of another, just as forensic science has become a tool in crime detection. To acknowledge the existence of disciplinary boundaries and to understand interdisciplinarity as the interlocking of different spheres with distinctive methods is not synonymous with being an enemy of interdisciplinarity. Nor does understanding interdisciplinarity as the interlocking of distinctive spheres with their own distinctive goals and methods entail a commitment to the view that science can in principle fix everything, that there is a purely technological solution to the problems of climate change.[13] The defence of the possibility of a humanistically oriented historiography is premised precisely on the assumption that scientism, understood as the view that science has the answer to all questions, precludes the possibility that the past could be understood as a response to self-given norms and thus that the future could be shaped through political agency, just as the historical past was so shaped. Undoing the nature/culture distinction that informs Collingwood's defence of the autonomy of historical understanding, could not be the key to solving the climate crisis[14] because it is only in so far as one acknowledges that the *idea of nature* has a history that one can reconceptualize humans' relations to nature and make room for the possibility that the future may be shaped by the adoption of environmentally friendly norms rather than simply anticipated, in much the way in which one expects rain after consulting the weather forecast.

Collingwood's defence of a distinctive historical past does not rest on a distinction between humans and the rest of nature as the new challenge suggests: the historical past is not the past of the human species. If the Slitheen, the Time Lords, the Daleks, and the Silurians had not been alien fictional creatures in the TV series Dr Who, but

---

[13] On the dangers of purely technological solutions, see Helena Paul and Rupert Read (2019).
[14] For a recent defence of the nature/culture distinction, see Malm (2019).

ancient civilizations predating the Egyptians and the Mesopotamians, they would be appropriate subject matter for history even if they did not belong to the biological species 'human'. What makes an explanation *historical* is neither the fact that it is concerned with understanding the past, rather than predicting the future, nor that it is concerned with the past of humans, rather than non-humans, but that it explains the actions of past agents by rationalizing them, in the way in which one would explain the behaviour of a driver who stops at a red traffic light, by invoking a traffic regulation rather than subsuming it under a natural law. The question that one should ask in order to establish whether certain life forms can be studied historically is not 'are they mammals?' or 'are they higher mammals?' or 'are they human?' but 'are they civilized?' And if they are, then they will need to be understood in different ways from the rocks and the waves, not because they have a supernatural 'inside' over and above a natural/observable 'outside' that the rocks and waves do not have, but because to the extent that they live by self-given rules or understandable social norms which they take to be binding, their behaviour cannot be explained like that of the sunflower which turns towards the sun, or that of the moon which orbits round its planet. Such is the nature of norms: unlike natural laws they can be disobeyed, but they will cast light on the behaviour of those who follow them, or fail to do so, in such a way as to render intelligible behaviour that might otherwise look wholly irrational.

The concept of the historical past, for Collingwood, is therefore neither that of a segment of time that lags behind the present and grows bigger with each passing day (the metaphysical view that time is a growing block), nor is it the time of the humans on planet Earth, the all too human past of kings and queens, of Queen Elizabeth rather than the queen bee: it is the correlative of sense-making rationalizing explanations. What is no longer present constitutes the historical past in so far as it is looked at through the lens of interpreting and self-interpreting beings. Historians tracing the rise and fall of civilizations are not palaeontologists seeking to date the evolution and extinction of a biological species through the study of its fossilized remains. While palaeontologists look at the fossilized remains of dinosaurs as providing evidence for the existence and evolution of a now extinct animal species, the mummified remains of ancient Egyptians are of interest to humanistically oriented historians *not* in so far as they provide evidence to document the existence and evolution of an ethnic group, but in so far as they symbolize the belief that the preservation of the body is required for the soul to find an appropriate home in the afterlife. The defence of the idea of a historical past is based not on an arbitrary divide between human and non-human animals, but on the assumption that to understand the past *historically* is to approach it as a *space of reasons* in which the actions of historical agents are understood as abiding by (as well as contesting) norms.

Before drawing to a close I should reiterate that defending a humanistically oriented historiography and a distinctive historical past (given the reciprocity thesis, the two go together) is not the same as defending an anthropocentric historiography that excludes in principle the possibility of ascribing historical agency to non-human animals. Lizards or aliens from a distant galaxy can be historical agents if they are interpreting and self-interpreting beings. Some animals – dolphins, elephants, higher primates – may have historical agency. Collingwood is not concerned with determining *who* exactly does or does not have historical agency, but with the more general point that the history of those beings (human or not) who do have a culture cannot be the same as the history of those beings (human or not) who do not have one: if there are beings who have a culture, then they have to be understood in a different way from beings who do not have one, as distinctive kinds of agents, and this is what distinguishes a humanistically oriented (which is not the same as *human*) history from other kinds of history. The objection that the nature/culture distinction rests on a form of human exceptionalism conflates the distinction between different types of inferences or explanations with the distinction between two kinds of beings, human and non-human. The attack on the idea of humanistically oriented historiography and of a distinctive historical past is yet another argument against the humanities and their distinctive way of knowing in the name of a new and subtler form of naturalism that seeks to deny the existence of methodological differences between forms of inquiry by undoing the distinction between nature and culture.

Humanistic history and the historical future

As we have seen, a *humanistically oriented* historiography is not the same as *human* history. The subject matter of a humanistically oriented historiography is not humans, understood as a biological species, and the time of humans on planet Earth, but the norms which govern any beings whose conduct can be explained as responding to certain normative demands rather than as conforming to natural laws. The new challenge to the possibility of a humanistically oriented historiography conflates the idea of the historical past with that of the human past. The historical past is *not* the human past; it is the past understood in a way that is different from the way in which it is approached by, say, the palaeontologist or the geologist. And because what defines the historical past is how it is explained, the historical past is not an insignificantly brief temporal segment of the geological past (the time of the humans) because it is not a segment of time at all, but a different way of approaching and understanding what happened in the past. It is the conflation of the historical with the human past that gives rise to the objection that traditional histories are premised upon a form of human exceptionalism.

While there is no denying that we should be challenged or even shocked by the reality of the Anthropocene, undoing the nature/culture distinction by undermining the idea of a distinctive *historical* past is not the right response to its onset since humans, *understood not as a biological species of featherless bipeds but precisely as interpreting as self-interpreting beings*, are the only ones who may be able to respond to the climate crisis. As Jeff Malpass said in a conversation at a recent conference on the role of the philosophy of history: 'the birds and the bees are not going to save us'.[15] There is no contradiction in describing humans (qua biological beings) as the cause of climate change and humans (qua historical agents) as the potential solution to it. It is just that when human activities are brought under the categorial description of events, their behaviour is explained like that of the sunflower which turns towards the sun, rather than like that of Roman legionaries who obey the commands of their centurion. We often switch seamlessly from one explanation to the other. When, for example, I reprimand my daughter for not picking the wet towels off the bathroom floor, I treat her as capable of responding to the norms of common living. When, on the other hand, I tell my partner 'Don't bother to reprimand our (lovely) teenager for banging the door: it is not her; it is her hormones', I treat my daughter as a force of nature. No parent of a teenage daughter needed to wait for the onset of the Anthropocene to learn that humans are forces of nature. What the Anthropocene has taught us is the extent to which these causal powers extend, *not* the fact that we have them. The recent challenge to a humanistically oriented historiography hypostatizes the methodological distinction between different forms of inference that Collingwood's explanatory pluralism seeks to accommodate and, as a result, erroneously identifies their respective explicanda with the ontological distinction between biological humans and the rest of nature. In seeking to combat human exceptionalism by rejecting the disciplinary boundaries between the human and the natural sciences it undermines the possibility of historical agency. In so doing, it inadvertently threatens to make the historical future as inevitable as the natural past. What appears to be a politically progressive argument motivated by the noble intention of curbing disrespect for the rest of nature (a clearly laudable goal) comes dangerously close to endorsing a fatalistic outlook that forecloses the possibility of taking affirmative action against climate change. Only if there is a historical past can there also be a historical future.[16] In

---

[15] Conversation with Jeff Malpas at the INTH conference in Stockholm, August 2018.
[16] See Retz (2021).

defending the distinction between the natural and the historical past Collingwood's philosophy of history makes room (philosophically speaking) for the possibility that the future climate of the planet may be shaped by responding to environmentally friendly norms, rather than merely forecast as the inevitable consequence of climate changes which humans have set in motion *qua forces of nature*. It is only *qua historical agents* that we can look to the future as something that can be *shaped* by changing the norms to which we responded in the past rather than as something that we can merely *facilitate* by playing a role analogous to that of yeast in the chemical process of fermentation.

Conceptual distinctions are not idle; they have real-life consequences.

9

The manifest and the scientific images

In this book I hope to have shown that to defend the autonomy of humanistic understanding as Collingwood undertakes to do requires nothing short of rethinking the task of philosophical analysis, of reconceptualizing what it is that we do when we think philosophically. On a widespread conception of metaphysics, philosophical analysis is concerned with identifying certain basic ontological ingredients (Jackson 1998), and showing how these ingredients combine to give rise to the familiar properties that objects possess, such as their colour, hardness, permeability, and so on. The task of philosophical analysis is to reveal the reality behind the appearances, to explain what the appearances are appearances of (Heil 2021). On this view, the reality that metaphysics investigates is like a cake, which is soft, moist and tastes sweet and possesses these qualities in virtue of some more fundamental ones, the basic ingredients out of which it is made (sugar, flour, butter, eggs) and how they are baked. On a rationalist conception of the role of philosophical analysis in metaphysics, the basic ingredients are knowable *a priori*, through reflection alone. It is from the proverbial armchair, without leaving his study, for example, that in the second Meditation Descartes undertook to establish what the real nature of material objects is, and that this nature is very different from the sensible qualities we experience (Descartes [1641] 2008). Using the analogy of a piece of wax fresh from the beehive, still smelling of honey, he argued that the wax's appearance conceals its real (and in his view, mathematical) properties, in the way in which a cloak covers up the body of the person wearing it. That the real properties of the wax are mathematical ones, such as size, extension etc., Descartes claimed, is known by means of reason alone, by reflecting on the consideration that even though the piece of wax could undergo many changes in its appearances (when melted for example), it would still remain the same piece of wax. While this conception of metaphysics has not altogether disappeared, it has come under severe pressure with the rise of the modern natural sciences. On an empiricist conception, the role of philosophical analysis is not that of establishing what the appearances conceal (as in Descartes' case), but rather that of explaining how the fundamental ingredients (the butter, eggs and flour), as discovered by physics, account for the appearances (the moistness and sweetness of the sponge). On this view it is the task of physics, not metaphysics, to determine what the basic ingredients are; philosophy should serve, in Locke's famous expression, as an 'under-labourer' to science ([1690] 2014, *Epistle to the Reader*). Although the task of philosophical analysis on the underlabourer conception is quite different from the way in which rationalist metaphysicians such as Descartes thought of the role of philosophy, the underlying conception of reality remains the same. Reality is still thought of as a cake, which is soft, moist and sweet and has these properties in virtue of the ingredients out of which it is baked. What changes is the role of philosophy. On the rationalist conception metaphysics limns the nature of being, it establishes what the fundamental ingredients are; on the underlabourer conception the role of conceptual analysis now simply becomes that of explaining how manifest objects have the macroscopic properties they exhibit (colours, textures etc.) in virtue of their underlying properties. Just as the moistness of a cake can be explained by the quantity of butter in the recipe, and its sweetness by the amount of sugar added to the mix, so manifest properties such as heat and hardness are shown to be entailed or accounted for (through the relation of supervenience) from mean kinetic energy or the lattice-like arrangement of the molecules (Jackson 1998: 3).

The way in which the basic or more fundamental level of reality is characterized has changed over time. Locke spoke of corpuscles. Talk of corpuscles gave way to talk of atoms and molecules, and talk of molecules to that of excitation patterns on quantum fields. But while the understanding of what counts as more fundamental has changed, the idea that the way in which one should characterize the relation between appearances and reality is in terms of the relation in which what is more fundamental stands to what is less fundamental has endured through these changes. This model of the relation between appearances and reality is shared widely by philosophers with very different ontological commitments. The questions that are normally addressed in this context concern how the appearances of macroscopic objects such as tables and chairs are accounted for by the underlying arrangement of the molecules, or, how conscious experiences such as the taste of mangoes or the smell of roses can be accounted for by the more fundamental particles, and which ontological commitments are best suited to explain the macro-level appearances. Physicalists and panpsychists, for example, may disagree about the nature of the fundamental elements, whether they are wholly physical or whether they bear traces of the mental, but they both endorse the idea that the appearances are to be accounted for in terms of elements which are more fundamental. The panpsychist rejoinder to physicalism (Strawson 2006) is precisely that it is not possible to answer Huxley's question concerning how consciousness could arise from neural tissue (see Chapter 4) without assuming that the fundamental constituents of reality are, in some very rudimentary sense, conscious, just as one would not be able to explain the sweetness of a cake without assuming that sugar was added to the mix.

The conception of reality as a cake which is baked out of certain fundamental ingredients generates a tension between the appearances and what they are appearances of, or between what Wilfrid Sellars (1963) calls the manifest and the scientific images of reality. One of the important questions that have arisen since the rise of modern science is whether the progress of scientific knowledge poses a threat to our everyday, ordinary descriptions of reality, such as the classification of objects into tables and chairs, or to the explanations of human doings which invoke reasons for acting rather than simply appealing to causes. Could it be the case that our talk and understanding of ordinary objects such as tables and chairs, or actions, understood in the manner of Collingwood, i.e. as *res gestae*, will wither away with the progress of natural science? While some may be content to simply abandon the manifest image and to regard everyday classifications of tables and chairs or explanations of actions in terms of motives as a kind of proto-scientific talk to be superseded by more sophisticated scientific accounts of what there is, the manifest image of reality is often deemed to be too important for it to somehow wither away with the progress of natural science. Yet most of the attempts aimed at saving such talk have tended to endorse the idea that the relation between the manifest and the scientific image is the relation holding between a basic list of ingredients, which are more fundamental, and the way the ingredients come to appear to us. But in so doing, they have failed to do justice to the sui generis nature of certain manifest objects and judgements.

As Heidegger ([1927] 1962) pointed out, manifest objects such as tables and chairs are generally or typically identified by referring to their point or function, their role in our practical engagement with the world, rather than their underlying material constitution. A table is for dining, or for writing on (if it is an office desk); a chair is for sitting on etc. The materials out of which ordinary objects are made, wood or metal for example, is insufficient on their own either to define what an ordinary object such as a table is, or to differentiate it from something else, such as a chair, since chairs, as well as tables, need to be hard and impenetrable in order to perform their characteristic functions. While hardness and impenetrability can be explained by invoking the underlying constitution of the wood out of which objects such as the tables and chairs may be carved or produced, the functional role of the objects cannot. In an analogous way actions, in Collingwood's sense of the *res gestae*, are identified by referring to their point or significance. A description of bodily movements does not capture the meaning or significance of the action since one and the same bodily movement could be the expression of many different actions: crossing a river, as we have seen, could be a declaration of war (if the river marks a border, as in Caesar's case) or simply taking a stroll on the other side of the bank. Just as the function of an ordinary object cannot be read off from the material constitution that is responsible for the object's hardness or its porosity, for example, so too the point of an action cannot just be read off from the behavioural description. As we have seen, it takes knowledge of Roman law to understand Caesar's crossing as an act of defiance against the Republic. Identifying the point of an action requires familiarity with what Collingwood calls the context of thought, just as identifying something as a table requires familiarity with the role that the object plays in the context of a practice (dining; writing and so on).

For this reason, Collingwood would argue, the attempt to find a bridge between what Sellars calls the manifest and the scientific images by showing what the appearances are appearances of, or how some fundamental constituents manifest themselves, as a great deal of metaphysics or scientific ontology attempts to do, is deeply misguided. The scientific image does not merely bring reality under a different description, in the way in which redescribing the action of opening a window as 'letting air in' rather than 'letting a fly out' does. The scientific image brings reality under an altogether different *kind* of description, one which requires the exercise of a different kind of judgement or the application of a different kind of inference, just as the application of a specific sense of 'cause' goes hand in hand with the identification of a distinctive explanandum. The role of conceptual analysis in metaphysics, for Collingwood, is to disambiguate claims that bring reality not merely under *different descriptions*, but under *different categorial descriptions*. His conception of metaphysics differs greatly from the one that has dominated so much philosophy, according to which the task of metaphysics is to identify the fundamental structures or basic list of ingredients out of which everything is made.

Collingwood rejects the idea that reality should be thought of as a cake which is baked out of certain basic ingredients that are responsible for the cake's appearance precisely because he rejects the conception of the role of conceptual analysis in metaphysics that accompanies this conception of reality, namely the view that the task of philosophy is either to identify the reality behind the appearances (as in the rationalist conception) or to explain how the basic ingredients, as discovered within the sciences, account for the appearances (as in the underlabourer conception). The relation explored by presuppositional analysis is not that between appearances and reality; it is rather that between different kinds of inferences which establish explanatory connections that address different questions. These different concerns are not mapped out along the lines of what is visible and what is invisible to the human eye, in terms of the macroscopic and the microscopic, of the more and the less fundamental, of the familiar (the shiny yellow appearance of gold) and the more esoteric (the chemical composition of gold) that requires specialized knowledge. According to Collingwood, there are plenty of scientific judgements which belong to our ordinary everyday familiar ways of explaining the world, such as, for example, when we claim that 'the cause of a boat sinking is her being overloaded' (Collingwood 1940: 299), that the sunlight and sea water bleached someone's hair, or that the lasagne burned because the oven temperature was too high (what Collingwood refers to as explanations in the practical sciences of nature that deploy sense II of the term 'cause'). We do not explain why the boat sank, why the hair was bleached or why the lasagne burned in the same way in which we explain why Paul went to the fishmonger, at least if Paul's trip is explained in a way that aims to show what the point of his doing so is. Of course, scientific explanations which invoke particles, molecules, or quantum fields are very remote from those which are used to explain that the boat sank because it was overloaded or that the lasagne burned because the oven temperature was set too high. But to the extent that esoteric scientific explanations, like their familiar counterparts in everyday explanations, aim to establish patterns for the sake of prediction and control, they answer the same kind of questions one asks when one tries to find out what it is that normally happens when one leaves the lasagne in the oven for too long or one spends too much time in the sun; they do not try to show what the point of spending a lot of time in the sun is (such as to get some free highlights courtesy of nature, or to acquire a nice tan, for example).

Collingwood rejects the understanding of the relation between scientific and humanistic explanations that characterizes a conception of the scientific image as being more fundamental than the manifest image in favour of a form of explanatory pluralism which argues that different forms of inquiry ask different kinds of questions and should not be ordered hierarchically as they are in the layered model of the sciences which assumes one kind of explanation to be more fundamental than another. He acknowledges the autonomy of humanistic explanations vis-à-vis scientific ones as well as the autonomy of scientific knowledge vis-à-vis humanistic understanding. Rather than advocating a new form of epistemic imperialism in which historical knowing takes over the position of epistemic privilege enjoyed by natural science whilst leaving the hierarchical structures of knowledge intact, he argues for a rebalancing of the epistemic power relations. This message is a particularly important one at a time when scepticism concerning the authority of science is rife, and the role of scientific experts and their expertise is increasingly being challenged or undermined. Unfortunately, Collingwood's nuanced claim that there is a proper time and a place for scientific explanations, just as there is a proper time and a place for humanistic explanations has been lost sight of, and his subtle defence of humanistic understanding has been construed as advocating one 'ism', namely (radical) historicism, rather than another, namely scientism. Collingwood, we have seen, is often assumed to be a radical historicist whose main contribution to philosophy consists in advocating the complete historicization of all knowledge, including scientific knowledge. This book has presented him as articulating *not* an argument for historical relativism, but an argument *against* scientism, i.e., a position which resists the reduction of humanistic understanding to scientific knowledge without committing the opposite error of denying the autonomy of science. To present Collingwood's philosophy as articulating a defence of humanistic understanding against scientism in the broad sense (as the attempt to reduce any form of knowledge to another) we found it necessary to revisit his conception of philosophy as a form of presuppositional analysis and of metaphysics as the study of the fundamental presuppositions which govern different forms of knowledge. These presuppositions, we have argued, are not relative to knowers; they correlate rather with the kind of questions one seeks to answer and the methodological assumptions which need to be made to find true and false answers to those questions. All explanations are 'because' answers to 'why' questions, but the kind of 'why' questions which are asked in one domain of inquiry are not the same as the 'why' questions asked in another. The mark of the thoughtful or properly reflective person is to discern the time and the place for scientific answers and the time and the place for humanistic ones, just as for Aristotle the mark of the virtuous person is to be able to judge what is the right thing to do in the specific circumstances. In so far as the main task of philosophical analysis is to align questions and answers philosophy does not teach us something that is completely new, but makes explicit what we in some sense already know (Collingwood 1933: 161).

Collingwood rejects both the conception of metaphysics as a form of armchair ontology which can deliver factual knowledge of reality and the conception of philosophy as the underlabourer of science. Knowledge, according to Collingwood, is something that is acquired within the sciences, once a set of presuppositions which provide the criteria for verifying and falsifying knowledge claims are in place. If you want to know whether silver dissolves in nitric acid, you should ask the chemist; if you want to know what is the cause of cancer, you should ask an oncologist. If you want to know who killed Alexander Litvinenko you should ask an investigative journalist (or a coroner, if what you are interested in is not who had motive to kill him, but what the physiological causes of death were). Philosophical reflection, on the other hand, tells us what the presuppositions that make knowledge in the first order sciences possible are; it disambiguates contested concepts in order to prevent conceptual confusion. Since philosophy makes no first order knowledge claims, it neither competes with nor undermine any of the first order disciplines. The end result of philosophical activity, so conceived, is not knowledge, but understanding of the presuppositions on which knowledge rests. There is no contest between philosophy and physics because philosophy, unlike physics, is not a form of knowledge. Nor is there any conflict between physics and other forms of knowledge because different forms of knowledge answer different kinds of questions.

Philosophers often assume that to make sense of things requires providing a unified picture of reality. Collingwood begs to differ. The art of philosophizing consists in the ability to make distinctions, to identify what belongs to a certain line of questioning and what belongs to another. This is not to say that because philosophy does not deliver knowledge as such, but rather an understanding of the presuppositions on which knowledge rests, that it has no value. By aligning 'because' answers with the right kind of 'why' questions philosophical analysis prevents the conceptual problems which arise when one mistakenly assumes that answers of one kind can be offered in reply to questions of another as in the scenario of the theoretical physicist and the AA mechanic we considered in Chapter 2. Re-aligning questions and answers is not an idle conceptual exercise; it has real-life consequences, as we discussed in Chapter 8, where we showed that only if one disambiguates the notion of 'past' and acknowledges a distinction between the *natural* and the *historical* past, can one also be entitled to speak of a *historical* future, one that can be shaped rather than merely forecasted, like the arrival of a storm.

References

Ahlskog, J. (2021), *The Primacy of Method in Historical Research: Philosophy of History and the Perspective of Meaning*, New York: Routledge.

Ahlskog, J. and D'Oro, G. (2021), 'Beyond Narrativism: The Historical Past and Why It Can Be Known', *Collingwood and British Idealism Studies* 27(1): 5–33.

Ahlskog, J. and D'Oro, G. (2022), 'The Leopard Does Not Change Its Spots: Naturalism and the Argument against Methodological Pluralism in the Sciences', in A. Tuboli and Á. Sivadó (eds.), *The History of Understanding in Analytic Philosophy: Before and after Logical Empiricism*, 185–208, London: Bloomsbury.

Anscombe, G.E.M. (1957), *Intentions*, Oxford: Blackwell.

Aristotle (2002), *Nicomachean Ethics*, Christopher Rowe (trans.), Oxford: Oxford University Press, with philosophical introduction and commentary by Sarah Broadie.

Ayer, A.J. (1934), 'Demonstration of the Impossibility of Metaphysics', *Mind* 43(171): 335–445.

Ayer, A.J. [1936] (1990), *Language, Truth and Logic*, London: Penguin Books.

Beaney, M. (2005), 'Collingwood's Conception of Presuppositional Analysis', *Collingwood and British Idealism Studies* 11(2): 41–114.

Benson, O. and Stangroom, J. (2006), *Why Truth Matters*, London: Continuum.

Boghossian, P. (2006), *Fear of Knowledge*, Oxford: Oxford University Press.

Bonneuil, C. and Fressoz, J.-P. (2016), *The Shock of the Anthropocene*, London and New York: Verso.

Boucher, D. (1997), 'The Significance of Collingwood's Principles of History', *Journal of the History of Ideas* 58(2): 303–25.

Broad, C.D. (1925), *The Mind and Its Place in Nature*, London: Kegan Paul Trench Trubner & Co.

Browning, G. (2004), *Rethinking Collingwood: Philosophy, Politics and the Unity of Theory and Practice*, London: Palgrave Macmillan.

Carroll, L. (1895), 'What the Tortoise Said to Achilles', *Mind* 14: 278–80.

Chakrabarty, Dipesh (2009), 'The Climate of History: Four Theses', *Critical Inquiry* 35: 197–222.

Chalmers, D. (1995), 'Facing up to the Problem of Consciousness', *Journal of Consciousness Studies* 2(3): 200–219.

Chalmers, D. (1996), *The Conscious Mind: In Search of a Fundamental Theory*, New York: Oxford University Press.

Clarks, C. (2012), *The Sleepwalkers: How Europe Went to War in 1914*, London: Penguin books.

Collingwood, R.G. (1929), Introduction to the Lectures on Moral Philosophy, unpublished manuscript, Bodleian library Collingwood dep. 10.

Collingwood, R.G. (1932), Introduction to the Lectures on Moral Philosophy, unpublished manuscript, Bodleian library Collingwood dep. 7.

Collingwood, R.G. (1933), *An Essay on Philosophical Method*, Oxford: Clarendon Press; revised edition, with an introduction by James Connelly and Giuseppina D'Oro, Oxford: Oxford University Press, 2005.

Collingwood, R.G. (1938), *The Principles of Art*, Oxford: Clarendon Press.

Collingwood, R.G. (1939), *An Autobiography*, Oxford: Oxford University Press.

Collingwood, R.G. (1940), *An Essay on Metaphysics*, Oxford: Clarendon Press, revised edition, with an introduction by Rex Martin, Oxford: Oxford University Press, 1998.

Collingwood, R.G. (1942), *The New Leviathan*, Oxford: Clarendon Press, revised edition, edited and introduced by David Boucher, Oxford: Oxford University Press, 1992.

Collingwood, R.G. (1945), *The Idea of Nature*, Oxford: Clarendon Press.

Collingwood, R.G. (1946), *The Idea of History*, Oxford: Clarendon Press, revised edition, with an introduction by Jan Van der Dussen, Oxford: Oxford University Press, 1993.

Collingwood, R.G. (1999), *The Principles of History*, edited by W.H. Dray and Jan Van der Dussen, Oxford: Oxford University Press.

Connelly, J. (1990), 'Metaphysics and Method: A Necessary Unity in the Philosophy of R. G. Collingwood', *Storia, Antropologia e Scienze del Linguaggio* 5(1–2): 33–156. Roma: Bulzoni ed.

Connelly, J. (2003), *Metaphysics, Method and Politics*, Exeter: Imprint Academic.

Crane, T. and Brewer, B. (1995), 'The Mental Causation Debate', *Proceedings of the Aristotelian Society*, Supplementary Volume 69: 211–36.

Crutzen, P.J. (2002), 'Geology of Mankind', *Nature* 415: 23.

Danto, A.C. (1965), *Analytical Philosophy of History*, Cambridge: Cambridge University Press.

Davidson, D. (1963), 'Actions, Reasons and Causes', *Journal of Philosophy* 60(23): 685–700.
Davidson, D. [1970] (1980), 'Mental Events', in *Essays on Actions and Events*, 207–25, Oxford: Oxford University Press.
Davidson, D. (1993), 'Thinking Causes', in J. Heil and A. Mele (eds.) *Mental Causation*, 3–17, Oxford: Clarendon Press.
Descartes, R. [1641] (2008), *Meditations on First Philosophy*, Oxford: Oxford University Press.
Donagan, A. (1962), *The Later Philosophy of R. G. Collingwood*, Oxford: Clarendon Press.
Donagan, A. (1972), 'Collingwood and Philosophical Method', in M. Krausz (ed.), *Critical Essays on the Philosophy of R. G. Collingwood*, 1–19, Oxford: Clarendon Press.
D'Oro, G. (2002), *Collingwood and the Metaphysics of Experience*, London and New York: Routledge.
D'Oro, G. (2007), 'Two Dogmas of Contemporary Philosophy of Action', *Journal of the Philosophy of History* 1: 11–26.
D'Oro, G. (2010), 'The Myth of Collingwood's Historicism', *Inquiry* 53(6): 627–41.
D'Oro, G. (2011), 'Davidson and the Autonomy of the Human Sciences', in J. Malpas (ed.) *Dialogues with Davidson: New Perspectives on His Philosophy*, 283–96, Cambridge, MA: MIT Press.
D'Oro, G. (2012), 'Reasons and Causes: The Philosophical Battle and the Meta-philosophical War', *Australasian Journal of Philosophy* 90(2): 207–21.
D'Oro, G. & Sandis, C. (2013), 'From Anticausalism to Causalism and Back', in G. D'Oro and C. Sandis (eds.) *Reasons and Causes: Causalism and Anticausalism in the Philosophy of Action*, 7–48, New York: Palgrave Macmillan.
D'Oro, G. (2014), 'The Logocentric Predicament and the Logic of Question and Answer', in A. Skodo (ed.) *Other Logics: Historical and Philosophical Alternatives to Formal Logic in the History of Thought and Contemporary Philosophy*, 221–34, Leiden and Boston: Brill.
D'Oro, G. (2015a), 'Unlikely Bedfellows? 'Collingwood, Carnap and the Internal/External Distinction', *British Journal for the History of Philosophy* 23(4): 802–17.
D'Oro, G. (2015b), 'History and Idealism: Collingwood and Oakeshott', in J. Malpass and H.H. Gander (eds.), *The Routledge Companion to Hermeneutics*, 191–204, London and New York: Routledge.

D'Oro, G. (2017), 'Collingwood's Idealist Metaontology: Between Therapy and Armchair Science', in Giuseppina D'Oro and Soren Overgaard (eds.) *The Cambridge Companion to Philosophical Methodology*, 211–28, Cambridge: Cambridge University Press.

D'Oro, G. (2018a), 'The Touch of King Midas: Collingwood on Why Actions Are not Events', *Philosophical Explorations* 21(1): 1–10.

D'Oro, G. (2018b), 'Why Epistemic Pluralism Does Not Entail Relativism: Collingwood's Hinge Epistemology', in K. Dharamsi, G. D'Oro and S. Leach (eds.) *Collingwood on Philosophical Methodology*, 151–76, Cham, Switzerland: Palgrave MacMillan.

D'Oro, G., Giladi, P., Papazoglou, A. (2019), 'Non-reductivism and the Metaphilosophy of Mind', *Inquiry* 62(5): 477–503.

D'Oro, G. (2020), 'In Defence of a Humanistically Oriented Historiography: The Nature/Culture Distinction at the Time of the Anthropocene', in Jouni-Matti Kuukkanen (ed.), *Philosophy of History: Twenty-First-Century Perspectives*, 216–36, London: Bloomsbury.

D'Oro, G. and Ahlskog, J. (2021), 'Imagination and Revision', in C.M. van den Akker (ed.), *The Routledge Companion to History and Theory*, 215–32, London and New York: Routledge.

D'Oro, G. and Connelly, J. (forthcoming), 'The Sense of the Past: Williams and Collingwood on Humanistic and Scientific Knowledge', in M. Queloz and M. van Ackeren (eds.), *Making Sense of the Past: Bernard Williams and the History of Philosophy*, Oxford: Oxford University Press.

Dray, W.H. (1957), *Laws and Explanation in History*, London: Oxford University Press.

Dray, W.H. (1958), 'Historical Understanding as Rethinking', *University of Toronto Quarterly* 27: 200–15.

Dray, W.H. (1963), 'The Historical Explanation of Actions Reconsidered', in S. Hook (ed.), *Philosophy and History*, New York: New York University Press.

Dray, W.H. (1980), 'R. G. Collingwood and the Understanding of Actions in History', in his *Perspectives on History*, 9–26, London: Routledge and Kegan Paul.

Dray, W.H. (1995), *History as Re-enactment: R. G. Collingwood's Idea of History*, Oxford: Clarendon Press.

Feigl, H. (1958), 'The "Mental" and the "Physical"', in Feigl, H., Maxwell, G., and Scriven, M. (eds.) *Minnesota Studies in the Philosophy of Science*, Vol. 2, Minneapolis: University of Minnesota Press.

Fodor, J.A. (1989), 'Making Mind Matter More', *Philosophical Topics* 17: 59–79.
Gadamer, H.G. [1960] (2013), *Truth and Method*, London: Bloomsbury Academic.
Gardiner, P. (1952a), *The Nature of Historical Explanation*, London: Oxford University Press.
Gardiner, P. (1952b), 'The Objects of Historical Knowledge', *Philosophy* 27: 211–20.
Goff, P. (2017), *Consciousness and Fundamental Reality*, Oxford: Oxford University Press.
Harding, S. (1991), *Whose Science? Whose Knowledge?* Ithaca, NY: Cornell University Press.
Heidegger, M. [1927] (1962), *Being and Time*, New York: Harper & Row.
Heil, J. (1999), 'Multiple Realizability', *American Philosophical Quarterly* 36(3): 189–208.
Heil, J. (2003), 'Levels of Reality', *Ratio* XVI: 205–20.
Heil, J. (2013), 'Mental Causation according to Davidson', in D'Oro, G. and Sandis (eds.), *Reasons and Causes: Causalism and Anti-Causalism in the Philosophy of Action*, 75–96, Basingstoke, Hampshire: Palgrave Macmillan.
Heil, J. (2021), *Appearance in Reality*, Oxford: Oxford University Press.
Hempel, C. (1942), 'The Function of General Laws in History', *Journal of Philosophy* 39: 35–48.
Hutto, D. (2013), 'Still a Cause for Concern: Reasons, Causes and Explanations', in D'Oro, G. and Sandis (eds.), *Reasons and Causes: Causalism and Anti-Causalism in the Philosophy of Action*, 49–74, Basingstoke, Hampshire: Palgrave Macmillan.
Hylton, P. (2007), *Quine*, New York and London: Routledge.
Jackson, F. (1986), 'What Mary Didn't Know', *Journal of Philosophy* 83: 291–5.
Jackson, F. (1998), *From Metaphysics to Ethics*, Oxford: Oxford University Press.
Kant, I. Groundwork [1785] (1964), *Groundwork of the Metaphysics of Morals*, translated by H.J. Paton, New York: Harper Torchbooks.
Kaldis, B. (2012), 'Worlds of Experience: Science' in Podoksik E. (ed.) *The Cambridge Companion to Oakeshott*, 64–85, Cambridge: Cambridge University Press.
Kim, J. (1988), 'Explanatory Realism, Causal Realism, and Explanatory Exclusion', *Midwest Studies in Philosophy* 12: 225–40.
Kim, J. (1989), 'The Myth of Non-reductivie Materialism', *Proceedings of the American Philosophical Association* 63: 31–47.

Kim, J. (1990), 'Explanatory Exclusion and the Problem of Mental Causation', in E. Villanueva (ed.) *Information, Semantics and Epistemology*, 36–56, Oxford: Blackwell.

Kim, J. (1992), 'The Non-reductivist's Troubles with Mental Causation', in Heil J. and Mele, A. (eds.), *Mental Causation*, 189–210, Oxford: Oxford University Press.

Kim, J. (1998), *Mind in a Physical World*, Cambridge, MA: MIT Press.

Kripke, S. (1980), *Naming and Necessity*, Cambridge, MA: Harvard University Press.

Kuukkanen, J.M. (2006), 'Meaning Change in the Context of Thomas S. Kuhn's Philosophy', PhD Dissertation, University of Edinburgh.

Kuukkanen, J.M. (2015), 'Historicism and the Failure of HPS', *Studies in History and Philosophy of Science* 30: 1–9.

Latour, B. (2000), 'On the Partial Existence of Existing and Non-existing Objects', in L. Daston (ed.), *Biographies of Scientific Objects*, 247–69, Chicago: University of Chicago Press.

Latour, B. (2017), *Facing Gaia: Eight Lectures on the New Climate Regime*, Cambridge: Polity Press.

Leibniz, G. (1686), 'Discourse on Metaphysics', in D. Garber and R. Ariew (eds.), *Discourse on Metaphysics and Other Essays*, Indianapolis and Cambridge: Hackett Publishing Company, 1991.

Levine, J. (1983), 'Materialism and Qualia: The Explanatory Gap', *Pacific Philosophical Quarterly* 64: 354–61.

Lewis, S.L. and Maslin, M.A. (2015), 'Defining the Anthropocene', *Nature* 519(7542): 175–6.

Locke, J. [1690] (2014), *An Essay Concerning Human Understanding*, Ware: Wordsworth Editions Limited.

Malm, A. (2019), 'Against Hybridism: Why We Need to Distinguish between Nature and Society, Now More than Ever', *Historical Materialism* 27(2): 156–87.

Martin, R. (1989), 'Collingwood's Claim That Metaphysics Is a Historical Discipline', *The Monist* 72: 489–525; reprinted with slight variations in D. Boucher, J. Connelly and T. Modood (eds.) *Philosophy, History and Civilization: Interdisciplinary Perspectives on R. G. Collingwood*, 203–45, Cardiff: University of Wales Press, 1995.

Martin, R. (1998), 'Editor's Introduction', in *An Essay on Metaphysics*, revised edition, with an introduction by Rex Martin, xv–xcv, Oxford: Oxford University Press.

McGinn, C. (1989), 'Can We Solve the Mind-Body Problem?', *Mind* 98: 349–66.
McLaughlin, B.P. (2013), 'Why Rationalization Is Not a Species of Causal Explanation', in D'Oro, G. and Sandis (eds.), *Reasons and Causes: Causalism and Anti-Causalism in the Philosophy of Action*, 97–123, Basingstoke, Hampshire: Palgrave Macmillan.
Melden, A.I. (1961), *Free Action*, London: Routledge and Kegan Paul.
Mill, J.S. (1843), 'A System of Logic, Ratinative and Inductive', in J.M. Robson (eds.), *The Collected Works of John Stuart Mill*, Toronto: University of Toronto Press, London: Routledge and Kegan Paul, 1963–91.
Mink, L.O. (1987), *Historical Understanding*. Edited by Brian Fay, E.O.Golob, and R.T. Vann, Ithaca, NY: Cornell University Press.
Modood, T. (1989), 'The Later Collingwood's Alleged Historicism and Relativism', *Journal of the History of Philosophy* 27: 101–25.
Moore, A.W. (2012), *The Evolution of Modern Metaphysics*, Cambridge: Cambridge University Press.
Murdoch, D. (2009), 'Descartes: The Real Distinction', in R. Le Poidevin, P. Simons, A. McGonical and R.P. Cameron (eds.), in *The Routledge Companion to Metaphysics*, 68–77, Abingdon: Routledge.
Nagel, T. (1979), 'What Is It Like to Be a Bat?', in *Mortal Questions*, 165–80, London: Cambridge University Press.
Oakeshott, M. [1962] (1991), 'The Activity of Being a Historian', in *Rationalism in Politics and other Essays*, London and New York: Liberty Fund.
Oakeshott, M. (1975), *On Human Conduct*, Oxford: Oxford University Press.
Oakeshott, M. [1983] (1999), 'Three Essays on History', in *On History and Other Essays*, 1–128, Indianapolis: Liberty Fund.
Oldfield, A. (1995), 'Metaphysics and History in Collingwood's Thought', in D. Boucher, J. Connelly and T. Modood (eds.), *Philosophy, History and Civilization: Interdisciplinary Perspectives on R. G. Collingwood*, 182–202, Cardiff: University of Wales Press.
Paul, H. and Read, R. (2019), 'Geoengineering as a Response to the Climate Crisis: Right Road or Disastrous Diversion?', in J. Forster (ed.), *Facing Up to Climate Reality: Honesty, Disaster and Hope*, 109–30, London: Green House.
Place, U.T. (1956), 'Is Consciousness a Brain Process?', *British Journal of Psychology* 47: 44–50.
Putnam, H. (1975), 'The Nature of Mental States', in H. Putnam (eds.), *Collected Papers* II, Cambridge: Cambridge University Press.

Quine, W.V.O. (1960/2001), *Word and Object*, Cambridge, MA: MIT Press.

Quine, W.V.O. (1990), *Pursuit of Truth*, Cambridge, MA: Harvard University Press.

Tyson, R. (2021), 'The Open Future in Peril: The Anthropocene and the Political Agent of Humanistically Oriented Historiography', *Rethinking History* 25(4): 440–57.

Rée, J. (1991), 'The Vanity of Historicism', *New Literary History* 22(4): 961–83.

Retz, T. (2017), 'Why Re-enactment Is Not Empathy, Once and for All', *Journal of the Philosophy of History* 11(3): 306–23.

Rotenstreich, N. (1972), 'Metaphysics and Historicism', in Krausz M. (ed.), *Critical Essays on the Philosophy of R. G. Collingwood*, 179–200, Oxford: Clarendon Press.

Roth, P. (2020), *The Philosophical Structure of Historical Explanation*, Evanston, IL: Northwestern University Press.

Rubinoff, l. (1966), 'Collingwood and the Radical Conversion Hypothesis', *Dialogue* 5(1): 71–83.

Ryle, G. [1949] (1990), *The Concept of Mind*, London: Penguin Books.

Saari, H. (1989), 'R. G. Collingwood on the Identity of Thought', *Dialogue: Canadian Philosophical Review* 28: 77–89.

Sellars, W. (1956), 'Empiricism and the Philosophy of Mind', in H. Feigl and M. Scriven (eds.), Minnesota Studies in the Philosophy of Science Vol I, Minneapolis: University of Minnesota Press.

Sellars, W. (1963), 'Philosophy and the Scientific Image of Man' in Sellars, W. (ed.), *Science, Perception and Reality*, 7–43, Atascadero, California: Ridgeview Publishing Company.

Schumann, G. (2019), 'Introduction', in G. Schumann (ed.) *Explanation in Action Theory and Historiography: Causal and Teleological Approaches*, 1–42, New York: Routledge.

Schumann, G. (forthcoming), 'Historical Explanation. An Anti-causalist Approach', in Habilitationsleistung, Hagen: FernUniversität.

Skagestad, F.P. (1975), *Making Sense of History: The Philosophies of Popper and Collingwood*, Oslo, Bergen and Tromso: Universitetsforlaget.

Skagestad, F.P. (2020), *Exploring the Philosophy of R.G. Collingwood: From History and Method to Art and Politics*, London: Bloomsbury Academic.

Smart, J.J.C. (1959), 'Sensations and Brain Processes', *Philosophical Review* 68: 141–56.

Stoutland, F. (2011), 'Interpreting Davidson on Intentional Action', in J. Malpas (ed.) *Dialogues with Davidson: New Perspectives on his Philosophy*, 297–324, Cambridge, MA: MIT Press.

Strawson, G. (2006), 'Realistic Physicalism: Why Physicalism Entails Panpsychism', in A. Freeman (ed.), *Consciousness and Its Place in Nature: Does Physicalism Entail Panpsychism?*, 3–31, Exeter: Imprint Academic.

Tamm, M. and Simon, Z.B. (2020), 'More-than-Human History: Philosophy of History at the Time of the Anthropocene', in Jouni Matti-Kuukkanen (ed.), *Philosophy of History: Twenty-First-Century Perspectives*, 198–215, London: Bloomsbury.

Toulmin, S. (1972), 'Conceptual Change and the Problem of Relativity', in M. Krausz (ed.), *Critical Essays on the Philosophy of R. G. Collingwood*, 201–21, Oxford: Clarendon Press.

Tosh, N. (2007), 'Science, Truth and History, part II. Metaphysical Bolt-holes for the Sociology of Scientific Knowledge?' *Studies in History and Philosophy of Science* 38: 185–209.

van der Dussen, J. (1995), 'The Philosophical Context of Collingwood's Re-enactment Theory', *International Studies in Philosophy* 27(2): 81–99.

Von, Wright (1971), *Explanation and Understanding*, London: Routledge.

White, H. (1973), *Metahistory: The Historical Imagination in the Nineteenth-Century Europe*, Baltimore, MD: Johns Hopkins University Press.

White, H. (2014), *The Practical Past*. Evanston, IL: Northwestern University Press.

Williams, B. (2006a), 'Philosophy as a Humanistic Discipline', in A.W. Moore (ed.), *Philosophy as a Humanistic Discipline*, 180–99, Princeton: Princeton University Press.

Williams, B. [1985] (2006b), *Ethics and the Limits of Philosophy*. London and New York: Routledge Classics.

Williams, B. (2006c), 'An Essay on Collingwood', in *The Sense of the Past: Essays in the History of Philosophy*, 341–58, Princeton: Princeton University Press.

Winch, P. [1958] (1990), *The Idea of a Social Science and Its Relation to Philosophy*, 2nd edition, London: Routledge.

Wittgenstein, L. (1963), *Philosophical Investigations*, Oxford: Blackwell.

Zalasiewciz, J. et al. (2015), 'When Did the Anthropocene Begin? A Mid Twentieth-Century Boundary Level Is Statisgraphically Optimal', *Quaternary International* 383: 196–203.

Index

AA mechanic 31–2, 37, 80, 93–4, 199
action(s) 11, 14, 17–20, 24–5, 27–8, 35, 37–8, 53, 61, 73, 75, 77, 80–1, 87, 89, 92, 100–3, 105, 107, 109–10, 116, 118, 122–3, 164, 166, 169–70. *See also* event(s)
    explanation of actions 58, 72, 74–5, 91, 105, 119, 168, 194
    humanistic explanations of 14, 24, 57, 82, 86, 94
    misunderstanding of 119
    rationalizing explanations of 55–60
adoptive parents 7–8, 10. *See also* biological parents
anachronism 158
analytic philosophy of mind 13, 61
ancient civilizations 9–11, 108, 172, 185
animals
    classification of 27, 101–2, 124, 186
    evolution of 108, 186
Anomalous Monism 72, 76–8
Anscombe, G. E. M. 73, 75, 103, 169
    Intentions 37
antecedent conditions 11, 35, 55–6, 59–61, 63–4, 74, 80, 82, 105, 124, 167, 167 n.1
Anthropocene 10, 23, 165, 170–7, 183, 187–8
anthropocentric/anthropocentrism 24, 151, 165–6, 186
anti-representationalism 144
Archimedes' 138–9
Aristotle 33–4, 100–1, 104, 198
Ayer, A. J. 16–17, 93, 104
    metaphysical pseudo-dispute 92
    verification/verificationism 17, 21, 47–9, 78, 91, 93–4, 131, 143–4

Baldwin, A. 6, 57
Beaney, M. 95 n.1
beliefs 14, 35, 55, 58, 60–1, 64–5, 67, 69, 73, 121, 153, 156, 161–2, 164, 186. *See also* desires
Benson, O., *Why Truth Matters* 129
biological parents 7–8, 10, 40. *See also* adoptive parents
biological species 9, 185, 187–8
biology 13–14, 40, 49, 58, 68–9, 170, 183
bodily movements 17–18, 60, 64, 74, 91, 112, 114, 116–17, 194
body, mind and 17–18, 63, 90–1, 95, 97, 99–101, 103, 105, 177
brain 5, 61, 64–5, 86, 95–6, 99
Broad, C. D., *The Mind and its Place in Nature* 62

Caesar's crossing of the Rubicon 1, 11, 19, 21, 112–15, 118–19, 123–4, 127–8, 135, 140, 147–9, 152, 168, 181–2, 195
carbon-dates 110, 120
Carroll, L., 'What the Tortoise said to Achilles' 95
categorial descriptions 51, 79–82, 100, 103, 107, 118, 169, 188, 195
categorial mediation 22, 150
causality 33, 65, 67
    causal efficacy 59, 65, 68–71
    causal exclusion 14–15, 37, 60–2, 64–6, 68–71, 76–81, 170
    causal explanations 15, 60–2, 64, 78–9, 169, 179–80, 182
    causal laws 68, 170
    causal relations 39, 64–5, 71, 76–7, 79
    causal responsibility 6, 11–12 (*see also* moral responsibility)

causa quod (belief concerning particular state of affairs) 35
causa ut (a goal) 35
cause/causation 7–9, 11, 13–15, 18, 28–31, 33–5, 38–41, 43–5, 47, 55–7, 59, 61–2, 70–1, 74, 78–9, 100, 109, 123, 129, 179–80
  causation conflict 38
  efficient causes 52, 73, 117
  heterogeneous notion of 28, 62
  homogeneous notion of 15, 61–2, 64, 81
  nomological sense of 63
  sense of causation 7, 15, 18, 28, 31–2, 34–5, 40, 43, 47, 52, 55, 57, 59, 63–4, 66, 76, 79–80, 89, 129, 170
ceteris paribus clauses 58, 68–9
Chakrabarty, D. 173, 183
chemistry 13–14, 39, 49, 58, 68–9, 170, 174, 183–4
Clarks, C., *The Sleepwalkers: How Europe Went to War in 1914* 182
climate change 170–1, 174, 183–4, 188–9
conceptual mediation 21–2, 145, 149, 156
consciousness 17, 90, 95–100, 103–4, 193
contemporary agents 19, 111, 136
contested concepts 6–12, 32, 49, 198
contextualism 104, 161–2
counterfactual causal explanation 180–2
counter-instances 115
crime detection 182–4. *See also* forensic science

Danto, A. C. 148
  narrative sentences 133–4
Davidson, D.
  Actions Reasons and Causes 72, 75, 79
  challenge to explanatory pluralism 72–80
deforestation 174, 182
Descartes, R. 63, 177, 191–2

desires 14, 35, 55, 58, 60–1, 64–5, 67, 69, 73. *See also* beliefs
disciplinary boundaries 166, 172, 179, 182–4, 188
disunity of science 14, 179, 179 n.10
DNA 10
D'Oro, G., *Collingwood and the Metaphysics of Experience* 4
Dray, W. H. 167–8, 182

Egyptians, ancient 5, 9, 11, 108, 121–2, 141, 143, 156–7, 171, 178, 185–6
Egyptologist 5, 108, 110, 121, 143, 178
electromagnetic discharge 96, 99
empirical classification 25, 27, 38–9, 100–3, 105
empirical generalization 83, 85, 115, 181
empirical verification 93–4
environmental humanities 183
epiphenomenalism 68–71, 77
epistemic relativism 13, 42, 161
  and explanatory pluralism 43–6
  and moral relativism 161–2
epistemology/epistemological 2–3, 76, 90–1, 99–100, 103, 105, 116, 118–19, 122, 132, 139, 141, 152, 163, 176–7
event(s) 14, 17–21, 28, 30, 35, 39, 52, 72, 77, 80, 100–3, 105, 107, 109, 112, 114, 119, 121–3, 148, 164, 168–70. *See also* action(s)
  historical 132–3, 145
  inside/outside of 112–16
  species of events 58, 119
evidence-based revisions 135–7
evolutionary history 10–11, 108
evolutionary past 9, 108
explanandum/explananda 5, 10, 18, 24, 35–7, 39–41, 43, 46, 55, 57, 59, 61, 63, 65, 68, 74–5, 77, 93, 100, 103, 105, 108, 116, 144, 152, 167, 167 n.1, 169, 179

explanation sketch 60, 166–7
explanatory connections 19, 32, 48, 74 n.1, 78, 80, 131, 143, 196
explanatory contexts 7, 9, 28, 34, 40, 45, 62–3, 65, 79, 81, 93, 109, 150, 160
explanatory gap 17, 91, 98–9, 105
explanatory pluralism 13–15, 25, 33, 42, 59, 62, 66, 70, 78, 80, 129, 144, 151, 155, 157, 188, 197
  Davidson's challenge to 72–80
  and epistemic relativism 43–6
  old and new challenges to 165–70
extinct species (fossilized remains of) 1, 9, 18–19, 108, 110, 120, 142, 185–6

familiarity 124, 127, 147, 175, 175 n.3, 195
feelings/sensations 21, 137–9, 141. *See also* thought, context of
Ferdinand, A., assassination of 22, 131, 133, 142–3, 147–9
Fodor, J. A 68–9
folk-psychological explanations 63, 65
forensic science 16, 36–8, 183–4. *See also* crime detection

Gadamer, H. G. 134, 136
gavagai 124, 126–7
Geisteswissenschaften 175–6, 177 n.5, 179
genetic ancestry 7–8
genuflection 125
geology/geological 58, 69, 165, 170–3, 176–7, 183, 187
global warming 143, 173–4, 182
God 16, 52, 91–2, 162
Goya, F. 92

Heidegger, M. 175, 177, 182, 194
Hempel, C. 63, 165–6, 167 n.1, 168, 172, 180
  explanation sketch 60, 166–7

hierarchical model of sciences 13–14, 39, 64–5, 154. *See also* layered model of sciences
historicism 153–5, 158
  radical 3, 25, 155–6, 161, 163, 197
history/historical 2–3, 9, 15, 18–20, 22–3, 36, 80–2, 107, 125–6, 143–4, 178
  of ancient civilizations 9
  evolutionary 10–11, 108
  historical agents 9, 11, 14, 20, 22, 110, 112, 115–16, 122, 124, 126–7, 130, 136–7, 141, 145, 147, 149–50, 152, 158, 160–1, 168, 172, 176, 179, 182, 186
  historical events 132–3, 145
  historical explanations 2, 42, 119, 144, 157, 163, 165–8, 167 n.1, 181–2, 185
  historical fundamentalism 3, 23, 153–4, 156–61, 164
  historical inquiry 22, 43, 105, 148, 150, 159, 163
  historical knowing 135, 152, 158, 197
  historical knowledge 2, 20–4, 26, 42, 46, 128, 131, 136, 141–5, 147, 149–50, 153–5, 160, 164
  historical misunderstanding of others 123–8
  historical narration/narratives 21, 130, 145–7, 173–4
  historical past 2, 9, 11, 14, 23–4, 107–11, 122–3, 129, 131–2, 135, 137, 142, 144, 146, 151–2, 158, 165–6, 170–1, 173, 175–7, 183–9, 199 (*see also* natural past)
  historical relativism 46, 152, 156, 162, 197
  historical revisionism 130–1, 135
  historical truth 129
  historical understanding 20, 42, 110, 116, 122–3, 128, 131, 138, 141, 150, 162, 166, 168, 170, 184

historical writing 133, 141, 145, 148–9
humanistic history 109–11, 114, 120–2, 126, 166
  and historical future 187–9
  natural history 11, 101, 109, 178
  scissors-and-paste histories 120–3, 158
  speculative philosophy, decline of 132–5
  traditional histories 171, 173–5, 187
Holocene 170–1
human exceptionalism 165, 186–8
humanistically-oriented historiography 26, 167, 170, 172, 177, 179–82, 184, 186–8
humanistic discipline 9–10, 36, 107–8
humanistic explanations 2, 5, 14–15, 24, 34–9, 42, 50, 52–3, 55–9, 61, 65–9, 72–3, 76, 78–80, 85–6, 101, 104, 119, 154, 170, 175 n.3, 197–8
  of actions 14, 24, 57, 82, 86, 94
humanistic understanding 2–4, 12, 25–6, 42, 78, 86, 116, 122, 125, 144, 152, 154, 161, 165–6, 191, 197
humanities 2–3, 5, 9–10, 16, 34, 40–2, 49, 60, 109, 132, 153, 173, 176–7, 179, 183, 187
human past 10, 165–6, 185, 187
human species, evolution of 108–9
Hume, D. 47, 91–2

Ibsen, H., *The Doll's House* 112
inductive inferences 47, 83–4
industrialization of farming 174, 182
insoluble mystery 16, 91–6. *See also* soluble mystery
interdisciplinarity 182–4
internal psychological process 56, 112, 116

inverted scientism 4, 23, 155–8. *See also* reversed scientism

Jackson, F., knowledge argument 97

Kant, I. 27, 40, 100–1, 146, 148
Kim, J., *Mind in a Physical World* 62
King Midas 89
  curse of 85–7
knowledge 1, 3–4, 7, 12, 15, 18, 25, 34, 40–6, 48–9, 51, 58–9, 62, 66, 80, 95, 127, 136, 155, 164, 198–9
  competent 136
  content of knowledge 130, 139–41
  empirical 47–9
  historical 2, 20–4, 26, 42, 46, 128, 131, 136, 141–5, 149, 153–5, 160, 164
  humanistic 156, 163–4
  insider 114, 114 n.1, 126–7
  knowledge argument 97
  knowledge claims 13, 25, 93, 131, 144, 151, 198
  objective 20, 132, 152
  presuppositionless 12, 50, 160
  of qualia 97
  scientific 2, 4–5, 9, 16–17, 21, 23–6, 41–2, 46, 51, 120–1, 131, 147, 153–6, 160, 163–4, 193, 197
Koch bacillus bacteria 157
Kripke, S. 97, 159

labour, division of 160, 162
Latour, B. 156, 172 n.2, 175
layered model of sciences 13–15, 39–40, 65, 77, 154, 197. *See also* hierarchical model of sciences
Leibniz, G. 46, 161
lightning 96, 99
limits of science 16–18, 90, 95, 103–4
Litvinenko, A., murder of 104, 198. *See also* murder mysteries

Locke, J. 50, 192
logical positivism 16–17, 91, 94–5, 95 n.1

mental states 17, 35, 55–6, 58–9, 65, 67–8, 70–1, 76, 90–1, 105, 117–18. *See also* beliefs; desires
Mesopotamians 178, 185
metaphilosophy 3, 27, 44, 71, 79, 90, 155, 177, 179
metaphysics 4, 6–7, 12–13, 16–17, 24, 40, 42–3, 46 n.1, 47, 49–50, 59, 65–6, 73, 77–8, 89–92, 104–5, 122, 132, 144, 159–60, 163–4, 170, 176, 191–2, 195, 198
   conceptual analysis in 12, 24, 192, 195
   metaphysical dualism 179, 182
   metaphysical (pseudo-) disputes 16, 92, 94, 104
methodological autonomy 14, 154, 162–3, 166
methodological unity in sciences 42, 67, 69–70, 153, 166, 168, 179–80, 182
microbes 172, 174–5
Mill, J. S. 57–8, 69, 166
   exact and inexact sciences 58, 69, 80
mind 5, 62, 85, 92, 107, 110, 112, 116, 126, 146, 177
   analytic philosophy of 13, 61
   and body 17–18, 63, 90–1, 95, 97, 99–101, 103, 105, 177
   environmental inputs and behavioural outputs 117–19, 123, 126
   philosophy of 7, 13–15, 17–18, 26, 59–63, 66, 71–2, 76–7, 85–6, 90, 95, 103, 117, 169–70
   place of mind in nature 15, 62–6, 68, 71–2, 86
   re-enactment and problem of other 116–19, 117 n.2

monism 63, 76–7
moral responsibility 6, 11–12. *See also* causality, causal responsibility
multiple realization functionalism 67, 69–71, 76
mummification (ancient Egyptians' ritual) 5, 11, 108, 122, 143, 186. *See also* Egyptians, ancient
murder mysteries 16–17, 90, 103–5, 183
mysteries/mysterious 16–17, 91, 95–6, 98–9, 103–4. *See also* *specific mysteries*

narration/narratives
   historical 21, 130, 145–9, 173–4
   narrative sentences 133–4
natural environment 173, 175
natural history 11, 101, 109
naturalism 23, 65, 151, 187
naturalistic dualism 70–1
natural laws 10, 19, 57, 115, 120, 123, 159, 185, 187
natural past 2, 9, 11, 23–4, 108, 110–11, 120, 123, 129, 132, 151–2, 158, 165–6, 171, 188–9, 199. *See also* historical past
natural science 2, 9–10, 14–15, 18, 23–5, 34, 36, 41–2, 50, 58, 62, 70, 84, 86–7, 90–1, 96, 104–5, 108, 110, 144, 153–5, 159, 163, 166, 167 n.1, 168, 176, 188, 192
nature/culture distinction 23, 164, 177–9, 183, 186–7
   Anthropocene challenge to 170–7
Naturwissenschaften 175–6, 177 n.5, 179
Neanderthals 10, 108
neural realizers 59, 65, 67, 70
neurophysiological explanations 5, 60–1, 63–5, 69, 97

neutral monism 76–7
nomological explanations 14, 18, 60–1, 63, 67, 68–9, 71, 73, 76–8, 80, 82–5, 87, 91, 100, 107, 166–9, 167 n.1, 180, 182
  of events 14, 55–60, 83, 91
non-reductive physicalism 66, 70–1, 76. *See also* reductive physicalism
non-reductivism 13–15, 58–60, 62, 66–72, 76–9, 81, 86, 155, 169
Novichok (nerve agent) 36–8

ontology/ontological 39–41, 50, 59, 64–6, 70–1, 73, 76–7, 80, 91–2, 98, 122, 126, 128, 160, 162, 176–7, 179, 182, 188, 191, 193, 195, 198
ordinary explanation 60–1

panpsychism/panpsychists 98
parent(s) 7–11. *See also* adoptive parents; biological parents
past 9–11, 107–10, 115, 126, 136, 147–52, 199. *See also* history, historical past; natural past
  evolutionary past 9, 108
  past agents 10, 14, 19–21, 23, 84, 110–12, 115–16, 118–22, 136, 139, 141, 144, 150, 154, 158, 161–2, 185
  scientific investigation of 110, 120, 122–3
period play 22, 112, 137, 141, 150
philosophy/philosophical 2, 4–6, 8, 12, 14–15, 23–5, 31, 43, 49–51, 58, 72, 101–2, 153–4, 178 n.9, 192, 195, 197–9
  contemporary 13, 16–17, 60–3, 66, 71–2, 95, 103, 105, 117, 169
  decline of speculative philosophy of history 132–5
  of mind 7, 13–15, 17–18, 26, 59–63, 66, 71–2, 76–7, 85–6, 90, 95, 103, 105, 117, 169–70
philosophical analysis 4, 7, 11–12, 23, 25–6, 27, 40, 47, 73, 76, 191–2, 198–9
philosophical belief 153, 164
philosophical disputes 7, 93
philosophical distinctions 28, 38, 90, 100–2, 105
physicalism 96–9, 193
  non-reductive 66, 70–1, 76
  reductive 64, 67, 69–71, 76
physics 1–2, 7, 13–17, 28, 39–41, 50, 58, 60, 71, 79, 90, 98, 104, 169–70, 174, 183, 192, 199
  explanations of 15, 39–40, 58, 64–5, 69, 71, 77, 154
  physical realizers 65, 68
power relations 3–4, 23, 154, 163, 197
practical sciences of nature 27, 29, 31–2, 34, 36–7, 39, 44–5, 47, 74, 82, 94, 196. *See also* theoretical sciences of nature
practical syllogism 56, 73
pre-Copernicans 155–7, 160
presentism 20, 122, 130, 132–7
presuppositions 4, 8–9, 12–13, 19–20, 22–4, 29–30, 33, 39, 43–4, 46–7, 51, 73, 77–8, 89, 93–5, 100, 110–12, 120–2, 129, 131, 143–4, 151–2, 154, 157, 160, 163, 170, 198–9
  absolute 20, 24, 32–3, 40, 42–8, 46 n.1, 65, 77–8, 95 n.1, 104–5, 129, 132, 144, 151, 159

of historical understanding 158
presuppositional analysis 15, 23,
    34, 39–46, 58–9, 65–6, 72,
    78, 86, 150, 154, 157, 164,
    196, 198
  source of dissatisfaction with
    47–51
  principle of uniformity of nature
    23, 47–8, 110, 120, 122,
    158–9, 163
principled revisionism 135–7, 141
propositions 30, 39, 43–4, 46–8, 56,
    91, 93–5, 138
pseudo-disputes 92–3
pseudo-mysteries 16, 94, 104
psychology/psychological 13–14, 18,
    40, 57–8, 68–70, 74, 81, 86,
    126–7, 169–70
  psychological explanations 61,
    64–5, 67–9
  psychological law 35, 56, 58, 60,
    64, 86
  psychological nature 56, 61, 73
psychophysical identities 97–8
pure being 12–13, 23, 49–50, 77–8,
    144, 156–60

Queen Elizabeth 185
Quine, W. V. O., radical translation
    124–7, 136–7, 181 n.12

radical conversion hypothesis 3
radical historicism 3, 25, 155–6, 161,
    163, 197
radical translation 124–7, 136–7, 181
    n.12
Rameses II, death of 156–7
rationalization 56, 69, 72–3, 75, 77,
    79–80, 82–6, 93–4, 109,
    162, 169
  prospective 83–4
  rationalizing explanations 18,
    55–60, 74–8, 83–4, 87, 91,
    100, 107, 169, 185

reality 6, 12, 17, 20, 22–5, 30–1, 33,
    40, 46, 49–51, 59, 61, 70,
    81, 87, 90, 96–8, 100–1,
    105, 107, 112, 115, 120,
    152, 156, 160, 163, 192–6,
    198–9
reasons 11
reciprocal relation 39, 59, 77, 86, 152,
    177 n.6, 179
reciprocity thesis 39–40, 51, 152,
    186
reductive physicalism 64, 67, 69–71,
    76. *See also* non-reductive
    physicalism
reductivism 65–7
re-enactment 117 n.2, 126 n.4, 141
    n.1
  and problem of other minds
    116–19
  and thought 137–41
reference invariance 158
relativism
  epistemic (*see* epistemic
    relativism)
  historical 46, 152, 156, 162,
    197
  value/moral 161
relativity 45, 160
responsibility 6, 11–12. *See
    also* causality, causal
    responsibility; moral
    responsibility
reversed scientism 164. *See also*
    inverted scientism
revisionism 21–2, 132, 135, 145, 147,
    149–50
  aprioristic 135–7, 141
  contemporary 130, 150
  historical 130–1, 135
  principled 135–7, 141
Roman law 113–14, 118, 123–4,
    127–8, 135, 140, 147, 149,
    181, 195
Rust film 6

sceptical/scepticism 20, 47–8, 119, 122, 128–9, 132, 150–1, 197
science. *See specific branches*
scientia 15, 41, 50, 80, 107, 154
scientific explanations 5, 14, 24, 34–9, 42, 50, 58–9, 61, 65–6, 79, 85–6, 89, 96–7, 101, 103, 151, 153–4, 157, 167, 196–7
scientific identities 97
scientific inquiry 94, 110, 150, 158–9
scientific investigation 42, 110, 120, 122–3, 143, 159, 168
scientific knowledge 2, 4–5, 9, 16–17, 21, 23–6, 41–2, 46, 51, 120–1, 131, 147, 150, 153–6, 158, 160, 163–4, 193, 197
and historical knowledge 141–4
scientific mysteries 103–5
scientific truth 50, 129
scientism 2–5, 12, 23, 26, 41–2, 152–5, 159, 184, 197
inverted 4, 23, 155–8
reversed 164
scissors-and-paste histories 120–3, 158
Sellars, W. 24, 145, 193, 195
empiricist myth of the given 145–7
semantic distinction 100–3, 105, 116
sense-making explanations 14, 35, 55–7, 60, 80–1, 83, 169, 185
Skripal, S. 17, 36–8
soluble mystery 91–5. *See also* insoluble mystery
spatio-temporal 21, 79, 137–9, 159
special sciences 13, 49, 68–70, 170. *See also* biology; chemistry; psychology
speculative philosophy of history 132–5

standards of evidence 43, 48, 50, 93–4, 121
standpoint epistemology 139, 141, 152
Stangroom, J., *Why Truth Matters* 129
supernatural/supernaturalism 57, 89, 172, 185

theoretical sciences of nature 28–9, 32, 34, 37, 40, 44–5, 79, 94. *See also* practical sciences of nature
thought, context of 137–41, 161, 163. *See also* feelings/sensations
Tolstoy, L., *War and Peace* 175
transcendent 16, 24, 89–92, 95, 148
transgression 10, 19–20, 82, 85, 114
tuberculosis 156–8

underlabourer of science 14, 50–1, 192, 196, 198

verification/verificationism 17, 21, 47–9, 78, 91, 93–4, 131, 143–4, 150
Vesuvius eruptions 18, 109, 120–1

White, H. 142
Williams, B. 3, 115, 161 n.4
Winch, P. 181–2
works of Collingwood
An Essay on Metaphysics 3–4, 28, 46 n.1, 79, 91
An Essay on Philosophical Method 4, 27–8, 39, 100
The Idea of History 9, 35, 119, 122, 137
Lectures on Moral Philosophy 27

yeast 174–5, 189v

www.ingramcontent.com/pod-product-compliance
Lightning Source LLC
Chambersburg PA
CBHW071835300426
44116CB00009B/1551